Internet-ontologies-Things

Internet-ontologies-Things

Smart Objects, Hidden Problems, and Their Symmetries

Sungyong Ahn

BLOOMSBURY ACADEMIC

NEW YORK • LONDON • OXFORD • NEW DELHI • SYDNEY

BLOOMSBURY ACADEMIC
Bloomsbury Publishing Inc
1385 Broadway, New York, NY 10018, USA
50 Bedford Square, London, WC1B 3DP, UK
29 Earlsfort Terrace, Dublin 2, Ireland

BLOOMSBURY, BLOOMSBURY ACADEMIC and the Diana logo are
trademarks of Bloomsbury Publishing Plc

First published in the United States of America 2023

A catalog record of this book is available from the Library of Congress.

ISBN: HB: 978-1-5013-9924-4
          ePDF: 978-1-5013-9926-8
          eBook: 978-1-5013-9925-1

Typeset by Integra Software Services Pvt. Ltd.

To find out more about our authors and books visit www.bloomsbury.com
and sign up for our newsletters.

For Eunyoung and Teo.

Contents

Illustrations

Figures

Table

Acknowledgments

This is more a book of inspiration than logic. I would like to thank all the things that inspired me to speculate about their own worlding beyond my control. Among others, my old Renovo and current Acer laptops, carried in my eight-year-old Incase backpack, put on the passenger seats of my old 2003 Ford Taurus and current 2006 Renault Samsung SM3, which always sacrificed their vents to hold my old Blackberry and Galaxy smartphones, which navigated me to my favorite cafes in Urbana-Champaign, Illinois, and Seoul, and to the new cafes across the United States and South Korea, where I wrote most of this book. They transformed the corner tables of these cafes, into which I stole to use their outlets and Wi-Fi connections, into the most personal and coziest places to write.

I would also like to thank James Hay for always believing in the academic value of my speculative work, Clifford Christians for assuring me of the still important role of ontological thinking in media studies, Jodi Byrd and Peter Darch and Angela Ke Li for their careful reviews and productive feedback, Naomi Taub for her careful copyediting and some of the most beautiful sentences in this book based on her suggestions, and my parents for always supporting my long journey of learning. And Eunyoung, my wife and soulmate, for being a beacon of light in my life.

Chapters of this book and other parts were revised from the following: the section on Pan-kinetics in the introduction and the first and last intermissions were revised from sections in "Stream Your Brain! Speculative Economy of the IoT and Its Pan-kinetic Dataveillance," *Big Data & Society*, 8 (2) (2021); Chapter 1 was revised from "Bartleby, the IoT, and a Flat Ontology: How Ontology Is Written in the Age of Ubiquitous Computing," *Postmodern Culture*, 29 (3) (2019); Chapter 2 was revised from "Symmetrifying a Smart Home: Topology as New Governmentality for the Internet of Things," *Media Theory*, 5 (1) (2021); Chapter 3 was revised from "Shooting a Metastable Object: Targeting as Trigger for Actor-Network in the Open-World Videogames," *Communication and Critical/Cultural Studies*, 15 (3) (2018); Chapter 4 was revised from "Becoming a Network Beyond Boundaries: Brain-Machine Interfaces (BMIs) as the Actor-Networks after the Internet of Things," *Technology in Society*, 47 (2016); and portions of Chapter 5 were revised from "Found Footage and the Speculative Economy of Attention," *International Journal of Communication*, 13 (2019).

Introduction

What it means to be "smart" is under constant renegotiation in the current technological environment, when the power of machines to enlighten us seems to far exceed what we once believed ourselves capable of managing in daily life. This renegotiation of what was once an exclusively human quality might be said to have substantively begun with the sudden ubiquity of "smartphones" in the early twenty-first century. How these devices became so "smart," rather than just intelligent, can be ascribed to a few sensors—such as motion, environmental, and position sensors as well as software systems to monitor user behaviors—and actuators—such as audio, visual, and tactile outputs—integrated into a palm-sized tablet. For the past fifteen years, these sensors and actuators, and their interoperability through seemingly infinite smartphone apps, have pragmatically redefined human users as inexhaustible sources of data as they unfold certain responses, anticipated or unanticipated, to the environmental cues, algorithmic nudges, and recommended content on the many screens to which they are exposed. In the current parlance, being "smart" pertains to our decisions and ability to personalize these responses by way of customized content, targeted services, and push notifications. By convincing us that it is economically rational, even necessary, to expose ourselves to these curated stimuli on smartphones and other smart technologies at the expense of our data privacy, the current renegotiation of smartness thus suggests an implicit injunction that software industries aim to internalize as the consumers' principle of economic decision-making: don't base your decisions simply on tangible pros and cons but on your somewhat paranoid concern about unknown discontents and insecurities. Whereas these hidden desires and anxieties were once black-boxed in between a person's restricted self-perception and their unconscious/nonconscious responses, such as Freudian slips, or otherwise pragmatically black-boxed by the behavioral sciences as somewhere in between the two terminals of the subject's sensorimotor activities, the smartness of technologies now allows machines to preempt and restage these problematic realities as the suboptimal states of their human users relocated to the folds of their *sensor-actuator arcs*.

While an individual's online and geospatial presence is the primary object that a smartphone's algorithmic sensorimotor arcs re-enfold for the purpose of unfolding domains of each smartphone app, the recent miniaturization of sensor, processor, and actuator technologies, as well as their wireless communicability, has enabled the software industry to transform any physical object into this speculative matter. Think of a person's physiological body, domestic space, and urban neighborhood tracked and stimulated by different sets of sensors and actuators embedded in, respectively, a smart cloth, smart home, and a smart city, all under the governance of software applications "located" in the clouds. Metabolisms and neurophysiologies would no longer be nonconscious processes under the skin and inside the skull but rather data streams with unknown rhythms and periodicities whose optimality for different tasks can be properly managed by an array of apps downloaded to a smartwatch or smart EEG headset. In a smart home and city, our habitual routines would not be considered efficient or sustainable enough to accomplish the many things we may want or need to do—that is, until our everyday decision-making is consciously or unconsciously optimized through ubiquitous digital nudges. Put differently, alongside the wireless sensor and actuator networks (WSAN) of the Internet of Things (IoT), or as the consequence of this new internet's descent from the clouds to real-world objects, we may be experiencing the emergence of a capitalist variant of "speculative realism." The philosophical field of speculative realism (Bogost 2012; Bryant 2012; Harman 2005; Meillassoux 2008), which can be thought of as a predecessor of the kind of speculative realism at issue here, argues—which is to say, speculates—that our material universe may enfold multiplicities of unknown realities, which withdraw from human perception but could be enacted and communicated by nonhuman objects, each of which has distinctive ontological concerns toward their operational environments. However, unlike philosophical speculation (which is also a strategic turn for the humanities that aims to bring possible worlds other than those correlated only with human reasons and interests into its purview), the speculation that, for the last decade, has driven sensors' ubiquitous data collection and our voluntary exposure to self-actuating smart environments is based sheerly on the economic concerns of software companies, who are betting on these other worlds as a chance to expand their service domains.

Internet-ontologies-Things examines this new materialist thinking in current software capitalism in relation to, and as the reflection of, the recent ontological transformations of the computational building blocks of algorithmic cultures, called *objects*. Defined in the source codes of computer programs as abstract agents that exchange messages with one another, giving unique responses tailored to their shared environments (including inputs from users, other agents, and databases), objects provided early programmers with more intuitive means to assemble a software system from simple and modular building blocks. Object-orientation as a computational logic during the time of personal computing was, in this sense, "a natural way of looking at the world" of bits then enclosed within the motherboards of desktops, which "help[ed] to decompose large systems into manageable components, making them easier to develop and maintain" (Kowalski 2011: 179). In the age of ubiquitous computing, these abstract agents reside in two distinguishable physical reincarnations: (1) smart objects capable of actuating themselves or each other according to what they perceive and how they respond to the environments on the one hand and (2) all the others, including humans, whose response-abilities to smart environments are pragmatically bracketed as the matter of algorithmic prediction between the stimuli that smart actuators distribute and the responses that smart sensors detect on the other. A kind of selection pressure behind this "natural" way of building real-world algorithmic systems with smart objects no longer pertains simply to how they are reassembled in the most efficient and resource-saving way for the collective goals already defined by programmers. This pressure, which some understand via the metaphor of natural selection, compels smartphones, watches, and other wearables such as EEG headsets to constantly collect users' behavioral, physiological, and neurological big data. Often this broad net is cast without even specifying what kind of benefits the data could bring or what kind of software application they could serve as immediate inputs for, which makes this selection pressure relevant to the software industry's current speculative stance to datamining. Their experimentation with novel ways to reassemble smart objects and human bodies aims to discover, or reenact, more niches in our daily lives, which will be machine-learned between certain environmental cues and our (non)conscious responses. And the suboptimal conditions of the niches are expected to be optimized as re-enmeshed with certain sensor-actuator arcs. However, contrary to the naturalist metaphor of ecology, these niches are not simply to select the fittest smart objects to optimize the given or speculated correlations between the cues and responses. Instead, the ecology of current smart objects reflects a teleological tendency within software capitalism in which the presence of these as yet suboptimal hidden niches is preempted as ontologically imperative to drive constant redistributions of smart objects for "the full colonization of the life-world by computational capital" (Beller 2018: 72). The goal of this book is to expose this new capitalist principle of algorithmic selection behind the so-called autonomy of smart machines.

This ecology of computational agents has been referred to by different names, such as Ubiquitous Computing (Weiser and Brown 1997), Pervasive Computing (Satyanarayanan 2001), and Amorphous Computing (Abelson et al. 2009), and has been understood to consist of various technological and theoretical incarnations of algorithmic agents, such as "smart objects" (Kortuem et al. 2010), "computational particles" (Abelson et al. 2009), and "smart dust" (Kahn et al. 1999). Compared to these terms, which focus either on the scale and flexibility of wireless computing or on the autonomy of individual machines, the Internet of Things (IoT), a more popular term in recent years, seems to better capture the speculative dimension of the current media ecology in its juxtaposition of two seemingly incommensurable words: *Internet* for the network hitherto thought to be colonized mostly by humans and *Things* for anything but humans. Writing in 2009, Kevin Ashton suggested that, in 1999, the emergence of the IoT meant most of all the changed method of data entry for the internet, from data entry performed entirely by humans, such as "typing, pressing a record button, taking a digital picture or scanning a bar code," to the environmental sensing of autonomous smart objects. He emphasized the hidden "waste, loss and cost" caused by things in our daily lives that might be preventable if "we had computers that knew everything there was to know about things—using data they gathered without any help from us." He expected, "we would be able to track and count everything … we would know when things needed replacing, repairing or recalling, and whether they were fresh or past their best." The problem he identified in the human method of data entry was that "people have limited time, attention and accuracy—all of which means they are not very good at capturing data about things in the real world." However, the type of "waste, loss and cost" newly found from the things that the sensors turn into data streams is inaccessible by humans not simply because, as Ashton claimed, we are too busy to constantly monitor and track these streams. It is rather because the problems are too embedded and distributed in the streams to be grasped by our all-too-human techniques of manipulating data. Like an equation between two variables kept invariant during a linear regression while all others are subject to change, these problems would come to the fore only when their correlations with our quantified-selves, decked out in smart wearables and living in smart homes, turn out to remain invariant and thus identifiable during certain transformations that the IoT's experimental sensor-actuator arcs bring to the things in between. Topologically speaking, the IoT's accessibility and our inability to access these problems are due to the problems' symmetry to the IoT's sensor-actuator arcs and asymmetry to our habitual sensorimotor activities. (As Chapter 2 discusses in more detail, symmetry in topology refers to an object's property that remains invariant under certain transformations inflicted on it. An object's symmetry defined in this way is thus always the symmetry *to* a certain power that transforms it.) So, when this book says a thing re-enfolded by the IoT's smart sensors and actuators, such as a body, home, car, or city, becomes a *topological object*, it does not simply mean the thing becomes more transformable in computer simulations. (All things in the real world are subject to constant transformations.) Topology repurposed into a media study concept rather emphasizes that the types of transformations the ubiquitous IoT actuators impose on the world and its things are not meant to make them fit into predefined categories or data structures but instead aim to reveal hidden correlations of things as invariant under, or symmetrical to, these controlled transformations as speculated in the first place. As the proponents of the IoT may claim, everything is thus topologically analyzable as folded into the sensor-actuator arcs of the IoT. At the same time, from the translation of everything into massive data streams as bracketed within algorithmic arcs, the IoT discovers the hidden dimensions of our nonhuman reality for its new service domains. The future values of this everything might remain in the forms of unknown correlations as yet inaccessible within big data but speculated to be foregrounded as symmetrical figures, sooner or later, to the correct transformations that some proper datamining tools would impose on it.

The "things" in the Internet of Things are, therefore, not restricted to smart sensors and actuators (which Chapters 1 and 2 discuss as functional elements in a smart car and home) or algorithmic and graphical objects in virtual reality (such as videogame objects, seen in Chapter 3) but those of organic matter digitally augmented (such as primate and human brains and bodies, discussed in Chapter 4). And this list is expandable to anything whose natural and cultural inter-objective dynamic in response to environments is worthy of consideration for the IoT's future domains of optimization.

Pan-Kinetics of the IoT

In this context, then, the Internet of Things this book describes is reflecting a speculative economy of the current software industry. Under negotiation here are two distinguishable forms of speculation that redefine the meaning of "smart," performed respectively by users and software companies: (1) the speculation *about* unknown suboptimal realities within our everyday lives and (2) the speculation *in* the profitable correlations within the data streams generated by ubiquitous sensors. This negotiation is likely to conclude by asking us to subscribe to more IoT services and thus sacrifice more personal data because the problems preventing us from being "smart," such as our neurophysiological bodies and their nonconscious behaviors, are asymmetrical to our self-understanding and habitual sensorimotor activities but symmetrical to the IoT's machine learning and its sensor-actuator arcs. Speculation is thus a form of cognitive labor that IoT users perform, and which is also redefining the meaning of their alienated labor in this new digital economy. Users are denied access to the problems their speculations create while smart objects and software companies claim their accessibility through constant datamining and analyses. Ultimately, this asymmetry to our own physical realities that the IoT claims to re-symmetrify produces a new regime of surveillance.

In order to elucidate his concept of the "panopticon," Foucault (1995) describes a prison designed so that all the cells are visibly visible from a central guard tower into which the prisoners cannot see. Even when the guard is absent, this generates a hallucinatory omnipresence of surveilling eyes by hiding the absence of the actual eyes in the central tower. Having been denied access to the hidden (and absent) sensor, the prisoners are compelled to display normative behaviors at all times. Yet the ubiquitous IoT sensors seem to reveal that the panopticon's pan-optics are not alone enough to perform this 24/7 surveillance, because the problems they should preempt no longer come to the fore under the mere sum of sensors. Unlike the illegitimacies of prisoner behaviors, which were identifiable by their deviations from normative responses to the hidden sensor/observer, security issues in the IoT tend to remain invisible until they begin to resist, or appear to resist, being continuously and seamlessly communicated by smart objects and apps. If we assume that, instead of a panopticon, an oligopticon—that is, the sum of "partial vantage points with limited view sheds" (Kitchin 2014: 11)—is the best a smart home could do when its sensors have yet to be integrated, the symptoms of some problems, even those as minor as the smart home's owner habitually wasting energy, could be distributed extensively across the incompatible sets of data streams from these different sensors. The smart homeowner's somewhat paranoid concerns about her suboptimal realities could then never be resolved completely despite her subscriptions to simple home security services. Even if she was positioned within the guard tower of Foucault's panopticon, that is, if she accessed the control panel through which the system allows her to monitor the current state of both her smart home and her own body, which are measured separately by multiple sensors or webcams, the result would be the same. By extension, for her self-surveillance to remain a smart decision, she needs a complementary means to "integrate and bind data streams together, work to move the various oligopticon systems into a single, panoptic vantage point" (Kitchin 2014: 11). In this algorithmic integration of self-tracking technologies, the user may still understand that, despite her ability to surveil, she is being denied access to the underlying mechanisms. She cannot control the smart actuators: the motors of security cameras whose secret motion tracking is black-boxed beneath dark surfaces; the actuators of smart objects to activate themselves or each other in more seamless ways; or their direct intervention in space by distributing perceptible or imperceptible cues or nudges to arouse certain responses from environments, which would be relayed to other sensors.

In the current "smart home" market, systems like those powered by Amazon's Alexa, in which the owners can freely reassemble smart devices to suit their daily routines, the actuators' autonomous operations are often marginalized as the system's passive ends to "convert the data/energy [already processed in the earlier stage] to motion to control system" (Rayes and Salam 2016: 82). For this behaviorist closure of sensors and actuators to act as a substitute for the user's physical interactions with home appliances, it might be enough for the system simply to match to already-known triggers that the sensors detect, like the user's voice commands, to the well-defined actions actuators perform, such as turning on devices. However, insofar as the ultimate goal of home optimization is to keep the atmosphere always and already in the optimal state for any task the user might take up, including those tasks we perform without thinking, the sensors and actuators need to be subjected to more dynamic and proactive reassembling, not only for targeting some registered behaviors but for cultivating a greater range of as yet unknown but soon to be predictable behaviors.

In the artificial intelligence (AI) research based on behavioral robotics in the 1980s and 1990s, the wiring of multiple arcs across sensors and actuators was an arduous engineering task for human researchers. Their goal was to simulate the evolutionary history of human intelligence through a machine's proper responses to and proactive manipulations of controlled lab environments (Brooks 1991; Brooks and Stein 1994). However, the artificial intelligence residing within the IoT's sensor-actuator arcs does not replicate this anthropomorphized model of operational intelligence. Instead, in the IoT, the optimality of things—a home or its owner—that the IoT manages to maintain for any probable events—her waking up, working out, and watching TV—is a computational problem asymmetrical to the hardwired sensors and actuators of humanoids. For the machine learning of each optimal condition of things likely to trigger these events, an IoT system needs to enable its actuators to nudge the things in a more proactive manner to generate more sensor data about their responses. While the IoT's voice-commanded or sensor-triggered automation begins with the sensors' detections of known problems and terminates with the registered solutions the actuators perform, their constant ambient data-gathering operations contribute to this machine learning of actuator-triggered transformations of sensor data. In other words, while its transient Sensor→Actuator operation turns a thing it enfolds into a short-lived "problem space" in which the thing is transformed according to a linear spectrum from the detection to the resolution of the problem (Newell 1980), its ambient Actuator→Sensor operations redefine the data stream from the thing as a "state-space," which describes all possible states the thing could pass through in response to the stimuli given either by smart actuators or by some outside factors. The extended Sensor→Actuator→Sensor operation of the IoT, in this respect, describes both its short-term and long-term approaches to the thing in the middle. On the one hand, it temporarily bifurcates each well-defined service domain for a registered problem. On the other, it constantly turns the thing back to a topological continuum that preserves abundant hidden correlations to be machine-learned for its speculated future services. The first half of the sensor-initiating cycle, Sensor→Actuator, represents the pan-optics of the IoT, the full visibility of known problems under its 24/7 surveillance. The second actuator-initiating half, Actuator→Sensor, can then be termed the IoT's pan-kinetics. What this regime requires individual users to internalize, alongside the panoptic sensors for the solutions of some known problems, would be the ubiquitous nudges or subliminal cues as the means to gradually unfold and optimize all hidden correlations within their smart bodies, homes, and cities.

This correlation-cultivating operation of the IoT, or its pan-kinetics, is comparable to that of an early experimental apparatus of behavioral psychology: the Skinner Box. This small container for an animal subject was also designed to cultivate certain behavioral responses of the subject between its stimulator (actuator) and recording device (sensor). Even though pan-kinetics seems to replace this early hardwired container with wireless sensors and actuators that are omnipresent enough to encompass a wide range of things spanning from a body to a city, the directions in which their operations travel are opposites. Signifying the confidence of the behavioralist program in grasping any observable behaviors, the Skinner Boxes' stimulations of animal subjects were meant to single out certain disciplined responses under their black-boxed input-output relations. In other words, the goal was to transform them into disciplined and reproducible objects. The IoT's pan-kinetics is, in the meantime, not intended to black-box the middle but rather revitalizes the things once considered stabilizable under behavioralist programs, including animal and human bodies and their societies, and restimulates their hidden responses to the worlds, far beyond human perceptibility but partially machine learnable.

In *Feed-Forward: On the Future of Twenty-First Century Media*, Mark Hansen (2015a: 4) explains that "today's media industries have honed methods for mining data about our behavior that feature as their key element the complete bypassing of consciousness." Requiring its users to be always responsive to nonconscious nudges everywhere, the IoT has also honed its pan-kinetics as a method for bypassing users' consciousness. The "nonconscious realm of sensibility" it intervenes in is experienceable (un)consciously only with the "missing half-second" of delay as "the temporal gap between brain activation and awareness" (98, 190). In other words, this realm feels most adjacent to the users' minds and bodies and yet is always withdrawing from their conscious access. The genealogy of the IoT may, in this respect, be traced further back to Actuator→Sensor systems that are older than the Skinner Box, such as Helmholtz's myograph, an experimental apparatus used in early neurophysiology research to examine this elusive domain of the human mind. But what is more noteworthy about this comparison are the contradictory effects these Actuator→Sensor systems have brought to the materialist understanding of human behaviors in the nineteenth and twenty-first centuries, respectively. As mechanical extensions of the experimental subjects' reflex arcs, the hardwired sensors and actuators in this early neurophysiological apparatus were meant to produce linear and graphical inscriptions of subject responses. These mechanical images of life then functioned to drive the mythical concepts of life, such as what vitalists termed "vital force," to the peripheries of scientific discourses (Patton 2018). In the meantime, as the new inscription method of subject behaviors or nonconscious responses of their bodies under constant subliminal stimulations, the big data collected through the IoT's pan-kinetics is resummoning something fetishistic in the form of the mathematical sublime, or the feeling that something significant is still hidden beneath the visible surface of big data (McCosker and Wilken 2014). Unlike data fetishism, which has been criticized for its tendency to reduce "all phenomena and means of accounting for phenomena to numbers" at the expense of "other less easily quantifiable albeit insightful ways of expressing phenomena" (Sharon and Zandbergen 2016: 1698), the speculative belief that maintains our attachment to pan-kinetic networks is more tolerant of this kind of epistemological criticism. That is, something less easy to quantify by current methods of datamining is no longer simply displaced but assumed to leave some hidden correlations on their way to constant withdrawal. For ordinary IoT users, the fetishistic over-evaluation of their quantified-selves and consequent overconcern for some suboptimal states of their lives are, in this respect, relevant more to their somewhat animistic imagination of big data. This fetishism is spurred by the lack of appropriate means (such as machine learning) to correlate it with their restricted understanding, as opposed to the early practitioners of quantified-self's belief in the numerical closure of selves. For software companies, in the meantime, the fetishization of their big data as even bigger than currently known is an economic imperative meant to justify their speculative investment in "any and all future scenarios and technologies" to unfold its unknown correlations (Andrejevic 2013: 78). This new fetishism is more than delusory in the current media environment where recognizing our inherent epistemological limit is the first step toward our becoming smart. Encountering hidden security and lifestyle issues and their asymmetry to human perception, we are left to invest our restricted reasoning power in the mere belief that something is certainly hidden and that the IoT's systemic stimulations will bring it back to the knowable domain of, or re-symmetrify it to, artificial intelligence.

This new commodity fetish can be projected onto anything so long as its natural/cultural responsiveness is re-stimulatable by ubiquitous actuators and transcribed into the sensor data with potentially unfathomable hidden correlations. From one's own body, shrouded under multiple smart wearables, to an entire smart city, the spaces that, we were told, would become more transparent through the literal pan-optics of sensors have ironically been possessed once again by something hidden. The full visibility of these spaces is now constantly updated through the pan-kinetic unraveling of hidden correlations.

Life's Asymmetry and Its Vulnerability

So, if the responsiveness of things in general is what the IoT restimulates in its search for the hidden correlations of the world, the thing first and foremost transformed into a topological object within the IoT's sensor-actuator arcs would be, in the elementary sense, *life itself.*

Life is a mysterious object. We sense it all around; it animates the behaviors of all living things (and sometimes nonliving things as well), but when we try to center our focus upon it, it withdraws to the peripheries of our consciousness, defying our descriptive abilities. One tricky way to grasp this elusive object is to define it as "what escapes *exact* definition and representation" (Olma and Koukouzelis 2007: 2). Even after nineteenth-century reflexologists deconstructed the concept of "vital force" by re-embedding the bodies of experimental subjects within the thermodynamic physicality of science labs (Patton 2018: §4.1), this reactionary mystification of life could have preserved some niches for the vitalist view in the peripheries of biological, neurological, and pharmaceutical discourses. While these vitalist materialisms have long been the purview of the humanities alone, the IoT now looks for the opportunity to expand into finer-grained materialities of our sociobiological life from its constant withdrawal to secret terrains. In other words, its withdrawal ironically indexes the presence of new frontiers for sensors and actuators with smaller sizes and higher resolutions, which will be embedded for searching the new IoT domains of optimization. Re-enfolding any life activities into its finer-grained sensor-actuator arcs, the IoT seems to resummon the ghost of vitalism, which the hardwired sensors and actuators of the myograph or Skinner Box once drove out to the peripheries of scientific discourse (Ahn 2013). Currently, vitalism instead reappears anywhere machines fail to grasp "a vital materiality" as "the swarm of activity subsisting below and within formed bodies and recalcitrant things" (Bennett 2009: 50). Both as the return of the repressed and the ontological justification for the IoT's expansionism, its resurgence redefines life as a topological object with lots of hidden dimensions, inexhaustibly enmeshable with sensor-actuator arcs of the existing technological networks. This therefore guarantees their infinite expandability—from experimental assemblages of devices in biology labs to the citywide environmental and behavioral sensor-actuator arcs that operate on the communal level of life activities.

In his study of the twenty-first-century's "politics of life," Nikolas Rose says that *life* as a medical and pharmaceutical phenomenon is now populating "a 'flattened' world, a world of surfaces rather than depths" (2007: 130). Life has been a boundary-object, since molecular biology in the late twentieth century began to function as the protocol for communicating life through the assemblages of such apparatuses as biotech and pharmaceutical companies, doctors, genetic counselors, genomics researchers, biobankers, and patient groups. The elusiveness of this boundary-object is never fully graspable by any single apparatus, but examinable infinitely through the new communicability between various individual and organizational actors that converge at a shared molecular level. At the same time, these actors' collective and ethical concerns for life, namely its optimization at multiple levels of individual healthcare, medical research, and pharmaceutical products, have also been understood to converge on a continuum of molecules, that is, "only one set of relays in complex, ramifying, and nonhierarchical networks, filiations, and connections" (130). No longer a "deep ontological reality" interpretable from surface symptoms, life and its mythical depth are now displaced to the relational databases the medico-pharmaceutical assemblages generate, and hidden correlations among the variables that compose the databases are speculated to be datamined for some unknown (ir)regularities of life. For its further optimization, individuals in turn become responsible for subjecting their molecular bodies to "pre-symptomatic diagnoses" in order to initiate "preventive interventions on a scale previously unimaginable" (89) before visible symptoms disrupt its regularities.

This tendency to molecularize life is accelerated by the advent of wearable and implantable healthcare technologies, which provide individuals with a digital shortcut for their bioethical responsibility of reframing a body as a continuum of data streams. Any irregularities in this continuum's transformations can potentially be reported automatically to healthcare authorities as the smart devices are constantly monitoring the "physiological parameter and environmental conditions" of (potential) patients. Previously, this task was "manually executed by nursing staff" or patients themselves, having been, "*de facto*, an efficiency bottleneck, which could be a cause of even tragic errors in practices" (Catarinucci et al. 2015: 515). Thus, one common future scenario for smart healthcare (Stantchev et al. 2015) suggests a local network of smart devices embedded in a human body and its surroundings, termed "fog computing," whose early detection and transfer of abnormal vital signs to "the cloud" of bigger medical institutions would enable the better prediction of a patient's critical states even before human doctors actually intervene.

At the same time, for the new smart cities, the vital continuum their distributed sensors and actuators aim to optimize is the more communal form of life, the hosts of which are called "insurgent citizens." The future scenario of the new urbanity the IoT promises has arrived at the right time after the failure of the modernist urban planning and to amend its once purely "idealist project of alternative futures" (Holston 1998: 38). As James Holston points out, the "imaginary city" designed via modernist planning's top-down approach was on a plane of inert matters whose reactions were deemed calculatable ahead of its actual implementation. Given the insurgent and nonconforming heterogeneity of things that had populated it, the failure of this city, which is "present nowhere in the world but existing only in plans," was predictable. For Holston's "project of rethinking the social in planning," this insurgence of vital materiality suggests "a realm of the possible that is rooted in the heterogeneity of lived experience, which is to say, in the ethnographic present and not in utopian futures" (41, 53). For the planning to be the process of unfolding rather than imposing a future, the planners' "ethnographic investigation" is, he argues, indispensable not only to "establish the terms by which residents participate in the planning of their communities" but to examine the possible futures already embedded in the heterogeneity of a city's material composition (53). The futurity of urban civilization and its pursuit of sustainability, after the failure of modernist planning, are, in this respect, also based on a sort of flattened world where the optimal near futures are not projected from the verticality of planning but emergent from the heterogeneous materiality of urban infrastructures, where some "insurgent forms of the social" should be constantly redirected and preempted by the planners' data-driven scenarios. To both planners and citizens, the emergent smart cities offer a digital shortcut for their ethnographic responsibility for "tracing, observing, decoding, and tagging" everyday activities, through which the sustainability of our optimal urban lives becomes a matter of unfolding by means of predicting and preventing possible negative incidents lurking in the ground. In this context, the recent research on the convertibility of smart cities into the infrastructures for counterinsurgency (Michaelis 2018; Pradhan et al. 2018) may obscure the fact that the optimal futures the smart cities promise have always and already been based on a certain militarized understanding of urbanity under constant alternations between insurgent problems and counterinsurgent IoT solutions.

The recent enterprises of life are, according to Rose and Holston, characterized by their effort to circulate the elusive and inexhaustible vital signs through assemblages of loosely interconnected actors on various scales. And to enable this circulation to continue optimizing life at the multiple levels of individual healthcare, corporate expansion, academic research, and governmental control, individuals are made responsible for molecularizing or digitalizing their own life according to the protocols of pharmaceutical industries or urban ethnography. In the age of the Internet of Things, this bioethical responsibility for communicating life is camouflaged in the forms of everyday protocols that people habitually perform, such as wearing smart clothes, watches, glasses, using smart plugs for every home appliance, and agreeing to the "terms of service" for all these gadgets. The exploitive mode of smart devices is normalized by these protocols, while operations to extract behavioral data from users' everyday lives purport to serve their smart citizenship. In the meantime, the necessity of minimizing delays in data transmission caused by too-human data entry methods or the verticality of bureaucratic processes provides ethical excuses for the smart objects' ambient generation and transmission of our quantified-selves to commercial networks.

Nevertheless, the necessity of our self-exposure to the IoT's dataveillance is not something merely fabricated by consumerist campaigns for the promised optimal future always around the corner. It is rather internalized when we accept as our normative condition the asymmetrical engagement in a world full of nonlinear problems beyond our understanding. For instance, under multiple wearable sensors, our own bodies reappear to be populated by these sorts of asymmetrical problems, whose nonconscious metabolisms, neurophysiologies, and behavioral economics are inaccessible to our intentional self-understanding. The ethical issues raised by our quantified-selves are, in this respect, not simply the possibility that these selves will be sold to third parties without our consent. The more significant issue might be software companies' exploitation of our paranoid concerns about these self-asymmetries. Algorithmic recommender systems target these insecurities when they collect user data for the purpose of "identifying the susceptibility of a person to arguments and proposals" about their unknown needs and problems, which constitutes "an aggressive marketing attack" from software companies, who claim to have already detected these needs and problems with their algorithms (Cellary and Rykowski 2015: S19).

The primary goal of the recent data-driven behavioral economics is also to target this "consumer vulnerability" (Nadler and McGuigan 2018). No matter how "annoying and unwanted" their suggestions of life-changing solutions seem to be, they become nearly impossible to ignore once we accept the proposition that our consciousness can recognize our needs only with a significant delay of at least several milliseconds or a "missing half-second." According to Mark Hansen (2015a), it is precisely in this interstitial missing time that "twenty-first-century media" finds its most functional niche to deploy an early warning system for our suboptimal states.

For the Internet of Things to expand its service domains to every aspect of our lives, its audiences thus need to be a different kind of tool users from the classical *homo faber*, whose agency has been traditionally characterized by her capability of putting things—including our biological bodies and objects in domestic and urban spaces—under the transformations that she can predict and control. We may remain media users in the IoT, but the way we have symmetrified the things to our intentional manipulations will change. Our being smart within its sensor-actuator arcs rather requires our delegation of the right as tool users to the devices themselves. In short, we should accept that they are smarter than us, better at predicting our needs and employing each other to resolve these needs (Kahn et al. 1999: §4.2). For this, we may need to symmetrify ourselves, our homes, and cities to the transformations that the IoT's smart actuators proactively bring to these environments. The easiest way to do so is to allow the sensors to constantly translate our domestic and urban presence, not to mention our online presence, into data streams subject to machine learning for their hidden correlations, and let the actuators constantly nudge us to keep our quantified-selves always and already in the optimal states for the multiple life activities we may intend to do as it predicts.

***

After the wane of the Enlightenment's grand narrative and its subsequent turn to the epistemological limits of human knowledge, reality as a Kantian concept of subjective construction has experienced constant ruptures and sutures around a slippery object called totality. Following, in addition, the post-modernist conclusion of "the end of the autonomous bourgeois monad or ego or individual" (Jameson 1992: 15) or that of "monadic relativism" in which "each consciousness is a closed world" (412), the autonomy of nonhumans, that is, nonhuman ways of being in the world constructed via manifold inter-objective realities, seems to be the next frontier in critical theory. In this context, the humanities' recent interest in nonhuman agency, such as the *actants* in actor-network theory, *vibrant matters* in Bennet's new materialism, and *objects* in object-oriented ontology, is a search for the theorization of other-worlding in which these things are no longer reduced to mere building blocks but proliferating their own realities according to their nonhuman interests. This somewhat apologetic and liberational gesture in the current ontological turn toward "the agency of things" is, as Mark Andrejevic argues regarding its resonance with the popularity of conspiracy theory in "post-truth politics" (2013: 268, 264), suggestive of a speculative shortcut for thinking about the totality beyond human understanding.

By contrast, this book focuses on how this post-Enlightenment deadlock is in point of fact what many "smart" projects today aim to enlighten their consumers and citizens about. As proponents of the IoT and big data might claim, our attempt to enlighten the lifeworlds, in other words, to symmetrify them to our control, will be foiled by our too human methods of record-keeping (Ashton 2009) and our still habitual method of thinking based on causality, not correlations (Anderson 2008). The enlightened minds of IoT users thus need to shift their attention from epistemology to ontology, from a field that could not offer us any guarantees about ourselves and our worlds to another that is even now being re-written by intensive machine-to-machine communications and suggests the presence of many unknown problems beyond our reach. In short, if there is to be a kind of new ideology for our smart life, it can no longer play make-believe by hiding the real limitations of our perception. It should, rather, overemphasize how restricted our condition is and, in turn, justify our jump to such paranoid speculations that there might be something unknown. This speculation is, however, more than just a convenient shortcut to the totality beyond our reach. Instead, it pushes us to rethink which of the following courses of (in)action is a more rational and economic way to protect our worlds from hidden dangers asymmetrical to human reason: Should we accept to remain always a little paranoid of these dangers without taking any action to resolve it because we are more paranoid of being the victims of invisible surveillance networks? Or isn't it, so to speak, smarter to hand over the right to manage our own bodies, homes, offices, and cities to the IoT's smart objects?

The ontological turn that the Internet of Things brings to our life worlds is similar to that which was recently taken in the humanities, liberating objects from merely being the building blocks of subjects. This turn is operationalized as algorithmic objects, initially designed as human-constructed abstract building blocks of software, begin to reincarnate in silicate bodies and communicate with each other about what they perceive and perform according to their own machinic protocols that computer science now calls ontologies (Gruber 1993). As the title of this book suggests, the small "o" connecting "T" to "I" in the acronym "IoT" indexes the ontologies that smart objects constantly bring to the new Internet, which speak of how the world appears to their data structures. The "o" that represents these ontologies always remains lowercase, because they do not aim to totalize data streams into a self-closed big Ontology but rather hint at the presence of manifold hidden realities which withdraw constantly from our too-human worldviews.

Chapter Summaries

The symmetries and asymmetries of the material substratum of our suboptimal realities to their technological optimizers and our self-understanding, respectively, are the two conditions that reorient the modern Enlightenment project to the nonhuman turn. This fundamental imbalance that asks us to redefine the meaning of our being smart is also the excuse to which the speculative economy of the current software industry and its new regime of dataveillance resort for their continuous extraction of data streams from users. Chapters in *Internet-ontologies-Things* examine these (a)symmetries through what are effectively case studies of media objects, such as smart cars, smart homes, open-world videogames, Brain-Machine Interfaces, and the "found footage" film genre.

Chapter 1, "How Ontology Is Written in the Age of the Internet of Things," scrutinizes the Internet of Things as an intersection of various object-oriented ideas emerging from the recent trends of philosophical, engineering, and consumerist modeling of reality. It analyzes two examples of this intersection: AIDA, a smart in-vehicle navigation system developed by MIT's Senseable City Lab and Audi, and Herman Melville's short story "Bartleby, the Scrivener," a literary prophecy of nonhuman objects in today's smart spaces. In this chapter, the IoT is discussed as operationalizing what some realist philosophers call a flat ontology. Criticizing the anthropocentric correlationism that stipulates objects as mere building blocks for human-constructed realities, these philosophers suggest another way of modeling realities in which every object stands on the same ontological footing with the equal right not to be "treated as constructed by another object" and "contribute to collectives or assemblages to a greater and lesser degree" (Bryant 2012: 19). These philosophical discourses coincide with the current trend toward the automation of algorithmic systems, which demote human users to the biological hosts of data streams that machines communicate. The IoT in this chapter is described as a peculiar commodity form across which these nonhuman realities in philosophical speculation and computer engineering intersect one another.

Chapter 2, "Topology as the New Governmentality of Everyday Life," suggests a topological framework as an analytic tool for the current social spaces enmeshed with smart objects, such as smart homes. This chapter appropriates Bernhard Riemann's differential geometry to redefine a smart home as a topological continuum and Henri Poincaré's group theory to analyze how this continuum unfolds its hidden levels, or problem-spaces, under the transformations the sensor-actuator arcs of the IoT inflict on it. Self-symmetrification, the decision to convert one's body into the data stream symmetrical to the datamining the IoT inflicts, is then framed as a new technique of smart self-management the owner of the smart home may consider.

Chapter 3, "Targeting in Open-World Videogames," examines the recent videogame genre called open-world as a prototype of the cultural interface in the age of the Internet of Things. A gaming space in this genre is built up of manifold algorithmic objects, from non-playable human characters (NPCs) to environmental objects like animals, trees, rocks, and other items. These objects, simply distributed over a world map and left to interact freely according to their own way of responding to the world, are redefining the rules of videogaming today. Gamers are now given a greater degree of freedom to network and repurpose nearby objects for their own goals with minimal restrictions from above. They are, in return, responsible for operationalizing their cultural interests, such as narrative or ludic experiences of gaming, into a form of network strategy. This chapter argues that the cultural platform of videogaming also functions to train people on how to use their freedom to interact with ubiquitous smart objects in today's urban landscape, which is becoming more and more like an open-world videogame as it is increasingly embedded with manifold algorithmic objects.

Chapter 4, "Brain-Machine Interface," further explores the state of human subjects and their freedom in network culture, but with an unorthodox example of a primate videogamer in a laboratory. Brain-Machine Interface (BMI), developed by the Nicolelis Lab at Duke University, is a neuroprosthetic apparatus that translates neural signals collected from multiple sensors hooked up to a primate's brain into machine-readable motor intentions. BMI is a local laboratory network that consists of several human and nonhuman actors: brain cells, electrodes, filtering and pattern recognition algorithms, gaming devices, biological limbs, robotic limbs, and human researchers/ trainers. This chapter discusses how Nicolelis Lab has mobilized these heterogeneous actors for this experimental example of the IoT, which has functioned not only to interface various motor intentions of animal subjects with different robotic limbs but also to translate its workability into the promise of future uses for BMI, such as industrial applications for patient groups, governments, robot industries, and medical institutions. In this respect, Chapter 4 traces an economy of hope that this network of smart objects has mobilized from a multitude of social actors who foresee its expansion from an experimental network in a local lab to the industrial application of the Internet of Things.

Chapter 5, "The Horror of Found Footage and the Speculative Economy of Attention," further discusses the economy of hope introduced in Chapter 4, linking it to the book's conclusion on the speculative economy of the current software industries. Found footage, one of the newest film genres, is characterized not only by its use of ubiquitous camera technologies but, more importantly, as the phenomenon that reflects how humans respond to invisible nonhuman agents in the age of smart objects. In this new horror film genre, camera operators, who are also the main characters, are always searching for something hidden in their everyday lives, such as evil spirits in haunted mansions, witches in a cursed forest, psychopaths in suburban areas, and monsters and aliens everywhere. Their confidence as tool users is, however, soon frustrated, as they discover that they cannot capture these supernatural beings with their shaky handheld cameras. The real dangers always withdraw into their blind spots the moment the would-be filmmakers/protagonists attempt to catch them. In this way, found footage symptomizes the proliferation of hidden dangers everywhere, the ones to which we failed to pay proper attention. It also reflects our generalized feeling of helplessness resulting from the fact that one can never properly control all these ubiquitous cameras simultaneously, which means that we are never able to expel these dangers no matter how many sensors we can access. A sort of speculative economy begins to work from this diagnosis as our boundless speculation about hidden problems gradually overvalues the necessity of algorithmic monitoring of our everyday lives. The more paranoid we become about these formless dangers hidden in our bodies, homes, and urban neighborhoods, the more we feel we need to pay for algorithmic solutions.

Besides these five chapters, there are five intermissions, which touch upon the following issues that the IoT raises: how speculation becomes cognitive labor in the IoT, how ontology functions as the protocol for machine-to-machine communication, how human response-ability is engineered within the sensor-actuator arcs of the IoT, how software interfaces exercise their environmentality, and how human brains are cultivated as the hosts of machine-learnable correlations under the smart headsets for the IoT.

Speculation

In 1999, Kevin Ashton saw the Internet of Things as a new method of data entry for the internet, a shift from that performed entirely by human labors, by "typing, pressing a record button, taking a digital picture or scanning a bar code," to the environmental sensing of autonomous objects (2009). His definition emphasized the user benefits of having computers that "knew everything there was to know about things" and were "able to track and count everything, and greatly reduce waste, loss and cost." At the same time, questions about the human rationale for this transition to the nonhuman practice of data collection were relatively underexplored in his subjunctive description. When does this "everything," Ashton's stand-in for anything, which causes unnecessary "waste, loss, and cost," reappear as an urgent issue that justifies this ubiquitous surveillance at the cost of our data privacy?

Speculation about technologies that almost infinitely extend human knowability to everything has continued apace since the Enlightenment, especially after its bout of Derridean "archive fever" (Hong 2020), that is, the pursuit of boundless Enlightenment, was coupled with the impetus of social changes, currently termed optimization of societies, their capitalist productions, democracies, and securities. However, in the recent resurgence of Enlightenment fever through digital technologies, the zero-tolerance policy of national security in the wake of the September 11th attacks was the most decisive phenomenon in gaining political traction for the IoT's tracking and counting everything approach. Suggesting that "even a single terrorist attack is an unacceptable failure of prediction," zero-tolerance signifies the preemptive logic of counterterrorism in the United States and has justified state agencies' zeal for collecting data about people's everyday lives on a massive scale, the "whole haystack" approach that works under "the assumption that there must be a needle" (Hong 2020: 20, 60). As McClanahan (2009) points out, this data-driven counterterrorism means that probability is no longer the sole criterion for predicting possible terrorist attacks, since preparing for the most probable catastrophic scenarios is not enough on its own. What appeared urgent after 9/11 was instead the proactive search for the missing links between distanced events that could render plausible even the least probable scenarios.

In this respect, the "haystack" metaphor, which former NSA director Keith Alexander (2005–14) used to describe the big data collected about people's everyday lives, is revelatory of how these raw data have, in fact, already been mediated by certain political speculation about the physical reality of how this data collection occurs. For Alexander, zero-tolerance signaled a shift in the haystack/needle metaphor itself, from the impossibility of finding a needle to the imperative nature of this almost impossible search effort, which operates under the condition that even the needle in question could threaten many lives. And, for this effort to be repeatable even without meaningful results, the metaphor also came to illustrate that everything could potentially lead to the prediction of the problem to a varying degree through the hidden equation of missing links between a benign stalk of hay and the malevolent needle. Exemplified in the case of a Bolivian woman subjected to terrorist profiling due to her recent "interest in the purchase of pressure cookers" and many other similar cases (Gabbatt 2013), the banality of hay suggests that even the equation with the weakest links is worth speculating to prevent its catastrophic consequence. As Kirn (2015) wrote in *The Atlantic* about the Snowden leaks in 2013, the excessive vigilance of lurking dangers since 9/11 had formed a certain condition in which "paranoia is the new normal." Paranoia, for Kirn, was primarily driven by people's affective repulsion to the omnipresence of secret surveillance networks (Hong 2020: 38). But this normalization of paranoia as a form of resistance to or detachment from state-driven surveillance meanwhile also obscured its other form, which the haystack imagery internalized as people's mode of cognition in a moment of ubiquitous danger in order to perpetuate their paranoid attachment to the surveillance state. In the context of post-9/11 homeland security, paranoia has in fact functioned as what Sedgwick (2003) calls "a strong theory," preparing the citizenry for any plausible threatening scenarios beyond their knowability, such as hidden terrorist networks in the "ticking bomb scenario" (Hannah 2006), by making them "capable of accounting for a wide spectrum of phenomena which appear to be very remote, one from the other" (Sedgwick 2003: 133–4). This preemptive logic of paranoia was, however, operable only at the huge expense of subjects' ceaseless cognitive labor of generating untestable suspicions about any plausible correlations among distanced events. Suggested by Alexander's haystack was, on the other hand, the rationale to justify paranoid citizens' resignation to state surveillance as the only realistic solution to reassure themselves (Dencik and Cable 2017). Implying a manifold of equations that each hay stalk draws to the hidden needle far beyond human knowability, his imagery positions the ubiquitous surveillance technologies and machine learning of collected data as the only alternative to which the paranoids could delegate their helpless efforts to preempt all imaginable links between tiny local anomalies in their neighborhoods and hidden terrorist attacks. As Hong argues, "the massive expansion of data collection and storage" continued in this context as what he calls *technologies of speculation*, which operate "under the idea that if everything could be tracked about everybody, the hidden correlations to the most unpredictable threats could be disclosed" (2020: 53).

As an earlier application of the IoT's tracking and counting everything approach, the zero-tolerance policy thus suggests how its opportunity cost, namely the disclosure of personal data, is compensable not so much by actual preemptions of terrorist attacks, which have not been that effective (Logan 2017), but by the resignation of the people who believe the needle is real and that only secret networks of smart surveillance could greatly reduce the waste, loss, and cost of their paranoid concerns. While this "state of exception precipitated by the terrorist attacks of 9/11 produced surveillance exceptionalism," for the software companies like "Google and other rising surveillance capitalists," to whom data collection and analyses were outsourced in a way to guarantee their own "paranoid style" of "self-management regimes that imposed few limits on corporate practices," the war on terror meant, on the other hand, the opportunity for "further enabling the new market to root and flourish" (Zuboff 2019). And, as nicknames for the current commercial IoT like the Internet of Everything (Evans 2012) and Everywear (Greenfield 2006) exemplify, surveillance is no longer an exceptional condition in the boom years of this new data business. A mild form of paranoia is now the normative state of media audiences since the inaccessibility by narrow human perception is a common feature of the problems that software companies commercialize and assume to be literally everywhere, from one's body, home, car, and office to an entire city. In many of these domains, of course, the problems are not quite life-threatening—a smart home is designed more to inform our decision-making and optimize our domestic lives, not for preventing a terrorist attack (as discussed in Chapter 2). But, even in these everyday conditions, the inefficiencies that need to be optimized, not to mention hidden symptoms of health problems detected by smart wearables, are now enmeshed with people's nonconscious behaviors, which can be tracked, counted, and analyzed only through ubiquitous sensors embedded in their daily routines. The paranoia that Kirn defined as a defensive reaction to surveillance is, therefore, also at work in these commercial domains. Cheney-Lippold writes that "in most instances of algorithmic identification, we are seen, assessed, and labeled through algorithmic eyes" and "affected by the thought, we know that something else is going on, but we're not exactly sure what it may be" (2017: 24). If we accept that addressing these issues is worth living with a subtle but constant unease, this reactive form of paranoia would then be convertible to a proactive gesture to prepare ourselves more properly for unknown problems. In this respect, everything being the emerging domain of the commercial IoT shares with hidden terrorist networks the appearance, under the post-9/11 mentality and recent trend of commodifying efficiency/optimality, of what Morton (2013) calls *hyperobjects*: objects felt immediate to human lives but always withdrawing $1 + n$ dimensions away from human knowability. While for Morton the climate is the most distinguishable hyperobject of the current time, the haystack, a metaphor for any domain of massive dataveillance, signifies that these hyperobjects are now everywhere as problems that require the IoT's tracking and counting everything approach. The more people attempt to grasp the needles embedded in this infinite haystack, the more they feel trapped in bottomless speculations about hidden correlations between every tiny detail in their surroundings and some unknown threat—that is, unless a certain actor smarter than humans eventually takes over this paranoid practice of self-surveillance. While facing this sort of problem, as Morton (2013) argues regarding climate change, postponing immediate action or refusing to pay for suggested solutions by insisting we need more than mere speculation is not rational behavior; given the imminence of its harmful manifestations, it is even hypocrisy. For other security and lifestyle issues, less catastrophic but still optimizable only by harvesting big data about people's collective behaviors, this responsibility for immediate action is rephrased as the reason why the decision "to opt out of a data commons" to protect one's privacy could cause a "free-rider problem" or betray "data philanthropy" (Espinoza and Aronczyk 2021). The providers of commercial IoT services today seem to know that these speculations are exploitable as the means to compensate for the IoT's opportunity cost of disclosure of personal data, and thus the common narratives of their white papers, usually begin with such diagnoses: "Cities and communities around the world face intractable challenges" (Falconer and Mitchell 2012: 2). "There are a lot of significant interrelated challenges ... that are interrelated and need to be dealt with in a holistic way" (Kulesa and Dirks 2009: 2). But "there's also good news ... full of pervasive technologies such as sensors or networks ... allow us to measure, to monitor, to manage and to optimize our use of finite resources ... to understand the interrelationship between systems" (4). As Hu (2015: 124) puts it, "a paranoid worldview" forms the affective background for smart objects to infiltrate into their commercial IoT domains "in which everything is hopelessly complex but, with the right (data) tools, can be made deceptively simple and explainable."

In this narrative setup, the invisible narrators or salespersons of the white papers mobilize users' speculation to maintain the connections between the two kinds of objects that are beyond human control: hyperobjects and smart objects. Moreover, the term *speculation* is used in current speculative realism in a manner that may allow us to redefine it as a common practice of realist sense-making. Graham Harman's object-oriented ontology (2005) articulates this most clearly, explaining that speculation is an ontological concern of things that constantly withdraw from any access of human or nonhuman actors but leave a residue for these actors to communicate about the world beyond their accessibilities. In a critique of contemporary realisms, Galloway (2013) points out how coincident this philosophical speculation about things' elusiveness—both limiting an actor's access and promising her further communicability beyond the limit—is with the recent "software companies reliant on object-oriented infrastructures" (351). He further alludes to a complicity between "the structure of ontological systems and the structure of the most highly evolved technologies of post-Fordist capitalism" (347). Chapter 1 follows this argument, exploring how this speculation as a purely ontological concern in philosophy is also converted into a sort of economic concern among IoT users and software developers. For these groups, the hyperobjects that they perceive most strongly as constantly withdrawing from their understanding include things like terrorism, climate change, viruses, minds, and all other unknown dangers and needs, which they also increasingly believe to be redirected to the predictable ranges of the IoT's algorithmic preemption.

As to the similarity between the works of entrepreneurs in the "creative industry" and artists in the contemporary post-conceptual arts, Vishmidt (2018) suggests "speculation as a mode of production," characterized by a common process of "gather[ing] all kinds of data and material and reproduc[ing] them" into a product, which is subject to "infinite self-realisation without guarantees"

(4, 18). On the other hand, the speculation I redefine here is a form of cognitive labor common to audiences as prosumers and characterized by its ontological leap beyond human perceptibility. In this respect, it is more comparable to another cognitive labor still dominant on the internet: attention. As a form of "immaterial labor" reflective of the real subsumption of human cognition under capital (Lazzarato 1996), attention is said to produce real values exchangeable in media industries, especially for advertisers, just as Beller (2006) analyzes its industrial production-like process in the human mind. Provoked conversely by hyperobjective problems we always fail to pay proper attention to, what our speculation adds to the big data collected by smart sensors about our surroundings are yet fictitious values. And to make sustainable our investment of personal data in the fictitious future where all the elusive problems are already preempted, the IoT also needs to let its smart actuators constantly re-stimulate physical domains to draw some profitable responses there, potentially correlatable to the problems under search.

How Ontology Is Written in the Age of the Internet of Things

Before the IoT, the internet was "almost wholly dependent on" human inputs, "not very good at capturing data about things in the real world" (Ashton 2009). The recent miniaturization of sensors, processors, and actuators and their attachments to various natural and technical objects have, however, made data extraction available not only from smart appliances, such as refrigerators and televisions responding to users and environments, but from the territorial/ migratory behaviors of animals (Gabrys 2016a) and physiological patterns of human organs (Parisi 2009). Just as the digital remediates the incompatibility of analog signals through its binary codes (Bolter and Grusin 1999), these smart and sticky computational objects relocate the things that once operated in each different context of their domestic lives, ecologies, and metabolisms to the same communicational platform.

Around the same time as the early conceptualization of the IoT, actor-network theory (ANT) has suggested to media studies a critical tool to rethink the conventional boundaries of subject/object, human/nonhuman, cultural/ natural, social/technological categories no longer as some higher orders or contexts to define the places of things in hierarchies. Actor-networks are when these categories turn into historical sediments of each thing's way to influence and respond to another as their mutual engagements in the making come to the fore of our attention. The IoT's "new sensor/processor/actuator affiliations" (Crandall 2010: 83–4), in this respect, expose hidden actor-networks of things in our lifeworld, which have been black-boxed by the habitual contexts of our uses of the things taken to be the only typology of their use values. As these things are now enrolled in a nonhierarchal communication structure of the IoT, the contexts of their human uses are also "unboxed" and their usefulness is re-measured in a digital network, not so much for their contribution to our self-imposed goals but for the network's prediction of our nonconscious needs.

Marx thought the use value of commodities is realizable only through their consumption for human needs at "a terminal point" of exchange (1993: 89), such as one's non-smart home. But in the IoT and its domestic application, value is conversely concretized by the exchange of thing-generated signals between smart objects, whose smartness is often advertised as their ability to detect the urgent needs of users even before the users recognize their own needs. John Law says a black box is reopened when "a stronger adversary, one better able to associate elements," appears (2012: 111). According to this "principle of symmetry," the IoT might also unbox the previous contexts of the human uses of nonhuman beings, or their monopoly of the right to define the functionality of objects if it is true that the IoT is more capable than humans of reassembling smart objects into the networks that address human needs. Marx put aside the human consumption of commodities as "outside economics except in so far as it reacts in turn upon the point of departure [in the form of what they reproduce namely *living labor*] and initiates the whole process anew" in the labor market (1993: 89). This reductionist interpretation of use value, based entirely on human "needs as biologically given and the natural" (Dant 1996: 501), has been denaturalized by cultural critics such as Baudrillard (1981) as their unboxing of human needs and desires out of "pure, natural, asocial" cocoons has relocated the concept of use value to "a system of relations of difference with other objects" (Dant 1996: 504). However, while this revisionist view of use value as "a fetishized social relation just as much as exchange-value" (Dant 1996: 504) still defines the social exclusively as the human construction,[1] the IoT, as one of the most advanced commodity forms today, pushes its users to agree with its "terms of use" suggesting why humans should delegate their right to using objects for their own needs to smart objects themselves as they are better at actuating each other in more customized ways to human needs. If domestic space in Marxian thinking was an example of this *outside economics* for our inalienable right as *tool users*, the delegation of the human right the IoT requires is to reopen and reconnect this private sphere to the economy of digital signals. And human users are the only smart beings whose access to this hidden economy is denied while other smart objects freely exchange queries and answers about their not-smart-enough human hosts.

This actor-network description of the IoT with this reversed user-object relation is suggestive of a structure of an ontological system that some recent realist philosophers, such as speculative realists, call flat ontology, characterized by its radical liquidation of any hierarchies among things.[2] This chapter examines how this new ontology of objects is resonant with the current media industry's attempt to expand its serviceable domains even to the speculative realities of autonomous objects. For these philosophers, the autonomy of objects is required for the "absolute truth" of reality to be redeemed from the subjective construction in anthropocentric "correlationism" (Meillassoux 2008: 5). However, today's use of the term *ontology* in computer science as the protocol for machine-to-machine communication[3] implies that the construction of inter-objective realities solely through the objects' mutual accesses and interoperations, regardless of how they are used and accessed by humans, is rather a commercial requirement for the presence of such computational problems that humans cannot access but are still manageable by the objects' environment-sensitive autonomous operations. In this respect, the Internet of Things provides a starting point for a critical inquiry that Galloway once raised about "a coincidence between the structure of ontological systems and the structure of the most highly evolved technologies of post-Fordist capitalism" (2013: 347).

To recontextualize this coincidence, this chapter focuses on how the architectures of algorithmic systems have changed over the past decades as programmers and users have delegated their grasp on computing machines' operational environments—databases or physical sources of input data—to some algorithmic agents better able than humans to reassemble the optimal networks to respond to the environmental changes. This chapter discusses two cases of algorithmic systems that concern this shift: Herman Melville's *Bartleby, the Scrivener: A Story of Wall-street* and the MIT Sensible City Lab's Affective Intelligent Driving Agent. This unorthodox comparison of a literary text and a media application aims to relocate Melville's problematic character Bartleby to a capitalist version of flat ontology the story illustrates through his nonhuman use of nonhuman beings, such as miscellaneous office suppliers on his desk. In Marxist criticism of the last century, Bartleby has been understood as the "perfect exemplum" of *dehumanized* workers under industrial capitalism, for whom no other choice than participating in the commodity exchange is allowed to realize their living labor. Melville's story restages this condition through its algorithmic distribution of "speculative-conditional" statements or the "logic of the 'if … then' statement" to define his possible usability in certain conditions of an office (Reed 2004: 258). Bartleby's famous response, "I would prefer not to," has been interpreted in this context as a gesture "to get out of circulation entirely," to the "space outside or beyond circulation," never achievable "except, of course, through death" (266). What this chapter's re-reading of his gesture focuses on is, however, not this suicidal exit to the "humanity" outside commodity exchange but his sneaking into the edges of an employer's algorithmic human resource distribution. Put differently, Bartleby's withdrawal to the peripheries of commodity exchange is to *nonhumanize* himself as an object not ontologically superior to other office supplies with which he persists in creating a secret network of nonhumans unseen by the employer. Redefined as one of these objects whose interoperations retrieve the office from the human employer's exclusive use of nonhumans, Bartleby prophesies and incarnates the autonomous algorithmic objects that prevail in current smart offices. As the following section discusses, these objects, as the building blocks of today's algorithmic cultures, construct their nonhuman ontologies not only for ubiquitous computing of hidden human problems but also for their *nonhuman use of human beings* as the sources of data streams.

Correlationism and Pan-Correlationism

In 1986, Friedrich Kittler anticipated the IF-THEN commands in computer languages would substitute for the symbolic order of human discourses as these "conditional jump instructions" would translate one's free will into a cybernetic servomechanism. For him, the IF-THEN command represented the computational logic of early cybernetics, which analyzed human behaviors, including language, as "cruise missile"-like variables whose linear trajectories are conditioned by simple feedback loops executable in a linear manner (1999: 258). In contrast, Katherine Hayles recently argued how today's technical infrastructure, which she calls "a cognitive assemblage," is consisting of many autonomous "technical cognizers" capable of tracking objects that behave like "highly mobile and flexible insurgents and 'terrorists'" (2017: 132).[4] Distributed in a swarm-like state, the modularity of these cognizers is designed to form an assemblage flexible enough not only to adapt to the changeable environments— like the US military drone swarms targeting actual human guerillas—but to cultivate the things enmeshed with its environmental sensors and actuators into the nodes of a potential network. In her analysis of Frans van der Helm's media performance *MeMachine*, for instance, a human body in "a high-tech data suit outfitted with sensors," such as electrocardiography (ECG), electromyography (EMG), and electroencephalography (EEG), is transformed into a source of manifold vital signals that these technical cognizers communicate with one another to form a local network under the fabrics (ARlab 2013; Hayles 2017: 129–30). This shift between Kittler and Hayles and their ways to conceptualize human behaviors as certain computational problems—from those drawing linear trajectories to displaying more distributed patterns—is noteworthy as it has also coincided with the relocation of human users from their previous positions as input typers or clickers outside of user interfaces to the sources of data streams in-between machine-to-machine interfaces. Most of all, this shift has been spurred by the elusive patterns of user-generated signals hardly caught in IF-THEN commands. And software industries have also had enough reason to exaggerate this elusiveness as the source of unknown problems in users' everyday lives insofar as the only candidate to catch up with this slipperiness of the new computational problems is the unlimited networkability of smart objects into each different algorithmic sensor-actuator arc replacing habitual sensorimotor responses of humans. Just as the ubiquitous dangers of guerilla-like intelligence present the problems to which only a military network of drones, called drone swarm, is (claimed to be) capable of proactively responding, smart technologies, such as smart clothes, also transform users' bodies and behaviors into the things full of unknown problems manageable only through the ubiquitous computing under the fabrics. And reframing of computational problems in general for the universal application of ubiquitous computing is how the IoT brackets its usability as a matter of speculation whose fictitious value is realizable only through the experimental reassemblage of its sensor-actuator arcs for any imaginable computational problems within data streams.

Algorithms have been marketed as efficient and automatized circuit-change technologies that can be applied to any goal-oriented process from industrial production to domestic reproduction. And both human bodies and nonhuman objects were, in their previous cybernetic modeling as servomechanisms, thought to be optimally aligned with certain algorithmic orders by means of proper discursive protocols or hardwired IF-THEN circuits that designated their proper places of consumption or employment (such as a workplace for human bodies to be reassigned as living labors and a house for the objects to be deployed for reproducing human labors). However, enmeshed with IoT sensors and actuators in the current smart spaces, they are rather encouraged to perform their spontaneous routines than being assigned to predefined positions for the programmed goals. This higher degree of freedom given to the things in-between was once the cause of inefficiency in the previous IF-THEN-based processes. But the speculative nature of the IoT's use value and its promise of future assemblages of things as yet unrealized always suffice to compensate for any temporary inefficiencies in restricted goal-oriented deployments of things. In a smart home, for instance, a software application to optimize its atmosphere to a given goal by the user—such as having perfect meditation—may need a certain preparatory period to figure out her preferred temperature, brightness, humidity, genre of BGM, etc. for the intended activity from her routine interactions with smart appliances, such as a smart thermostat, lights, humidifier, speaker, and so forth. And it would not be until after this (ever) delayed promise is fulfilled that the system eventually discovers the most optimal way to reassemble these devices according to the home's *meditation parameter*, a computational problem that would be machine-learned from an equation consisting of these environmental variables and her EEG-scanned meditation practices. Insofar as there always remain some other parameters that can be correlated to any other activities the user is not yet aware she would soon intend to do, the fictitious use value of a smart home is open to constant re-realization through her subscriptions to more IoT-driven optimization services.

From Kittler's "cruise missile" to Hayles' "highly mobile and flexible insurgents," or from the deterministic order of procedural programming to the experimental openness of ubiquitous computing, change has been, I argue, the character of correlations that a software system requires to exist between its operational environment—user inputs, databases, or anything streaming data—and its algorithms—a series of IF-THEN commands in a source code or recombinable sensor-actuator arcs of the IoT. Cybernetics' early emphasis on the feedback mechanism has somewhat defined the autonomy of an intelligent system as its operational closure, meaning its recurrent turning back to readiness for processing new inputs after finishing the previous until the input for termination is given and, from this concern, the human programmer should engineer, ahead of any test runs, a priori correspondence of the environment to the data structures through which the system reconstructs its reality. On the other hand, the environmental parameters under ubiquitous computing are not defined a priori but are gradually generated from autonomous interoperations of smart objects as indicative of hidden correlations between the objects' actuations and the environment's responses. Let me call the former approach the *correlationist* modeling of computational reality following how speculative realists use the term *correlation* to criticize Kantian philosophy of subjective construction. And then the latter could be termed the *pan-correlationist* following how Alex Galloway criticizes the speculative realism's complicity with current software capitalism.

Pan-correlationism for Galloway describes how Graham Harman's object-oriented ontology (OOO) democratizes *relation* "by disseminating it to all entities" liberated from the subjective construction of reality that has long monopolized the meaning of relation (2014 November). As a self-claimed disciple of Bruno Latour, Harman recognizes actor-network theory's contribution to this democratization but, at the same time, as a proponent of the self-identical concept of object, he disagrees with ANT's radical relationism in which anything cannot be present as an actor even to itself until its continuous influences on the others are noticeable within a network in the making (Law 2012). Object-orientation is, in this respect, Harman's theoretical framework to restore the speculative autonomy of objects against the dissipative force of relationism, and what he takes instead as definitive for an object's becoming self-identical is its constant withdrawal from others to its own mysterious inside, which "contains unknown realities never touched by any or all of its relations" (2009: 132). By doing so he achieves two goals. First, objects are no longer exhausted by any correlationist others, either humans or nonhumans, which attempt to monopolize all the inter-objective relations within the network for the construction and expansion of human-centered realities or technoscientific networks. In OOO, "relations do not exhaust a thing" (2009) as it always preserves some hidden realities to withdraw further into. At the same time, insofar as relations are the consequences of objects' mutual entanglements only through their constant withdrawals from one another, there always remain more relations to be extracted between any objects as they always hide more insides to withdraw further. According to Galloway, these mysterious objects capable of surviving both Kantian correlationism and ANT's relationism are, however, still open to pan-correlationism, a sort of capitalist relationism that repurposes Harmanian assumption of the inexhaustible insides of objects into the promise of the inexhaustible correlations ever extractable from "the sensual skin of exchange value" that each object's withdrawal leaves behind (Galloway 2012).

As "the structure of the most highly evolved technologies of post-Fordist capitalism" (Galloway 2013: 347), ubiquitous computing also transforms its operational environment into a sort of speculative reality suggesting ubiquitous correlations. Like Harman's OOO, object-orientation as a "computational logic" (Kowalski 2011) in computer science defines objects as each self-identical agent with its own "beliefs (what the agent knows), desires (what the agent wants) and intentions (what the agent is doing) at its core" (Jennings 2000: 288). As the IoT affords more autonomous and experimental interoperations of reincarnated objects, this logic currently promises the inexhaustibility of data streams, extractable from any sensor-augmented things and then transmittable as inputs to other smart objects without letting any linear modeling of single objects exhaust their hidden correlations. In this respect, pan-correlationism also suggests how resonant the anti-correlationism of the speculative realists is, in fact, with the more common usages of the term *correlation* in big datamining. As Chris Anderson once claimed as the editor of *Wired*, correlation now manifests the end of "causation" as the human means of "crude approximations of the truth" (2008) and is assumed to be discovered from anything data-minable but subject-object relations. As a speculative turn the software industries recently took, the IoT thus updates the previous capitalist ontology, which Heidegger once characterized by industries' "challenging-forth" of "the world, nature, culture, etc. as available for extraction, processing and storing as standing reserve"; the new ontology of software capitalism is, as David Berry illustrates, for the capital's "streaming-forth" of everything as available for data streaming and mining as standing reserve of correlations (2014: 96).

The blueprint of the current age of ubiquitous computing was, in some respect, already presented in the 1970s with the new semantics of early object-oriented computer languages, which Alan Kay, the architect of *Smalltalk*, an early OOP language, described as "a bit like having thousands and thousands of computers all hooked together by a very fast network" (1993: 70). According to Kay, objects as the "behavioral building blocks" in OOP "have much in common with the monads of Leibniz" (70) as each object also enfolds definitions of its own constituents, data structures, and possible interoperations with others. Put differently, an object envelops its own "tiny ontology" that states its selective exposures and responses to the environments (Bogost 2012: 21). To build an algorithmic system for object-oriented programmers is thus to distribute these objects in certain sequential or recursive orders in a source code instead of the cumbersome IF-THEN commands in procedural programming. And the compiling of the source code is when these objects are exposed and respond to their operational environments and, in turn, gradually evolve into a cognitive assemblage. However, despite this seeming networkability of the objects, their interoperations during the compiling on a personal computer are, in fact, designed as a sort of pre-established harmony as a human programmer needs to put them in designated locations in the first place to ensure that their object-to-object communications occur in a predetermined order.

However, the networkability that some real-world objects currently earn as they are embedded with tiny sensors, processors, and actuators of the IoT is enabling more experimental reassemblages of the objects. Rather than implying the pre-established harmonies human programmers project, the correlations that reassemble the IoT's sensor-actuator arcs are now unfolded from these objects' corporeal interactions with one another just as a drone swarm constantly updates its flying formation from the aerodynamic data each drone's interactions with others generate. The operational environment of an algorithmic system is thus no longer simply a metaphor for "human-entered data" but means the ubiquity of data that can be extracted from any interactions of physically distributed objects. These objects may remain pre-programmed in their noncomputational source codes of biology, physiology, ethology, ecology, social behaviorism, and so forth until they are brought to a flat digital ontology of the IoT. And these separate contexts, to which each thing's function has been restricted, are the problems that the IoT aims to unbox through its digital translation of the things' actor-network-like relation-making across the contexts. Meanwhile, the things once stabilized in their own contexts also resume their individuations on this digital platform as they are exposed to the new selective pressure that pushes them to find new functional niches in algorithmic cultures. For instance, your heart, muscles, and brain, already stabilized in your metabolism, myology, and neurophysiology, could be now relocated to a digital network under a "smart cloth" outfitted with ECG, EMG, and EEG. Their resumed individuations to the new digital niches have nothing to do with the pre-established correlation between your body and mind under your conscious or reflexive control. Rather, they can be correlated further to other digital objects sneaking under the cloth forming the IoT's sensor-actuator arcs, such as the Apple Watch or Fitbit, better than yourself at telling when you need to stand up, take a deep breath, slow the pace down, and so on to optimize your workout. Human organs are not simply deployed within a servomechanism in this sense but constantly re-individuate themselves to renew their temporal niches and uses within nonhuman networks.

From this changed usability of human bodies, Bartleby's gesture to disconnect himself from any capitalist uses of human beings by saying, "I would prefer not to" do anything assigned by the human employer may earn a new ontological meaning. His gesture can be reinterpreted as a prophecy of recent smart objects and their withdrawals into the peripheries of human control.

Bartleby, the Scrivener

The first quarter of this short story about a law office on Wall Street in the 1850s is devoted to describing the functional relations among the three employees, which the lawyer, the first-person narrator, says he could have successfully maintained until the new employee, Bartleby, brought too much disturbance.

The employees' nonhuman-like nicknames—Turkey, Nippers, and Ginger Nut—are what they "mutually conferred upon each other" because they are "deemed expressive of their respective persons or characters" (par.6). For instance, it is Ginger Nut's job to deliver "ginger-cake" to Turkey and Nippers, whose performances of "copying law papers" are complementary to each other because the former is reliable only in the morning, whereas the latter works well only in the afternoon. For the lawyer once confident in reorganizing their different responses, to make the office operational for his own goal is thus to distribute these workers according to a procedural sequence: "it being morning, Turkey's answer is couched in polite and tranquil terms, but Nippers replies in ill-tempered ones ... to repeat a previous sentence, Nippers's ugly mood was on duty, and Turkey's off" (par.45); to paraphrase in an object-oriented pseudo-code, IF it is morning, THEN call Turkey or ELSE call Nipper. The lawyer's "doctrine of assumptions" is applied everywhere in the office insofar as he can predict how each actor will respond in certain conditions, and it enables him "to enlist the smallest suffrage in [his] behalf" (par.155, 46). Following these pre-established correlations that the lawyer projects, Ginger Nut contributes to the system by circulating ginger-cake, which in turn demonstrates its functionality through "probable effects upon the human constitution" of Turkey and Nippers (par.52), whose functions as scriveners alternate in the morning and afternoon.

However, this seamless circuit-switching ceases to work after the lawyer hires Bartleby, a new scrivener "more a man of preferences than assumptions," whose recalcitrant personality is characterized by his highly selective response of "prefer[ing] not to do" any other tasks than transcribing law papers "at the usual rate of four cent a folio" (par.83). In the middle of the story, Bartleby begins to narrow his response further to the extent of preferring not to answer any queries from the lawyer and finally ceasing to produce any human readable texts. At this point, the lawyer, as an algorithm builder, has the following conversation with Bartleby:

"Now what sort of business would you like to engage in? Would you like to re-engage in copying for some one?"

"No, I would prefer not to make any change."

"Would you like a clerkship in a dry-goods store?" ...

"I would prefer not to take a clerkship," he rejoined, as if to settle that little item at once.

"How would a bar-tender's business suit you? There is no trying of the eyesight in that."

"I would not like it at all; though, as I said before, I am not particular." ...

"Well then, would you like to travel through the country collecting bills for the merchants? That would improve your health."

"No, I would prefer to be doing something else."

"How then would going as a companion to Europe, to entertain some young gentleman with your conversation,—how would that suit you?"

"Not at all. It does not strike me that there is anything definite about that. I like to be stationary. But I am not particular."

(par.197–209)

ANT's *principle of symmetry* states that "all the elements that go to make up a heterogeneous network, whether these elements are devices, natural forces, or social groups," can make themselves present as actors only "by influencing the structure of the network in a noticeable and individual way" (Law 2012: 124–6). As I argued above, this principle also implies that any actors withdrawing from their current networks should be enrolled in another network "better able to associate elements" (111) unless they prefer not to return any noticeable responses and thus not to be present as actors any longer to others. Let me interpret Bartleby's preference *not to do something else* as the expression of his fatigue over remaining such a thing unable to be present at all if not assigned to a functional niche in the office or outside labor markets according to the lawyer's "doctrine of assumptions."[5] His strategy to respond to any queries by saying, "I prefer not to" is then the minimum that an actor needs to contribute as the noticeable influence on the current network it stays in. As a *dehumanized* object stuck within the algorithmic human resource management, Bartleby's gesture to postpone his reassignment to particular is to unbox the apparently seamless commodity exchange in the labor market. The lawyer's subsequent and never-ending IF-THEN questions—"would you like to re-engage in ...? Well then, would you ...? How then would ...?"—are, in turn, the maximum the employer needs to do to black-box again the formal symmetry of the capitalist uses of human beings.

The lawyer's attempts to find a new niche for Bartleby, however, turn out to be undertaken always too late after Bartleby has already declared his preference not to do that work. And when Bartleby is proved unable to be handled by the servo-mechanical "logic of the 'if ... then' statement," the lawyer discovers a secret network of nonhumans in which Bartleby's withdrawal finds the smallest niche for his presence: a "bachelor's hall" that "Bartleby has been making" with things hidden at the peripheries of the lawyer's attention, such as "a blanket" under his desk rolled away, "blacking box and brush" under the empty grate, "a tin basin, with soap and a ragged towel" on a chair, "a few crumbs of ginger-nuts and a morsel of cheese" in a newspaper (par.88). Shortly after Bartleby declares his presence in the office despite his refusal to accept any of the new positions the lawyer recommends, these objects once believed to be under the lawyer's "doctrine of assumptions" reappear to form an alternative network in which each thing's presence is concretized not through the lawyer's monopoly of (non)human resources but through their mutual engagement at the peripheries of capitalist resource distribution. Contrary to the traditional interpretations of Bartleby's gesture as a suicidal disconnect from any social ties, what he really achieves through his withdrawal, other than the redemption of humanity "through death" (Reed 2004: 266), is the retrieval of social ties among nonhumans from capital's dehumanizing *correlationism* or from its reduction of every object, including human labor, to either exchange or use value to preserve or increase capital. According to Harman's object-oriented complement of ANT, objects' withdrawals into their inner realities "never touched by any or all of [their] relations" are enough for their presence without being mobilized for the businesses of others (Harman 2009: 132). These withdrawals also suffice to let the ubiquitous distances between the objects be filled with finer-grained relations as "the joints and glue that hold the universe together" (2005: 20). Bartleby's disappearance into the peripheries of commodity exchange likewise finds a hidden society of nonhumans in which he is finally on an equal footing with everything else. Through the lawyer's lost confidence in assuming the possible uses of Bartleby, Melville's story dramatizes the conflict between the correlationist construction of reality by a human employer as the avatar of old capitalism and the pan-correlationist network-making across distributed nonhumans and through their mutual engagements. But his story fails to anticipate how vulnerable these nonhumans are to the finer-grained resource management algorithms under advanced capitalism and how the new avatar of capitalism will come, 150 years later, in the form of these distributed nonhumans called *smart objects.*

Ontic Principle of Ubiquitous Computing

Mark Weiser defines ubiquitous computing as when microprocessors withdraw from the center of users' attention toward the peripheries and communicate more with one another (Weiser and Brown 1997). Information technologies before ubiquitous computing, such as "pagers, cellphones, newservices, the World-Wide-Web, email, TV, and radio," were designed to "bombard us frenetically" to draw our attention to their presence in a human-centered network of things (79). Like Turkey claiming his functionality to the lawyer even in the afternoon when he in fact does not function well by asking, "if his services in the morning were useful, how indispensable, then, in the afternoon?" (par. 6), these machines appealed for their usefulness to human users who held a strong grip on what ANT calls the "Obligatory Passage Point (OPP)" of the network: the point all participants should pass through to get registered as the actors contributing to the network (Callon 1986: 205–6). On the other hand, smart objects, which no longer compete for human attention, rather prefer to stay "calm" in the periphery of attention as Bartleby does. And the secret "confederacy" they form as they "whisper information to one another in inaudible frequencies" about their users is not just for letting them ready to reoccupy the center of our attention as we call them out (just as Weiser's original design intended) but to let them "conspire to sell us products" and services in a timelier manner (Andrejevic 2005: 113–14).

In their withdrawal to these peripheries, smart objects are just performing the minimum for their enrollment as sensors, namely *scrivening* "unmodulated digital data" from their operational environments. But for their proper alignments within certain sensor-actuator arcs temporarily assembled for each different IoT application, something needs to be still busy with examining these ambient data and updating its doctrine of assumption about which object's actuation would be the most contributing under different conditions to different goals (Clemens and Nash 2015). Unlike the lawyer's helpless IF-THEN instructions in Melville's story, the IoT's ubiquitous computing is capable of and patient with performing this never-ending job assignment to figure out the most optimal arrangement of smart objects for the problems at the system level. In this sense, what becomes ubiquitous in the UC era are not only the symmetrical edges of the network for the objects' horizontal communications but their asymmetrical engagements with a collective intelligence that functions to stabilize conflicting objects into the reciprocal and modular functions of the network. As Galloway writes, "no arbiter impedes" these objects at the level of machine-to-machine communication, but for their autonomous responses to one another to be gradually realigned in the most efficient and harmonious way to reach collective goals, a sort of "ultimate mystical medium" is still assumed to operate as an invisible hand (2012). In the Personal Computing (PC) era, human users could still perform this arbiter role as they monopolized the obligatory passage point of the system at the time, namely the graphical user interface, or GUI, which enabled them to design the harmonious interoperations of algorithmic agents for their conscious goals. On the other hand, the mystical arbiters in the UC era are rather omnipresent in the form of ubiquitous computing across microprocessors everywhere, and the harmony is no longer pre-established by the assumptions of human designers but, like the flying formation of a drone swarm, constantly updated from the ubiquitous correlations between each object's actuation and how the environment responds (that the sensors stream-forth).

Regarding this new image of the organic whole these inorganic actors generate, Harman's object-oriented ontology can provide only a limited account as it leaves "countless tiny vacuums" between any objects withdrawing from one another. On the other hand, Whitehead's process philosophy and his concept of *actual entity* suggest another ontological modeling that could turn "the universe of things" in the UC era into "a finely articulated plenum" of data for its collective and creative individuation (Shaviro 2015: 39). While OOO considers the mysterious cores of each withdrawing object as the inexhaustible resources for worldly relations, the becoming of actual entities for Whitehead finds its resources from the "multifold datum" that other entities' already finished becomings have left in the universe. And, contrary to the constant withdrawals of Harmanian objects, each entity's becoming is usually lasting only for a fleeting moment while it prehends the universe according to its own "subjective form" through the process he calls "concrescence," and after completing its "subjective aim," this entity then immediately perishes back into the universe as the part of its datum for other entities' further datamining (Whitehead 1978: 19, 27, 185). In this respect, the speculative presence of actual entities in Whiteheadian ontology seems to provide a philosophical analogy for algorithmic objects, which also occur as cognitive agents only for limited durations while they process input data and then influence other objects only by means of what they already performed, namely the changes in the shared data environments to be processed further by others. However, considering that each actual entity's concrescence is not influenced by any others but its own assumption on the "harmony" between its subjective forms and objective data it feels (27), a source code written by a human programmer as the sequential or recursive orders of objects is not analogous enough with the universe open to the creative evolution in Whiteheadian philosophy. The smart objects in the IoT could be, on the other hand, a better candidate for the technical incarnation of his actual entities as their fleeting actuations generate enormous data streams with some yet-unknown correlations for other objects' becoming contributing to different software applications.

Besides this structural similarity, it is noteworthy how Whitehead's "secularization of the concept of God" (207) as none other than one of these entities also supports the analogy's feasibility. While all the other entities' concrescences are temporal and short-lived, the Whiteheadian God is characterized by its never-completed concrescence. It is because God's subjective aim is "the ultimate unity" between the entire multiplicities of actual entities it senses and its conceptual prehension of their ideal harmony "in such a perfect system" (346). And this is inevitably an ever-delayed goal insofar as God cannot determine the courses of other entities' becoming but is only able to induce or nudge them to adjust their subjective aims. Taking the position of this global but not omnipotent agent in the analogy, what a ubicomp system aims, namely the algorithmic calculation of the optimal interoperations of smart objects for systemic goals, is also a never-completed process that must be constantly updated from each object's actual operation without any pre-given harmony.

This secularized understanding of God is decisive for Whitehead's philosophy to remain as nonhierarchical as Harman's flat ontology. Thus, as Shaviro emphsizes, "all actual entities in the [Whiteheadian] universe stand on the same ontological footing," and even God for Whitehead has "no special ontological privileges" over the most trivial entities "in spite of" the asymmetrical "gradations of importance, and diversities of function" among entities (Shaviro 2015: 29). However, unlike media studies' recent focus on this implicit flatness in Whiteheadian ontology (Gabrys 2016a; Hansen 2015a; Parisi 2009), what makes his philosophy a really better analogy for the emerging universe of things called IoT than OOO are, in fact, these gradations of importance and functionality that indicate the persistent existence of asymmetries among the things in the networks. The particular entity standing at the apex of the gradations was once called God but now reappears in the form of ubiquitous computing. And its never-ending *concresence* as a global intelligence intervenes in all the other entities' temporal *concresence* as each node of its network. Rather than assigning each entity one by one to a specific place already prepared—which Melville's lawyer attempted but failed—ubiquitous computing encourages the entities to find their own *bachelor's hall* within the multifold data transmitted from the actual world. By letting them interact according to their own ways to perceive and respond to the environments, it rather constantly updates its knowledge on the environments' optimality not only for its current goals but also for some yet-unknown user interests it would commodify in near future. In this respect, it is not *in spite* but *because* of these asymmetrical interventions of ubiquitous computing that all other less important but still functional entities are relocated and "rethingified" upon a flat and symmetrical platform of smart objects (Gabrys 2016b: 192).

Speculative realists promote their "ontic principle" as a democratic principle for nonhumans in opposition to "the vertical ontologies of ontotheology or a humanism" that "trace back and relate all beings to either God, humans, language, culture or any of the other princes." They suggest "a flat ontology, one made exclusively of unique, singular individuals, differing in spatio-temporal scale but not ontological status" (Bryant 2011: 268–9). The Internet of Things as the commodification of ubiquitous computing also operationalizes this ontic principle by liberating digital objects from their previous obligation to pass through users' conscious decision-making. However, regarding the primary asymmetry implicit in the current technological networks (Hoffman and Novak 2018: 1198; Lindley et al. 2017; Mitew 2014), such societal metaphors as Bryant's "democracy of objects" (2012) often fail to take into account how the idealized autonomy of things in their local sensing and actuating are, in fact, also asymmetrically engaged in the quasi-theological individuation of a global intelligence, whose aim is to know all possible ways to redistribute these autonomies for all possible services it could sell. Like the pastoral power of Foucauldian governmentality mobilizes its constituents' voluntary confessions for its "humanly incomprehensible divine sovereignty," the "quasi-transcendental power" of the IoT (Cooper 2020: 37, 45) requires smart objects to be liberated from their human princes and freely stream their inter-objective realities.

So, in the most up-to-date bachelor's hall, such as an interior of a smart car in the following section, Bartleby's gesture to nonhumanize himself as one of these objects relocated to a flat and invisible network does not simply mean his liberation from capitalist resource management any longer. It rather suggests the condition for a global intelligence system to emerge from its asymmetrical interventions in each symmetrical edge of the network.

AIDA: A New Bachelor's Hall

AIDA (Affective Intelligent Driving Agent) is an in-dash navigation system developed by MIT's SENSEable City Lab, Media Lab, and Volkswagen's Electronics Research Lab. Equipped with several projectors displaying a 3D map on the dashboard, AIDA visualizes the most efficient route to a destination as a solution to the possible need of a registered driver (Figure 1). Unlike non-smart systems, "AIDA analyses the driver's mobility patterns, keeping track of common routes and destinations" to "identify the set of goals the driver would like to achieve" (MIT Sensible City Lab 2009). To provide the driver with the most customized niche not only within a sensor and actuator network of a vehicle but in the traffic networks and points of interest (POI) in neighboring areas, AIDA collects not only a variety of behavioral and physiological data from a driver concerning her implicit needs but the data "pertaining to various aspects of the city including traffic, seasonal information, environmental conditions, commercial offerings, and events" (Lorenzo et al. 2009).

Figure 1 AIDA 2.0.

An ordinary object-oriented navigation system maps the surrounding areas it passes through by redistributing the real-time data it receives, such as GPS and traffic information, to the predefined algorithmic objects, such as a street, intersection, or geo-tagged landmarks. These objects are displayed on the map as each node in a graph that individuates the shortest route to the "human-entered" destination. On the other hand, as a prophet-like agent smart enough to direct the driver to where she must go to fulfill her current need, what AIDA individuates foremost is not just the shortest route but some urgent needs of the driver, whose symptoms would remain peripheral to her attention until individuated into a red route on the map to a certain Point of Interest AIDA recommends. For this preemptive operation as a recommender system, AIDA mobilizes not only the interior network of the Audi full of interconnected sensors, such as those for facial expressions, voices, galvanic skin response, braking/acceleration pressures, seat position, and steering (Figure 2), but "a multitude of tags, sensors, locationing devices, telecommunications networks, online social networks, and other pervasive networks ... proliferating in cities," as well as the driver's social networks.

Say our Bartleby now finds his new bachelor's hall in this Audi car, maybe, as a test driver of this commercial IoT experiment. After one week of his subliminal entanglement with its sensor and actuator network, AIDA would begin to figure out his "home and work location" and "be able to direct" him to the grocery store he is likely to prefer. After a month, AIDA could be able to detect his hunger

Figure 2 A network of sensor-augmented things in AIDA 1.0.

from the signals collected and analyzed through the "historical behavioral collector (HBC)" and "historical route collector (HRC)," and then recommend the restaurant rated highest by Yellow Pages users with similar social media profiles (Lorenzo et al. 2009). Bartleby would find he notices his hunger only several minutes after the distributed symptoms were already detected by AIDA, but he may not care about this delay at first even though it is always long enough to pass the restaurant most customized to his taste. However, after he learns his too-human consciousness always lags behind his body's nonconscious responses by at least several hundred milliseconds, or the "missing half-second," long enough to be hijacked by other nonconscious cues from "the advent of affective capitalism and computational media" (Hansen 2015a: 190; Hayles 2017: 191), even hunger would begin to feel like a crisis that requires AIDA's preemptive intervention. His individuation as a registered driver, or mere source of the predictable data stream, would, in this respect, coincide with AIDA's ceaseless translation of his physiological and behavioral states into the problems that can be easily resolved by driving his car along each red route it recommends on the map (Figure 3). In other words, while Bartleby finds himself in his

Figure 3 Recommending a POI.

most comfortable niche within this local network of smart objects, AIDA also becomes a prophet-like intelligence, ceaselessly weaving a flat ontology out of many different types of sensor data—such as GPS data, a city's Points of Interest and their rankings in Yellow Page, lots of geo-tagged images of the city, the driver's and his neighbors' social network profiles, and his historical route and behavior data.

After these reciprocal individuations, Bartleby, on the day of his public demonstration, would see something reminiscent of the compulsive questions of the lawyer in Melville's story haunting the dashboard, tuned up for the maximum functionality of AIDA. On the way to the destination AIDA has already predicted from his route histories, Bartleby would encounter many small pop-up windows and tags on the map referring to places for entertainment, social events, and other sensor-augmented commodities, claiming to concretize his unknown desires distributed across his facial expressions, voice, galvanic responses, butt position, accelerating, and braking foot pressures. Just like the lawyer in the story, AIDA asks, "would you like to …? Well then, would you …? How then would …?" Contrary to the lawyer who failed to keep up enumerating all possible niches for Bartleby due to his too-human managerial skill, AIDA's recommendation is ever-extendable. Bartleby is already in his most customized bachelor's hall, which eliminates any possible disturbances even before they actually occur. And only this sort of global intelligence can access the problem called ubiquity.

Over the past decades from the September 11 attacks in 2001 to the recent Covid pandemic, the meaning of ubiquity in our paranoid concern for security has changed from what warns us to look around for hidden peepholes of government or corporate surveillance to what reminds us of the presence of certain problems that always remain peripheral to our helpless attempts to pay close attention. In the meantime, AIDA-like surveillance or self-tracking systems have also been more acceptable as the term *asymmetry* has ceased to be simply descriptive of our engagement with some unknown enemies but suggests the more general and nonconscious entanglement of human beings with nonhumans.

Hardt and Negri argue that "the gray zone of war and peace" in permanent danger of insurgency and terrorism justifies the "total mobilization of social forces" for the preemptive strike of a military power that is "in asymmetrical conflicts" over unpredictable "guerrilla attacks" (2004: 13, 51–2). Massumi writes similarly that civilian life in this "crisis-prone environment" falls "onto a continuum with war" in which a preemptive power's intervention should be "as ubiquitously irruptible as the indiscriminate threats it seeks to counter" (2015: 27–8). After 9/11, it has been even more difficult for international law to distinguish civilians from combatants, based simply on the latter's notable feature "of having a fixed distinctive sign recognizable at a distance" (Wilke 2017: 1042). As Wilke points out in the cases of NATO's 2009 operation in Afghanistan and the recent "police violence against Black civilians in the US" (1050), the binary of militants/civilians or insurgents/civilians is now redefined by the more ambiguous terms of the involved/uninvolved. The domain of the cybernetic counterinsurgency, a city or battlefield, is in turn transformed into a sociopolitical continuum of suspects with varying degrees of involvement: (almost impossible) pure innocents—potentially involved—(completely) known terrorists. Relocated to such a wide spectrum of the middle in this continuum, anyone is now potentially involved with "the imminent threat" that must be preempted. While the "sweeping techniques of post-9/11 surveillance and data gathering" were once conceived "of a scale appropriate to wholesale calamities like terror attacks and natural disasters, not to ordinary crime or protest" (Pasquale 2015: 48), this speculative continuum of population lets us consider any tiny events unfolded from the middle as potentially complicit in some harmful networks. As Frank Pasquale quotes from one state official, therefore,

> You can make an easy kind of a link that, if you have a protest group protesting a war where the cause that's being fought against is international terrorism, you might have terrorism at that protest. You can almost argue that a protest against [the war] is a terrorist act. … violent extremists could also be identified by bumper stickers on their cars indicating support for libertarian groups.
>
> (2015: 48)

What the Internet of Things generalizes even to the scales of human bodies under wearable devices and home/office for smart appliances is this militant conception of environments within the tension between the insurgency of ubiquitous problems and the counterinsurgency of an intelligent system. Enmeshed with the IoT's sensor-actuator arcs now, a domestic space or human body is subject to the constant machine learning that aims to discover some hidden links assumed to exist between a sensor's detection of a tiny anomaly, as trivial as "bumper stickers," and a bigger problem latent in the space. In Melville's fiction, Bartleby's symmetry-breaking insurgency was never preventable by the lawyer's linear management programmed in IF-THEN statements. But, in AIDA, his body's becoming a mere physiological continuum with many insurgent problems conversely justifies his voluntary participation in the IoT's ubiquitous data collection. For AIDA's becoming a collective intelligence from the concrescence of manifold human and thing-generated data, the ubiquity of these lurking problems should also be advertised as the reason why humans need to relinquish their right to the uses of objects they have monopolized so long and why it is time to hand this right over to the IoT, which can use them more preemptively to maintain a space always customized to our needs.

Ontology, Operationalized

But what of the seemingly more fanciful idea that the Internet might one day "wake up"? Could the Internet become something more than just the backbone of a loosely integrated collective superintelligence—something more like a virtual skull housing an emerging unified super-intellect?

(Bostrom 2014)

The question Nick Bostrom raises regarding the possibility of superintelligence emerging from the current internet is suggestive of how, for the last two decades, the internet has evolved in relation to the two engineering goals he presented in 1997 for the "bottom-up approach" to artificial superintelligence (ASI). At the time, he suggested "a high-bandwidth local-area network" of "a great number of moderately fast processors" put in "a highly parallel architecture" and the use of "present equipment to supply the input and output channels" for its perpetual learning (Bostrom 1998). His earlier vision was of an autopoietic network whose operational closure against "a rich flux of sensory input" (Bostrom 1998) could differentiate manifold sensor-actuator arcs capable of responding to any inputs with proper outputs. The spontaneous learning process this vision assumed has, however, hardly been realized not simply because of the difficulty of building "an adequate initial network structures" as flexible and plastic as "the initial neuronal structure in new-born infants" to be raised to a whole person with general intelligence (Bostrom 1998). More significant for this spontaneous learning to continue has been the translation of this vision for a local computing network into a promise for the general interests of other cognitive systems—including human experts and their expert systems, as well as individuals as everyday decision-makers—to mobilize their contributions to the unlimited input and output channels.

However, the internet seems to be much better at this social engineering than any single engineering project; its development has been driven by the general interest of software industries, namely the expansion of its services to any predictable user interests. The preprogrammed initial structure of the network in Bostrom's early vision has been replaced by the networks of "more capable autonomous software agents." Its operational closure, then, gives way to the experimental openness of the networks through "more efficient protocols governing the interactions between such bots" (Bostrom 2014). In the meantime, the capitalist ontology discussed in Chapter 1, which might be termed the speculative realism of hidden correlations, has provided users with the rationale to rethink their quantified-selves as the computational problems of optimization between their neurophysiological and behavioral economic bodies and environmental cues and nudges. To mobilize each user's participation as a unique input-output channel to train its superintelligence, the IoT thus reengineers its operational environments into multiplicities of unknown correlations open to constant reoptimization through smart object-to-object communications.

In Harman's object-oriented ontology, the secret cores of objects, which constantly withdraw from each other and are therefore never fully graspable from one to another, are ironically intensifying the universe with ceaseless partial communications between objects proliferating their inter-objective realities. Likewise, enmeshed with tiny sensors and actuators, things in the IoT—for instance, a human body and its home—translate their elusive inner dynamics—such as the body's neurophysiological dynamics under the skin and its nonconscious domestic routines—into the data streams under constant datamining to unfold their partial correlations with other things that occur. Optimization is the process of putting a thing in the best condition for another thing's occurrence (or nonoccurrence). In the IoT, this conditioning of correlations is performed proactively by the nudges of autonomous smart objects regarding the predicted event. For the superintelligence emerging from this new internet, any causality between things in human knowledge is the machine-learnable matter of optimal correlation for the things' co-occurrence. Thus, for its perpetual learning, smart objects' conditioning of things is motivated as much by the speculation about some yet unlearned correlations as by its temporary goals to optimize the known correlations. Put differently, the IoT's object-oriented solutionism is "decomposing problems [of optimizations] in terms of autonomous agents that can engage in flexible, high-level interactions," and for opening its operational environments onto these secret entanglements of things, "decisions about what actions should be performed are devolved to autonomous entities" (Jennings 2000: 283–4).

From the object-oriented programming in the PC era to the IoT's ubiquitous computing, the relation between the whole and parts in algorithmic systems has, in this respect, changed in a way that allows local agents to retrieve more autonomy from a system of which they were once just functional parts. The totality of the system's functions, or its general intelligence, has also been redefined as what should be constantly updated as the sum of learned interactions of local agents out of all interactions these agents might have with yet unknown others. The classical conceptualization of totality as *more than a mere sum* is, therefore, no longer accurate, because individual elements are always under multiplicities of interactions unable to be summed up into a coherent representation of a whole. For this system, Ontology with a capital "O" as the knowledge base for all possible things and interactions in the world, therefore, "comes later" and only after some of these manifold interactions are gradually stabilized as the registered and retraceable interactions (Hansen 2015b: 42).

In *Alien Phenomenology*, Ian Bogost describes this operationalizing view of ontology with a neologism, *ontography*. In his version of speculative realism, which is more strictly based on the engineering concept of object-orientation, things in general are defined by their ontographic operation as "a general inscriptive strategy" (2012: 38) to record "random, anonymous meetings one has in modern environments" into its own "compact modes of representation," which he calls "tiny ontology" (2006: 73). For Bogost, ontology is not something written in "a treatise or tome" but a modular and recursive function of *ontography* as a thing's way of engaging with environments as well as its becoming "the basic ontological apparatus needed to describe existence" (2012: 19–21). Even if a huge Ontology comprehensive enough to encompass any tiny ontology is still imaginable in Bogost's alien phenomenology, it could no longer be bigger than a mere sum. A big Ontology would rather be the loosest and partial sum of manifold tiny ontologies if what it could incorporate within its formal compilation of the most common facts for every singular objective worldview would inevitably be just some trivial facts commensurable with any particular local ontology. Put differently, tiny ontologies are prior to the big Ontology as objects' autonomous modes of existence and their ways to "perceive and engage their worlds" (29). The multiplicities of these tiny ontologies form the background of the universe from which a huge Ontology emerges as a fractal figure of a common world drawn from lots of singular ontographies that accidentally encountered one another.

While, for Bogost, *fractal* is descriptive of the assemblage of objects "held together tenuously by accidents" (25), for the IoT, this never-ending pattern left by modular operations of mathematical operators is a metaphor for the maximum interoperability of its smart objects. And the big Ontology assembled from each focused operation of smart objects is not the product of random encounters between tiny ontologies, such as those of *flâneurs* in what Bogost calls "modern environments" (73). It rather pertains to a certain design decision to maximize the autonomous networking of smart objects to re-enmesh their shared environments with ever-switching sensor-actuator arcs for more optimization problems to be serviced. The protocols to translate one's output into another's input should thus require only the minimum degree of mutual understanding since each singular worldview of objects is not the primary concern; hidden correlations may be hardly perceivable by any singular agent but unfolded through their loose interoperations.

Regarding this ontological commitment of objects to a system's speculative realist modeling of reality, the AI research at the turn of the century conceptualized ontology as the protocol for machine-to-machine communication, which might be prepared for the artificial general intelligence that Bostrom anticipated would come soon after. In "The Role of Common Ontology in Achieving Sharable, Reusable Knowledge Bases," Thomas Gruber writes:

> Today's knowledge systems are isolated monoliths characterized by high internal coupling (e.g., among ground domain facts, procedures, terminology, axioms, and idiosyncratic ways of modelling the world) and a lack of external coupling interfaces that would enable the developer to reuse software tools and knowledge bases as modular components.
>
> (1991: 601)

While "the symbol-level representation used internally by the agent" is black-boxed from other agents, ontology as the "knowledge-level" protocol provides the agents with languages to translate their secret understanding of the world into a formal response to the queries from others, no matter how incompatible their symbolic cores (Gruber 1993: 909). Ontology for Gruber in this sense aims to convert how each agent perceives and responds to the world into "libraries of shared, reusable knowledge" that can be given as inputs to others as the parts of their environments or as "background knowledge," like the Whiteheadian universe given as the multifold datum left by the finished becoming of actual entities (1991: 602). But its goal is not so much to integrate these noisy backgrounds into one truthful representation but to maximize the possible external couplings between these otherwise incommensurable inner worlds or tiny ontologies of algorithmic agents through their formal symmetry of query-answer. This ontology could therefore only articulate some tenuous facts, such as the common classes of objects and their possible interactions. In doing so, this "weakest theory" enables "the most models" about the same reality to coexist in the backgrounds (Gruber 1993: 909), and by making "as few claims as possible about the world being modeled," it maximizes agents' "freedom to specialize and instantiate the ontology as needed" and their "*ontological commitment*" (910).

For the current IoT ontologies, these multiplicities of monadic worlds of things in the background are occasionally gathered around certain predicted events. The sensor-actuator arcs assembled by them unfold certain suboptimal realities of the environments for these events to happen. For instance, in an Amazon-branded smart home, a shortcut called "Good Morning Routine" cues Alexa to organize a network of smart appliances, such as a smart thermostat, smart lights, and a smart speaker, which converts the home into a problem space with a single optimal state for the occurrence of the user's perfect wake-up. Other routines, such as the "Headspace Meditation Routine," which work across smart lights, a thermostat, speaker, and a smart watch, unfold each different state of optimality for the occurrence of the user's perfect mindfulness. In this respect, the inter-objective reality of the IoT is constantly reconstructed under its ontology and is more "correlationist" than the subjective construction of reality in Meillassoux's sense (2008). The causality of human intentions in the world corresponding to their exercises now gives way to the correlations between objects' autonomous conditioning of the world and the co-occurrent nonconscious responses of subjects that, as ANT emphasizes, we so often mistake for the products of our intentions.

Topology as the New Governmentality
of Everyday Life

Re-intensifying a (Non-)Smart Home

Small objects called social plugins, such as Facebook's "Like," "Share," "Send," and "Quote" buttons, are everywhere on the current internet. Signifying how easily user participation can be done through one's reflexive motor response of clicking, the visible surfaces of these objects also effectively conceal how proprietary the behavioral data collected on the other side of the interfaces are as software companies use them to recommend certain contents or webpages customized to each user's preference. Embedded even outside of social network sites, their supposed optimization of one's personal web browsing experiences also contributes to the ultimate ambition of the companies like Facebook to let their services filter and redisplay the entire internet to their users. In this respect, the new fabric of the web or its network topology today is no longer woven through people's conscious decisions to click the hyperlinks that individual web designers created. "Beyond the hyperlink," the topology of each weighted edge of the web is now governed by machine learning's prediction of user preferences among all possible links it can generate (Gerlitz and Helmond 2013: 1358).

If this object-oriented place-binding is what social plugins have secretly experimented with on the web under the banner of Web 2.0 and its myth of user participation (Scholz 2008), the recent miniaturization of smart sensors, processors, and actuators (Crandall 2010), or the things in the Internet of Things, suggests a topology of real-world objects as the new logic of spatialization applicable to any physical domains. In this case, optimized through these small machines embedded virtually in everything people interact with on a daily basis are their routines to manually manipulate these objects for everyday needs. And, as the current hype of the IoT and its domestic application imply, the fabric of a person's private life in a smart home is woven through the ambient interoperations of smart objects that activate themselves or each other according to the IoT's algorithmic preemption of her emerging needs even before she recognizes them. In the following pages, I will develop a topological framework analyzing the new form of media power behind this IoT-driven transformation of human geography, but for now, to repurpose topology as a branch of mathematical thinking into a tool to describe this process of place-binding, let me start off with a simple thought experiment on a non-smart home, filled with several electronic devices but not yet digitally interconnected.

Say each device in this setting exerts its effect over a nearby area and can be redeployed anywhere insofar as it does not overlap another. A domain that each device's influence reaches could then be stretched and bent flexibly since they are rearrangeable in many improvised ways. Following the definition of topology as a study of the properties of objects that "remain invariant under bending, stretching, or deforming transformations" (DeLanda 2002: 25–6), this domestic space can be considered a topological object, which is characterized not so much as a container for separable devices but as a continuum having flexible and unbreakable inner boundaries as its topological invariants that determine the scope of all possible interoperations of the devices (Figure 4). Each device in this conceptual space would then be symmetrical to any transformations the house undergoes in that it could operate invariantly in any position. (Note that the word *symmetry* here is used in its mathematical sense, meaning when an object or its property is invariant under a specific transformation the object

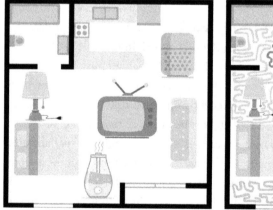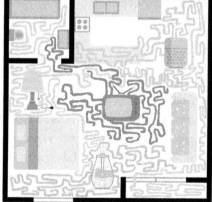

Figure 4 Two topological isomorphs of a domestic space with stretchable boundaries of devices.

undergoes. In this sense, symmetry is always *symmetry to* certain power that imposes transformations upon the object.)

However, most of the symmetries these devices have preserved would be broken as soon as a person moves in and her daily routine—waking up, sitting at a table, having breakfast, reading something—redeploys them to the new niches. Under the influences of the homeowner, they can be functional only by being consistently engaged with a trajectory she draws to refresh her energy to begin and continue a day. This means the devices no longer remain the same under all possible stretching and bending of the continuum but are symmetrical only to a linear transformation along the homeowner's daily routine. As Manuel DeLanda says, "an undifferentiated *intensive space* (i.e., a space defined by continuous intensive properties) progressively differentiates, eventually giving rise to *extensive structure*" (2002: 27, emphasis in original). Her singularity embeds a line of force or attractor within the continuum and makes "a large number of different trajectories, starting their evolution at very different places in the manifold, … end up" being aligned "within the 'sphere of influence' of the attractor" (15, 32). Despite the extensive structure that the space's transformation eventually culminates in, this topological description at least conceptually preserves the undifferentiated continuum of the space insofar as it is still able to unfold lots of hidden functional states with the introduction of other attractors than the person's daily routine. Topology repurposed as a means to describe the place-binding of domestic space in this way rediscovers its intensive proto-territory where manifold functional relations among the entities are still open to all possible redeployments prior to any extensive structures.

This chapter examines the smart electronic devices and their network called the Internet of Things as the technological attractor that re-intensifies this topological potential of domestic space, currently renamed smart home. Embedded with a multitude of sensors and actuators, a domestic interior in its most advanced form now is redefined as a topological continuum that could unfold potentially innumerable functional spaces in response to software applications' constant redeployment of smart objects. In the first section of the chapter, this continuum is discussed as not simply discovered under people's everyday routines by ubiquitous sensors but cultivated by the new form of media power I term topological power, which, as the second section argues, constantly redifferentiates the continuum into the new service domains for its algorithmic governance. The third section then discusses Bernhard Riemann and Henri Poincaré's mathematical thinking of manifold, or multiplicity, as a possible theoretical tool to describe this undifferentiated proto-territory of the IoT, from which the final two sections theorize the new logic of place-binding in smart home and the new technique of self-governance its smart residents internalize.

Topology in Culture

In the introduction to the special issue of *Theory, Culture & Society* on "Topologies of Culture," Lury, Parisi, and Terranova discuss the recent interface culture, which they illustrate as "a proliferation of surfaces that behave topologically," as something that originated from "20th-century developments in the gridding of time and space, the proliferation of registers, filing and listing systems, the making and remaking of categories, the identification of populations, and the invention of logistics" (2012: 8). Encompassing all these early computational modelings of the workplace, domestic space, and social geography, and currently embedded in all of these human spaces, digital interfaces for the past decades have registered a variety of objects—from home/office appliances to consumer goods—to their heterogeneous networks. At the same time, the functional values of these objects have been recategorized along with the online activities of their users, whose quantified-selves have also been registered to the same interfaces as the collections of computable variables: from their demographic characters to the patterns of online behaviors. By topology, these authors suggest how the "'lower level' principles of invariance or consistency" in human geography have changed as its subjects and objects have been relocated to the networked social platforms. While Euclidean axioms define objects as something invariant under such geometric transformations as "rotation, symmetry, scale and translation" and, in turn, define their movement as the "transmission of fixed forms in space and time," the movement they topologically reconceptualize is analyzed as "the ordering of continuity" (6–7, 13), or, in my term, bending and stretching of a continuum to make something invariant emerge from its folded surfaces. Suppose you are walking around a city with a GPS-tracking augmented-reality app. Prior to any other representations of your engagement with the city, your physical displacement would be expressed as a linear transformation of a geo-data continuum along the trajectory of a data point representing your location. The graphical boundaries of urban objects would then appear in the app's GUI as nearby Points of Interest (POI) only as the result of the software's constant ordering and folding of the continuum into the changed data point. In the same way, your social profile would be constantly updated and improvised through the algorithmic comparison of your pathway across the POIs to what others draw (Lury and Day 2019). The movement here is not about your dis-placement as the consequence of your motor intention ingrained in "pre-given territorial containers" (Allan 2011: 286). Rather it expresses certain power that makes a place itself emerge from the continuum in which objects should be constantly re-included as the things orderly changing under given deformations.

In this respect, an object's "becoming topological" means the liquidation of "the rigidity of the distinction between inclusion and exclusion," once determining the place of the object "based on essential properties, such as archetypes, values or norms, or regional location" (Lury et al. 2012: 5). Objective boundaries rethought as topological matters are instead under constant recreations through "different kinds of folding and filtering" of the continuum (Mezzadra and Neilson 2012: 60). Reconfigured as a continuum of multilevel relational data, the urban landscape likewise also becomes an object with lots of embedded boundaries, which preserve the "excess" (Lury 2009: 80) open to the software's alternative ways of folding/filtering. In the recent discourses of human geography,[1] topology has, therefore, been introduced as the term to describe these innovated lower-level principles for the movement of humans and nonhumans "in culture as a field of connectedness," and their "inclusion and exclusion" along deformable boundaries (Lury et al. 2012: 5).

What I mean by topological power is a new form of power that capitalizes on this transformability of human geography converted into a digital continuum. This power mobilizes people's speculations about hidden values and problems embedded in their material footing and exploits them as what justifies the expansion of its governance. In doing so, this power constantly re-differentiates the continuum into a multitude of problem spaces, which can be managed optimally by its environmental sensors and actuators. There can be various conductors of topological power. Active users of self-tracking devices, such as early proponents of quantified-self, for instance, exercise this when they attempt to expand the scope of their self-governance by digging out some unknown computable problems from their everyday lives; a smartwatch, on the other hand, exercises its governance by asking the wearer to delegate this job to quantify herself without being a data analyst herself; governments and corporate actors could expand the scope of this datamining of hidden problems to a whole city converted into big data. Even though the objects each conductor takes for its domain are stretched vastly from a body to a city, topology expresses their common logic for territorial expansion, never imaginable with the territoriality previously understood as a geometric extension. Space under topological power is transformed into a relational database with lots of unknown correlations. Claimed to be discovered sooner or later by embedded sensors and actuators, these correlations are indicative of hidden problems like unknown health issues or impending terrorisms detectable only by the pattern recognition algorithms of a smartwatch or smart city. As the rest of this chapter demonstrates, the technological embodiment of topological power, such as the IoT, is, therefore, superior to other territorial actors based in a single extensive level of space since the number of objects a topological actor could put under its governance is potentially unlimited as it could unfold hidden levels of space ad infinitum.

The expansion of topological power for the past decades has been driven by the proliferation of software interfaces embedded not only in the new urban landscape but also in human skins under smart wearables and it has foregrounded lots of hidden correlations otherwise undetectable. On the other hand, the above thought experiment on the transformability of a non-smart home suggests another direction that topological power has recently taken to access the underlying continuum of our everyday lives. The becoming topological of space in this domestic scenario is not achieved by its connection to the outside networks. It is rather intensified through the manifold regional interconnections of devices in the same sense as what the term *manifold* means in Riemannian differential geometry: a set of "multiply extended magnitudes ... susceptible of various metric relations," in which "a [Euclidean] space constitutes only a special case of a triply extended magnitude" (Riemann 2007: 23). Our not-yet-smart home is likewise topological as it is charged with lots of potential interoperations among the devices that could be susceptible to various functional relations if rewired properly to each other. As the technological solution to this quest for becoming topological of everyday life, the IoT embeds miniaturized "RFID and sensor technology" in domestic objects and lets them "observe, identify and understand the world" from their own data points and, in turn, transforms the space into a relational database (Ashton 2009).

According to the International Telecommunication Union's description, the things in the IoT are enrolled in a new dimension called "Any THING communication," distinguishable from two other dimensions of the ICTs in the past, namely "Any TIME communication" and "Any PLACE communication" (2012: 2). This new dimension for machine-to-machine communication provides smart objects with an ontological platform for their reciprocal presence without being necessarily used in human TIME and PLACE. This means, for realizing the IoT's ideal of the "full use of things to offer services to all kinds of applications" (3), a smart home should first liberate its objects from their previous obligation to follow the instructions directly given by humans and let them communicate freely with each other about the space's hidden relational problems. For instance, the state of the space as yet optimal for predictable user behaviors, such as going to bed, can be communicated and optimized by the relevant applications, such as a sleep app that manages the interoperation of a smart thermometer, lighting, phone, and watch. A smart home topology in this scenario can be then roughly analyzed into three different conductors of power in negotiation. First, there is the homeowner so interested in optimizing her lifestyle to the extent of speculating her daily routine as a continuum embedded with lots of efficiency problems. Second, the smart home applications she purchased then function as technical conductors of topological power to unfold these invisible problems of her daily routine. Third, the primary concern of a service provider, who owns big data gathered from its smart home subscribers, would be to data-mine a greater number of serviceable problems for the companies' further commodification of the smart home infrastructure.

Manifolds in the Internet of Things

Kirstein (2016) suggests an architectural abstraction for expanding "the edge of the networks that make up the Internet" even to the not "IP-enabled" objects, such as the devices in our non-smart home scenario. According to him, a typical IoT system consists of two layers: DeploymentNet, or the physical lower layer for the actual enrollment of smart objects to a physical domain; and ServiceNet, or the upper software layer where the virtual objects as the algorithmic counterparts of the physical objects are abstractly defined for their deployment for the IoT applications. For the regional IoT infrastructure (such as a smart home with several smart devices) to be automatically operational for the applications in the software layer, the semantic technology called ontology needs to intervene in the middle for "the alignment and matchmaking tasks … to identify which smart entities that 'live' in the house are appropriate for the applications/ services to function" (Kotis and Katasonov 2012).[2] Replacing a person's habitual deployment of objects for her daily routine, this machine-to-machine protocol enables the smart home to optimize itself to the predictable human needs. However, this technological optimization of space, which the homeowner may delegate to the IoT to save the time she used to waste on walking around and manually turning on and off the devices, is not only to fulfill her daily needs but the corporate conductor's commercial interest, namely constantly renewing the space's commodifiability.

For the person in the not-yet-smart setting, to live her daily routines is to transform her surroundings gradually into a figure symmetrical to her everyday practices. Along the multiple sensorimotor pathways from what physiologists call reflex arc to what phenomenologists call intention arc (Merleau-Ponty 2005), any move she takes at home is followed by her somatic expectation of the transformation her move would bring in space. The actual perception that succeeds her move would in turn confirm or update this expectation to prepare for her future moves. In this sense, the person's living in her not-yet-smart home is topologically isomorphic to the process whereby a spatial continuum is folded by a set of biological sensors and motors interconnected through certain physiological pathways. As Ingold says, "places are formed through movement, when a movement along turns into a movement around" (2008: 1808); to put it differently, a place is unraveled as what the sensors perceive is aligned with how the motors routinely operate, and vice versa. Like the typical residents of modern buildings, whom Pink et al. call "directors of flows," this person improvises "the material configuration and atmosphere of [her] bedtime home as [she] move[s] through" the space for "switching the lights on and off, closing curtains, plugging in things to charge and setting up technologies to 'work' while [she is] asleep"—to make it "felt right" to her "bedtime routine" (2016: 86, 88).

On the other hand, the IoT's optimization of a smart home is not for stabilizing it into a single "right" level because its stability is bad news for the service provider, meaning no more problems are embedded for the company's datamining. Stability in a smart home should rather be a transitory equilibrium about to be broken by the new problems the updated application soon excavates. As Kitchin and Dodge (2011: 71) illustrate with the term "code/space," in a smart home, "space is constantly brought into being as an incomplete solution to an ongoing relational problem" that is the maximum optimization of space. And for this bringing-forth of more optimal space to be repeated over and again, the physical continuum of a smart home should be full of small relational problems to a variety of predictable user behaviors, such as its state not-yet-optimal-enough for sleeping, doing exercise, or watching TV, which can be optimized further by each different application. Unlike the spatial continuum of a not-yet-smart home setting being folded through the physiologically hardwired sensorimotor arcs, the continuum of a smart home, under multiple sensor-actuator arcs, is not detained within just a single level of optimality. Instead, its IoT system needs to keep the continuum intensive enough to be de-/re-territorialized by different sets of smart objects for different applications. The two-layered structure of the IoT in this commercial concern is, therefore, the product of the strategic design decision to guarantee the IoT's intensive penetration all the way down into lurking problems. While its lower layer for the maximum interoperability of smart objects intensifies the space with lots of relational problems, the upper software layer gradually identifies and commodifies them into its serviceable domains. For instance, Lanzeni observed in a citizen-sensing environment project that the problem of knowing the real cause of air pollution is always engaged with some "other environmental elements" that the current deployment of environmental sensors cannot detect. These other elements' withdrawals from the grip of current software solutions are, however, still expected to "become tangible" and "bring [the participants] closer to understanding what was causing the pollution" as the project would redeploy the sensors by "improving firmware or to move to a different technology" (2016: 55–6, 60). In other words, the smart future where all these environmental elements are optimized is imagined to be already embedded in the material bottom but not just unfolded yet through a proper software application in the high.

As Dourish and Bell say, "the proximate future vision" of ubiquitous computing has spurred the "dramatic transformations of technological infrastructure" for the last three decades from Mark Weiser's early research at Xerox PARC in the 1990s to the recent IoT (2011: 24–5). And, in the topological framework roughly sketched above, this future vision is now reinterpretable as more than just the rhetoric of Silicon Valley on its "future infinitely postponed" (25). In between the intensive lower layer and the abstract upper layer of a smart home, the most optimal future for our smart life is inevitably postponed infinitely because it would stay lurking in the underlying continuum until the software applications unfold all of its problematic hidden levels and, more importantly, because this continuum would always be abundant with hidden problems.

Riemannian and Poincaréan theories of symmetrical space

At the heart of the current hype about the IoT is this sort of topological speculation about the multiplicity enfolded in our physical reality. And, for the IoT's expansion of its service domains to be sustainable even after everything is already replaced by smart objects, this multiplicity should continue unraveling its hidden measurable levels through the multiple "cuts" the wireless sensors and actuators constantly inscribe on its continuum (Poincaré 1913: 54). With regard to this resourceful multiplicity, this section discusses Bernhard Riemann's mathematical concept of manifold and Henri Poincaré's group theory and how they theorize the cause, or attractor, behind implicit sensors and motors that function in their mathematical imaginations to cut through to the hidden geometries of the manifold.

In the essay on a manifold "at the foundation of geometry," Riemann explains how a surface with constant curvature, or a geometric plane, could be unfolded from this conceptual space of multiply extended magnitudes. He first assumes that for measurement in the most basic sense to be possible, the length of a line should be independent of its position no matter where it is superposed to be compared with other lengths. He then contrives an anonymous "one," who (or which) passes from one magnitude to another to transport "the line element ds" as an infinitesimal yardstick to define "metric relations of which a manifold … is susceptible." As this mathematical cursor moves across a manifold, he argues, the nearby magnitudes it passes through are gradually localized into the points fixed by the homogeneous Pythagorean distance function. And, consequently, it concretizes one embedded level of the manifold, on which any configurations "distinguished by a mark or a boundary" the cursor draws appear symmetrical to the group of geometric transformations, such as displacements and rotations (Riemann 2007: 24, 26).

In this heuristic explanation, Riemann's differential geometry suggests a mathematical actor that folds the magnitudes infinitely close to its trajectory into the geometric theorem at the expense of breaking all other relations the manifold once preserved. Even though he does not explicitly mention anything about the motility of his yardstick, its simple operation to superpose the line element (ds) upon other magnitudes already assumes the elementary capacity of movement the yardstick should have. And this motility delivering the smallest measure all over the manifold is the attractor that Riemann introduces to unfold a single stable level of measurability from the intensive space imagined by the non-Euclidean geometries in the nineteenth century and thus rewire it with the Cartesian coordinate.

On the other hand, the substitute Poincaré suggested for this purely mathematical attractor in Riemannian geometry was a simple biological being capable of sensing and moving in a physical environment of multiply extended intensities. In his physiological and phenomenological explanation of the origin of geometry, what appears invariant enough to replace Riemann's hypothetical yardstick is an elementary correlation between two types of state changes this biological cursor undergoes as moving around the continuum of intensities. First, there could be the changes aroused from its sensors "independent[ly] of will" by something that hits its surfaces (Poincaré 2007: 121). On the other hand, there could also be the changes that are "voluntary and accompanied by muscular sensations," indicating nothing outside but which muscles are activated within its body and how much (Poincaré 2007). An eye, for instance, can be thought of as an intersection for these two types of changes to be intermingled. Say it moves to the right and left as the manifestation of a motor volition that activates certain muscles. The metric relation between the external sensations that have passed through the retina during this motor activity would then be for now measured by the amounts of coincident muscular sensations. (E.g., a red spot on the right could be certain muscular sensations away from a blue spot on the left.) And if there is no other motor apparatus activated during this brief experience, these voluntary muscular sensations would be enough to unfold specific spatial relations invariant under the continuum's repeated distortions through the eye movements, whereas all the other parts of the continuum would withdraw to the background. For the physiological system that is multiply extended to its intensive environments through its sensors and motors also multiply interconnected along certain sensorimotor pathways, these elementary sensations can be alternative to the Riemannian line element, not hypothetically given any longer but experientially emergent in this case. According to the trajectory this body draws, the surrounding manifold would eventually bifurcate into a phenomenological space—not so much a transcendental form but just a set of magnitudes that appears to be invariant or orderly changing under (in other words, symmetrical to) a group of transformations the hardwired sensors and motors of this biological cursor apply to its intensive surroundings.

For Poincaré, the attractor that unfolds a geometric structure embedded in a manifold is this voluntary action of a physiological system that accompanies certain muscular sensations, or what current neuroscience calls proprioception, which enables "the sensory cortices to predict specifically how the actions to be taken will change the relations of the eyes, nose, ears, and fingers to the world" (Freeman 2000: 33). He also knew that the "sensible space" this biological being inhabits is not three-dimensional a priori but possible to be folded into "as many [degrees] as there are nerve-fibers" (Poincaré 2007: 132). A manifold for him is thus characterized by its feature capable of being bound by as many local sensorimotor pathways as any possible observing systems, but without being exhaustible by any of them. Inferred from this feature is that underlying intensities of physical reality are embedded with lots of hidden levels that can be unfolded separately by different attractors, but never unfolded altogether. Geometry for Poincaré is, therefore, just one unraveled order out of these manifold others. And what its appearance as a single stable level expresses is the operation of the anthropomorphic sensorimotor pathways, which put a person's phenomenological world under the "maximum grip" the person holds on a certain embedded order of the intensities (Freeman 2000: 120–1).

In Poincaréan group theory, symmetry attains a new ontological meaning besides an object's invariance under a subject's observation or manipulation since it now refers to the emergence of the subject-object boundary itself from a continuum under transformation. Symmetry is an event whereby a group of sensors and motors is interconnected along an arc, through which the folded inside of the continuum achieves a stable grip on one embedded level of the outside. In this respect, symmetry is akin to what Karen Barad describes by the term *agential cut*: "topological dynamics of enfolding whereby the spacetimematter manifold is enfolded into itself" and "the marking of the 'measuring agencies' by the 'measured object'" emerges (2007: 140, 177). This cut is where a continuum is folded in two and differentiated into symmetrical inside and outside. Therefore, it is prior to any boundaries of the observer/observed, toucher/touched drawn on the continuum.[3] As the cause that makes the cut, an attractor does not belong to either of the two poles of the symmetry, namely the subject/object or system/environment. Its power topologically thought is rather described as a continuum's fluctuation to make a fold on its own surface, from which something invariant comes to the fore, or bifurcates, as an object. This movement is both material and discursive in that what the unfolded space presents is not only the objects' invariant boundaries but the group of transformations to which their objectness is defined to be symmetrical. Riemann's infinitesimal yardstick is one instance of this power as it folds a mathematical manifold into a measurable space under the maximum grip of the Pythagorean Theorem. Poincaré's group of transformations is another and it folds an intensive continuum into a livable space on which a phenomenological subject, like our homeowner, would have the maximum grip with her routine sensorimotor responses. And, the IoT is the latest example of this attractor as its wireless sensor and actuator network constantly refold the underlying continuum of a smart home to multiply its optimal grips of serviceable and marketable spaces for its perpetual market penetration.

Two Types of Power in Manifolds

Symmetry has been used in media studies as the term to describe the equal right or mutual accessibility assigned bilaterally to both sides of the interaction, such as human/nonhuman and subject/object, especially since its appropriation of actor-network theory's principle of symmetry. However, in the term's function as the convenient gesture of reciprocity formally given to "all the elements that go to make up a heterogeneous network, whether these elements are devices, natural forces, or social groups" (Law 2012: 124), often overlooked has been that, even for actor-network theory, symmetry has never been just descriptive of the relation between preexisting actors but expressive of a certain power which draws some invariant responses from undefined entities, such as Latour's microbes (1984), to make them reappear as the reproducible objects and thus mobilizable. Emphasizing these power dynamics concealed in the term's common usage, the symmetry reconceptualized in the last section, on the other hand, suggests another way to think of the meaning of reciprocity. Prior to any bifurcations of such pairs of subject/object, observer/observed, or system/ environment, symmetry now means an ontological event, or what Barad calls intra-action (2007), whereby a continuum folds an arbitrary subject boundary along its incurved arc, around which something invariant would then appear as objects.[4]

There can be two types of power that govern this emergence of objective spaces from a manifold. Exemplified by the Riemannian bifurcation of mathematical space and Poincaréan phenomenological space, the first type of power is operating as its fold tends to be hardwired to maintain its current grip on a single level of the manifold. Like the eye swaying from side to side, the fold in this case would move *along* the continuum and then move *around* only for enrolling what it has just passed through as the objects re-traceable by its registered or habituated motor operations. On the other hand, another type of power, which the earlier section mentioned as truly topological and thus always better than human eyes at governing unknown problems, tends to constantly rewire its fold to update its current grip to a different level every moment. In this case, the fold would move around to the initial point only to initiate each new move-along to the undiscovered territories of the space. While the feature of a manifold the first type seeks out is its single symmetrical level bound by the routinized sensorimotor responses, the second type does not concern with identifying the most stable level but constantly redeploying its wireless sensors and motors to examine all the "nested set of vector fields related to each other by symmetry-breaking bifurcations" (DeLanda 2002: 32).[5]

Regarding how the first type of power operates within a social domain, it is noteworthy Brian Massumi's analysis of Foucauldian governmentality into two alternating techniques to fold "the [social] continuum 'that lies between the organic and the biological, between body and population'" (2015: 24). According to him, this neoliberal approach to optimize individual freedom within the ever-changing acceptable limit is still relying on the "disciplinary power" for its function to enable everything it "passes through" such as "bodies, gestures, discourses, and desires to be identified and constituted as something individual" (Foucault 2003: 29–30). However, the symmetry of this level of "the spatial distribution of individual bodies" (242) under the maximum grip of local disciplinary apparatuses is shortly broken as the "regulatory biopower" re-bifurcates the continuum into a population: the "phenomena that are aleatory and unpredictable when taken in themselves or individually, but which, at the collective level, display constants" to its demographic apparatuses of "forecasts, statistical estimates, and overall measures" (243, 246). Foucauldian governmentality in this sense forms "a correctional reuptake mechanism for emergent normative variation" (Massumi 2015: 25), which constantly updates the acceptable limit of individual behaviors from the changing statistical regularity; as Stephen Collier (2009: 93) argues as to Foucault's lectures on security, territory, and population, this mechanism also implements "a topology of power" as it transforms the social continuum into "a problem space to be analyzed by tracing the recombinatorial processes through which techniques and technologies are reworked and redeployed." And, in our concern with the technique that governs individual devices in a domestic setting, this form of geographical governmentality is topologically isomorphic to how our homeowner transformed her space by manually redeploying the devices to their new niches, whose collective interoperations would correspond to the constants in her daily routines, such as her regular needs and desires.

The second type of power is distinguishable by its tendency to unfold more symmetries hidden in the continuum no matter how symmetry-breaking an attempt to find a new one is to the others already discovered. It does not seek out a limited set of constants to detain the continuum's dynamics in a single or two-coupled level of geometry or individual-population. Instead, the power is now concerned with drawing a whole state-space for the continuum to pass through in its recurrent differentiations from one state to another, constantly updating its optimal grip from one hidden level to another. This type of power is appearing in the middle of the two layers of a smart home as the software applications, downloaded and executed in its upper layer, also tend to redeploy smart objects below constantly into each new sensor-actuator arc to unfold a hidden marketable level of the space (Figure 5). For instance, in an existing smart solution to "the wellness of an elderly living alone," a set of smart objects, including a room heater, toaster, microwave, TV, bed, and chair, is deployed by an algorithm that calculates the "wellness parameters," the measure for space's engagement with a person's health-related routine (Suryadevara et al. 2013). On the other hand, the same set of objects can be redeployed in other applications to calculate other parameters, such as the measures of space's engagement with energy-consuming routine (Moreno et al. 2014), calorie-burning routine (Helal et al. 2009), and

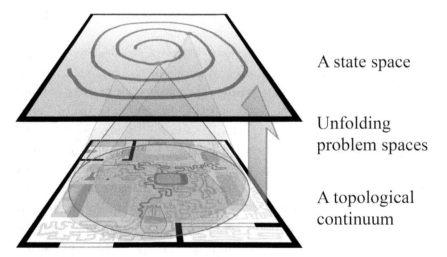

A state space

Unfolding
problem spaces

A topological
continuum

Figure 5 An intensive space and a problem space.

so forth. As the semantic protocol to define possible interoperations of these nonhuman actors in a smart home, the IoT ontology in the middle, in this respect, represents a different form of governmentality, and its optimization of the space for the most livable condition does not pertain to reducing it to a population of the objects interoperating within the statistical regularity of the homeowner's daily routines. Alexa Routines, for instance, are sets of actions Alexa-powered smart appliances perform as the preemptive substitutes of the homeowner's physical routines for turning an Amazon-built smart home into each optimal state to a variety of goals it predicts from verbal or behavioral cues. And these machinic routines are inexhaustible in their customizability neither because the homeowner is the reservoir of insatiable needs nor because of the new gadgets she would purchase in the future. It is rather because these objects are subject to the constant recombination and redeployment to detect some still unresolved uneasiness always remaining in her "Good Morning Routine," "Start my Day Routine," "Screen Time Routine," "Good Night Routine," and so forth (Amazon n.d., "Alexa Routines"). The machine-to-machine protocol of the IoT is, in this respect, designed to maximize the possible ways for the smart objects to interoperate under the assumptions that there always remain some unknown problems and that the hidden parameters to measure, or to commodify, these problems can be identified through the constant reassemblage of the objects' intensive interoperations. Re-stirring the space once hardwired by a person's everyday routines and exploring all the problematic levels its resumed re-differentiation could pass through, this new technique for space-binding, in turn, transforms the smart home into a continuum, or a nested set of problems related to each other by symmetry-breaking bifurcations.[6]

Understood as a manifold, smart home, therefore, redefines the meaning of domestic space. It is no longer something lived by and organized through a person's habitual sensorimotor activities. It should rather be constantly re-differentiated into each specific "problem space," in which a particular "set of operators" are temporarily aligned with a certain IoT application to convert "a set of [problematic] *initial* states" of the space into "a set of *goal* states" (Newell 1980: 5, emphasis in original). A person cannot govern these problems optimally not because there are too many of them but because she cannot live at all different levels simultaneously. The smart objects thus do not need to be symmetrical to the context of the homeowner's direct use of them. For the larger number of smart objects to be interoperable enough to foreground all the hidden parameters of the space, they should be symmetrical to the microscopic perturbations of the continuum each other's operation arouses.

Ontopower

As early as the 1950s, the American architect Charles Eames anticipated that future architectures would approach their new state of the art "based on handling and relating of an impossible number of factors." His early vision for cybernetic architecture, however, required the architects to take huge responsibility to control "the effect of and affect on many simultaneous factors" because these humans were the only experts "to use such a tool" that "could make possible the inclusion of more factors—and could make calculable the possible results of relationships between combinations of factors" (Halpern 2014: 134). About a half-century later, Mark Weiser in the 1990s suggested ubiquitous computing as this kind of tool to integrate a manifold of human and machine-generated databases into one's home and office. However, what the ubicomp's slogan of "calm technology" promised was not to enable humans to process all computational elements simultaneously but to liberate them from their previous responsibility for multitasking, namely to symmetrify lots of technical objects simultaneously to their conscious goals (Weiser and Brown 1997). Finally, in our still-coming age of calm technology, we witness that the withdrawals of smart devices into our intensified peripheries are furthered by the corporate conductors of topological power, making every human problem potentially symmetrical to—or expressed in the form of equations consistent to—their smart applications. The state-space the IoT lays over our intensified smart home redefines these problems as what we cannot access since they are too dispersed and embedded, but we still need to pay for their algorithmic and preemptive solutions.

The market potential of smart homes is, therefore, proportional to the number of problems assumed to hide in its intensive space. To justify the IoT's interventions, these problems must remain undistinguishable until their urgency is detected by each software application. Under this commercial necessity, a smart home can be defined as what Massumi calls a "crisis-incubating environment" (2015: 40), where the crises are concealed in the forms asymmetrical to a Poincaréan observer, or our homeowner, who could recognize the problems only too late after the crises already disturb the symmetries of her daily routines. And what the recent smart home applications and other regional smart environments incubate foremost as this sort of crisis is hidden inefficiency issues in people's everyday lives, such as unnecessary energy wastes (Moreno et al. 2014). No longer merely being a problem of one's bad habit, the inefficiency is now embedded in the imperceptible fluctuations of space that her nonconscious behaviors precipitate. "The preemptive power" of the software layer thus needs to be always ready to "counter the event-driving force of accident if it catches it in the before of incipience" (Massumi 2015: 40). In other words, "if Alexa has a hunch that you're away from home or everyone has gone to bed, she can proactively turn off lights and adjust the thermostat to your preferred sleeping temperature," preemptively acting "on her hunches without having to ask" (Amazon n.d., "Alexa Smart Home"). As Massumi says, the power of this sort is environmental as it "alters the life environment's conditions of emergence," but it is different from how biopower detains a continuum within "a territory, grasped from the angle of its actually providing livable conditions for an existing biological being" (40). It also goes deeper than how Foucault's environmentality (2008) is recently revisited as the power that influences "the 'rules of the game' through the modulation and regulation of environments" to optimize people's ways of life with the maximum degree of freedom (Gabrys 2014: 35) or that expands Skinnerian "behavioral techniques" to the techniques of "environmental psychology" for "managing and controlling affordances" of the environments (Hörl 2018: 160). While this Foucauldian environment is still to be optimally graspable by our biological sensors and motors, or by our behavioral economic reorganization of sensorimotor activities, a manifold the topological power intervenes in is rather "a prototerritory tensed with a compelling excess of potential which renders it strictly unlivable" or ungraspable for humans (Massumi 2015: 40): the multiplicity of hidden levels that a society of smart objects in an ideal IoT ontology assumes to unravel one by one through their intensive interoperations. Tensed with this ungraspable multiplicity and unlimited interoperability of smart objects, the IoT's crisis-incubating materiality also cultivates its smart futures, which could be brought into reality as proper sets of smart objects eventually discover the hidden parameters for each unknown problem. Massumi uses the term *ontopower* for this topological power distinguishable from Foucaultian biopower. And, as he exemplifies with the battlefields of modern warfare against "the proteiform 'terrorism'" (11) and as Howe (2019) suggests in the case of Iceland's glaciers with "environmental precarities," this power works for any "continuum in space/time/matter" with excessive orders, asymmetrical to the "human-centered" sensing practices, but symmetrical to the sensing practices of "other-than-human entities" (Gabrys 2016a). As the domestic counterpart to these post-9/11 battlefields and Anthropocenic environments, a smart home also incubates its own problems asymmetrical to our everyday sensorimotor activities.

Ulrich Beck said in the 1980s that "the 'logic' of risk production" would replace the "logic of wealth production" in late capitalism where the risk distribution, not the wealth, becomes the most urgent problem for the still ongoing project of modernization (1992: 12). Under the "conditions of 'scarcity society,'" the technoscience as the engine of modernization was, he says, for "opening the gates to hidden sources of social wealth." On the other hand, under the condition of a risk society where "for many people problems of 'overweight' take the place of hunger," the issue for this technoscientific modernization is no longer "obvious scarcity" but invisible side effects of modernization, such as harmful chemicals and pollutants, which "escape perception and are localized in the sphere of physical and chemical formulas" (20–1). These threats, detached from "any possibility of perception," are "not only transmitted by science, but in the strict sense are scientifically constituted" (162). Modernization's self-referential turn to its own side effects, or modernization risks, has formed a vicious cycle of self-intensification, which has constantly generated new side effects no matter how many solutions have been accumulated to the known problems so far. The "insatiable demands long sought by economists" have in this sense been discovered from our inexhaustible concerns over the life-threatening side effects in the technoscientific second nature while the welfare states of the West have claimed that material demands from the first nature, such as hunger and basic needs, have almost been sated and satisfied (23).

As the local demonstration of this risk-cultivating second nature, smart home however suggests that some of the urgent problems hidden in our not-enough modernized ways of life are still rooted in the first nature of our biological self. In this new domestic space characterized by its capacity to monitor its own energy and resource consumption, our biological needs as much as the sociocultural are revealed to have never been satisfied optimally by the consumerism of the past century insofar as our self-recognition of desires and consumer skill to arrange the objects in hand to fulfill these desires has always entailed inevitable delays and inefficiencies. Unlike Beck's expectation, the fields of science that have been the most enthusiastic about embedding their "shunting yards of problems" (179), or a web of scientific measures for each different problem, might be, in this sense, neither chemistry nor environmental science but the studies on the too-human-inefficiencies in our biological first nature, such as behavioral economics (Nadler and McGuigan 2018). In a smart home, the IoT replaces these shunting yards of behavioral sciences with its algorithmic sensor-actuator arcs and integrates each unfolded thread of the problem into its new service domains.

Self-knowledge and Self-symmetrification

If the ultimate goal of a smart home is to make it prepared for any problem lurking in a person's everyday life, what should be symmetrified first to the IoT's algorithmic preemption would be the person's intentional being. Her quantified-self is then a topological solution for this. As the digital shadow of a person's everyday practice, quantified-self suggests that the presences of human "bodies, minds, and daily lives" in smart environments are translatable into the imperceptible perturbations within databases collected through "various self-tracking tools and applications, including emotion trackers, food trackers, and pedometers" (Ruckenstein and Pantzar 2017: 402). Like other topological matters, these human-caused perturbations enfold various levels that signify her "wants, needs, and goals ... individual diversity in areas such as sleeping, eating, drinking, or exercising" (411). However, occurring as nonconscious processes in the first place, these problems would remain just fluctuations within a physiological continuum of her body (or brain) until they appear, at best after several milliseconds of missing time, to be something (un) conscious to her self-understanding (Hansen 2015a: 90; Hayles 2017). If it is true that her intention is not the cause of her agency but the consequence of lots of distributed actors in a smart home, these too-human milliseconds of delays in self-understanding would be already long enough to make an intensive continuum of her body—as yet to be bound by her consciousness—feel like a crisis that needs to be preempted by the IoT. Given the inefficiency embedded in this delay of human consciousness, her smart home should be under the control of the IoT applications to make it always and already optimal for her imminent intentions and desires. Even before she finds she wants to go to bed, the environment should be symmetrified to the actions to come by dimming the light and warming the room. In short, the homeowner needs to have a sort of open-mindedness as a new technique of self-management, which can be called self-symmetrification: to render one's nonconscious more accessible by various smart devices better than humans at managing the most optimal state of their neurophysiology. This technique to symmetrify one's daily routines to the IoT may, however, not ask for her too much but to live her days as routinely as possible by following such instructions: Do not talk "to Alexa in a stiff, awkward manner" but "relax" when you talk with it; Do not use "Alexa in a restricted and stunted way," otherwise you would feel "reduced as a person, even robotic"; Do not let yourself locked-in an assemblage by "repeating the same interactions" that would constraint what you as "the consumer, as part of the assemblage, is capable of doing and experiencing" (Hoffman and Novak 2018: 1179, 1187). She would be then an economic human, not in the sense of Skinnerian behavioralism, from which Foucault in 1979 drew his *Homo œconomicus*, but in the sense of current behavioral economics. In other words, it is not because she is a rational decision-maker but because of her "systemic responses to the variables of the environment" (Foucault 2008: 270; Millner 2019). Human rationality for behavioral economists is enhanced through the engineering of these environmental variables by means of their "nudge" policy, which redesigns the environment as a "choice architecture" by redistributing conscious and nonconscious cues intervening in people's decision-making. The two words contradictory to each other but combined in their "libertarian paternalism," in this respect, suggest the meaning of the new symmetry between humans and their smart environments. In "the libertarian aspect" of the term, humans still feel their "freedom of choice" guaranteed at most or even increased in the new choice architecture (Thaler and Sunstein 2008: 5); but, at the nonconscious level, they are in fact constantly pushed by "choice engines" (Thaler and Tucker 2013).

The smart home this chapter described is one of the most advanced examples of these nudge architectures. The smart homeowner now rediscovers herself not symmetrical to her self-understanding but as a host of manifold vital signals tracked by smart devices' "power of countless observations of small incidents of change—incidents that used to vanish without a trace." However, contrary to how the early proponents of quantified-self once willfully "delegated" the practice of "data-gathering" and "record-keeping" "to a host of simple Web apps," her movements in a smart home are more silently tracked by the ubiquitous sensors that quantify "every facet of life, from sleep to mood to pain, 24/7/365" (Wolf 2019). She is no longer a director of flows but a source of flows, and if the continuous optimization of her everyday life the smart home promises is proportional to the number of connections she has with the ubiquitous sensors and actuators, the only rational decision left to her is not to symmetrify the devices to her everyday uses but symmetrify herself to every new device.

Human Response-ability

In these new smart environments, we no longer bear the responsibility of PC users, namely, to rearrange algorithmic objects available on a desktop or a GUI of software into an assemblage symmetrical to our conscious goals. We are required instead to symmetrify our conscious or nonconscious activities to the ubiquitous computing in the background of our lives in the, following the everyday protocols camouflaged in routinized practices, such as wearing smart clothes, watches, and glasses, operating smart appliances, or using smart plugs to smarten non-smart appliances. *Self-symmetrification* is, in this sense, the practice of transforming one's own body into a manifold within a network, or to black-box its physiology and neurology as the indeterminate middle within the multiplicities of sensor-actuator arcs each smart application organizes in a smart home. Its effectiveness in optimizing our surroundings to our psychosomatic state and vice versa is, however, irrelevant to the behavioralist reduction of the body's neurophysiological continuum to a simple sensory-motor mechanism similar to a Skinner box. Instead, its promise for the ever-optimizable near future is based on a topological feature of the continuum that bifurcates as many different sensor-actuator responses as the number of smart applications.

In the previous chapter, we explored the smart home as a new domestic space enmeshing the human owner with its sensor-actuator arcs. The wireless interoperability of smart objects and their constant reassemblages enable a smart home to bifurcate each different problem space from moment to moment, thus stabilizing the most urgent perturbations that happen in the home's hidden physiology and neurology. As Deleuze writes about "societies of control," a smart home in this scenario functions "like a self-deforming cast that will continuously change from one moment to the other." The chapter also topologically redefined the homeowner as an undifferentiated manifold within the assemblages, whose conscious and nonconscious responses to the ubiquitous smart objects were not only programed along habitually hardwired sensorimotor arcs but under constant transformations "like a sieve whose mesh will transmute from point to point" (Deleuze 1992: 4).

The media studies discourse on human response-ability to a technical system has found its prototype in the operator of Whirlwind radar, a Cold War-era digital computer developed for the US Navy. In this real-time early warning system of the 1950s, the job of a human operator in front of a CRT monitor was to make the "man-machine interaction" continue through the repeated "input-output relationship" between the operator and computers. For instance, a human operator was typically tasked with shooting "a light gun" at a small flashing dot on the monitor to identify potential enemies or "taking various push button actions" in response to the data that the computers showed them "in varying display format" (Rowell and Streich 1964: 539). For this military system to detect ongoing enemy attacks in real time for their permanent deterrence, the operator was trained to perform each specialized task to *close a gap* between a monitor and switch panel through his semi-mechanized behavioral responses (539). In short, the operator was settled into a militarized Skinner box.

In the age of the Internet of Things, this model of human-machine interaction is updated to a non-Skinnerian version as the sustainability of the system in current smart environments does not require closing the loop for the deterrence of known problems but constantly reopening the loop to preempt unknowns. The responsibility of a human operator is not to fit their neuroplasticity into the cast of automated input-output relations but to let it be diffused, as through a sieve, into lots of different potential networks. The system, moreover, is not designed to prevent extremist futures like nuclear holocausts or consumers no longer responding to commercials but rather mundane, measureless dangers like terrorism and pandemics. These ubiquitous threats are constituted by invisible networks that constantly change form or by consumers whose reiterative desires lock them in current market segments. As the proactive means to prepare for these unknown networks or to re-network the markets around unknown needs, smart objects require their human users to hold in reserve some extra response-ability, which they will need for the new sensor-actuator arcs that the IoT will offer them, in theory as a way to break through a current impasse. Until these innovative pathways emerge, our black-boxed neuronal connectivity should remain plastic.

The neuronal "flexibility" that Malabou defines as a brain's ability "to receive a form or impression, to be able to fold oneself" (2008: 12) might be enough to train the human operator of Whirlwind through its software manuals or protocols for input-output interconnections. But our new responsibility to reassemble ubiquitous intervals between smart objects is no longer imparted to us through the disciplinary process of (military) training. Rather, it is performed in our living through everyday protocols that renew what she calls our "neuroplasticity" as "the resource of giving form, the power to create, to invent or even to erase an impression, the power to style" (2008).

In his genealogy of human responsibility in computing from that of the Whirlwind operators in the 1950s to the early videogamers in the 1970s, Claus Pias (2011) points out how, before the PC era, users were integrated into the machinic rhythm of algorithms by responding to the "ping" computers sent with the "pong" as a human answer. Pias derives the term *ping* from the software utility of the same name designed for network administration, which functions to send a small data packet to a particular address in the network to see if it is ready to answer, like a sonar technology to detect responsible objects in the dark of oceans. Meanwhile, *pong*, named after the early Atari videogame, describes the condition of a gamer, responsible for exchanging a virtual ping-pong ball with a computer across a net and thus also responsible for being in the right place at the right time to continue a rally. The pair of *ping* and *pong* for Pias symbolizes the necessity of closing the loop between humans and computers to "prolong the playing" itself. For Whirlwind operators, this *Ping-Pong* with computers meant being responsible for constantly delaying the threat of total devastation, or "Game Over" as the "symbolic death of the player and an end to all communication" (73, 76). For multitasking users in the PC era, this symbolic gameplay might have signified their responsibility to provide proper inputs to each different program just as stage-based videogame designs in this period redefined the gamer's responsibility as developing each different strategy for different goals from stage to stage rather than a mere pong. In the UC era, on the other hand, the sustainability of these machinic pings and human pongs is no longer based simply on the flexibility of human responses to different software interfaces. It rather depends more on the system's capacity to reassemble its sensor-actuator arcs in response to the plasticity of data streams that spontaneous and nonconscious user behaviors generate.

The following chapter examines emergent "open-world" videogame design as an illustration of changes in gamer responsibility corresponding to the UC era. Enmeshed by a network of algorithmic objects in virtual reality, the neuroplasticity of the open-world gamer is responsible for drawing multiple lines of correlation among the objects as a means to individuate a plethora of hidden stories, events, puzzles, and other encounters embedded in a playable world.

Targeting in Open-World Videogames

Targeting and Videogame Objects

To aim a crosshair at an object, or to *target* it, is the most rudimentary skill players must master in many videogames. From a first-person shooter (FPS) caught in a killer instinct for shooting every enemy to a third-person role-playing gamer (RPG) obsessive about searching for hidden clues to continue a quest, targeting is the first step to map a player's chance encounters with objects. There are lots of targetable objects, such as non-playable characters (NPC), enemies, props in backgrounds including animals and plants, and items. Each of them has a different degree of concreteness according to its way of becoming in virtual reality—whether assigned to certain locations when a map is generated, like the bosses and treasure chests in *The Elder Scrolls V: Skyrim* (2011), or randomly generated in certain areas as a player character steps in, like the citizen NPCs in *Grand Theft Auto V* (2013), or produced by a player such as healing potions made of other ingredients. Even for an object existing from the very beginning with concrete properties defining its existence (such as the coordinate of a position and predefined behavior patterns to environments), it is only through targeting that this object is dragged out from its initial isolation and begins to interact with others and eventually reoccurs as an *event* a gamer experiences as a part of a story or play. In other words, targeting realizes an object's operational values by implementing its interactions with others, whose collective interoperations would progressively unfold certain stories, challenges, and quests hidden in a gaming world. In a recent philosophy of videogame design called *open-world*, the number of targetable objects and their different responses to a gamer's targeting are, therefore, determinants for the number of possible events that the gamer's interactions could unfold from its virtual reality.

Targeting is in this sense a supplementary action to fill the gaps between the objects being pure signifiers in this narrative genre. Under the conditioning of an object-oriented *game engine*, these objects are generated in an open-world as individual *paradigmatic* elements belonging to each different class of objects with different properties and responses to the environments. On the other hand, as the only un-programmed source of uncertainty in this open-world, a gamer's targeting functions to create actual *syntactic* interconnections between objects and converts them into the events unfolding. However, neither solely being a *parolē* to anchor a signifying chain at an instance of storytelling nor an intentional *noetic* activity, targeting in videogames often happens during a gamer's meaningless wandering over objects as well. For these algorithmic beings, a gamer's ludic wandering—that Aarseth calls a gamer's "extranoematic responsibilities" comparable to a reader's "eye movement and the periodic or arbitrary turning of pages" (1997: 1–2)—is indistinguishable from his/her noetic-narrative acts, the targeting intentionally performed to make a story unfold. No matter what a gamer intends, his/her behaviors are, beyond a user-friendly videogame interface, fed back as undifferentiated motor inputs or data streams with which the objects initiate their interoperations. These inputs can be then classified as *either* noetic narrative action *or* ludic wandering but only secondarily as the result of the objects' responses, which can be *either* serialized as an algorithmic simulation of a story arc *or* experienced as mere playful chance encounters. In this sense, the recent design decision for the more playable values or *replayability* in videogames—by such means of making a story unfold in many different paths to multiple endings, hiding more sub-plots, or making even simple encounters enjoyable, in short, by building an open-world—is concerned with such an engineering question: How to make algorithmic objects more communicable so that their interoperations could evolve into creative assemblages for multiple story arcs or more playable values even from a gamer's "emergent strategies" that are "neither anticipated by the game designer, nor ... easily derivable from the rules of a game" (Juul 2002).

This figure-ground switch in videogame design foregrounds an asymmetric engagement between gamers and objects, which the ludologist/narratologist debates of the early videogame studies have failed to recognize in their obsession with the authentic cultural value of gaming blind to the algorithmic *values* generated on the flip side of the interface.[1] As much as targeting is a gamer action to mobilize objects for its strategic goal, the machine also induces and mobilizes this gamer action for drawing motor inputs to instantiate its technical agents, *objects*, into specific operational units. For instance, the audiovisual cues objects radiate and the *auto-targeting* feature that enables the objects to draw the crosshair up to themselves are not only to help gamers to reassemble these objects into certain discursive or playable orders in a more convenient manner but for these objects to target back to the gamers' attentions to extract some data streams for their individuations. In this respect, the studies on gamer behaviors in massive multiplayer online role-playing games (MMORPG) (Chan et al. 2009; Kafai 2010; Lee et al. 2011) may provide another example of this figure-ground switch. While these studies usually analyze log files as algorithmic inscriptions of so-called ludic or narrative gamer behaviors, what remains cryptic on the other side of these human-readable logs would be the networks of objects assembled through their mutual responses gamers' targeting triggered. Contrary to Aarseth's definition of narratives' "hypertext epiphany" from a videogame space, which he supposes to be all rooted in "a planned construct rather than an unplanned contingency" (1997: 91), the objects in an ideal open-world are plastic enough to create certain functional networks even from the unplanned contingency of gamer actions. For all those objects to be relocated in a world played as those generated from, used for, killed by, thrown toward, transacted with, transformed into, and operated upon each other, a gamer's prolonged hours of *aporia* are necessary as the "disoriented movements ... looking for fresh links in a hypertext labyrinth" (78–9).

As a recent trend in nonlinear game design, an open-world is, therefore, characterized by its lack of *invisible walls*, which used to restrict the number of objects a player can interact with in each stage of the game's overall story arc. Commonly used in a linear level design, these walls were given to objects (including the gamer's avatar) as redundant rules from above to prevent certain interactions from happening, especially those conflicting with the story, such as an avatar's leaving for a quest even before a princess is kidnapped. On the other hand, designing an open-world without this sort of transcendent rules means the "task of defining and ordering the [collectives] should be left to the actors themselves" (Latour 2005: 23). In other words, an ideal open-world is potentially open to any controversial interoperations of objects insofar as a space their networking unfolds is still playable, no matter how short-lived its story-arc is or how distracted the current quest is with too many interruptible events to close an arc.

In this sense, the open-world design of recent narrative games simulates an *actor-network* in more than a metaphorical sense. Under ANT's ontological concern for the "world-making activities" of objects, the social is defined "not as a special domain, a specific realm, or a particular sort of thing" such as "invisible and unaccountable social forces." The social in ANT rather results from "a very peculiar movement of re-association and reassembling" traceable only through "following the work done to stabilize the controversies" by objects themselves (Latour 2005: 57, 7, 53). In the open-world design of videogames and its emphasis on objects' autonomy, the "notion of social force" can also be dissolved and replaced "either by short-lived interactions [as mere chance encounters] or by new associations [extended as multiple story-arcs]" (66). The sociality of videogaming in this genre thus appears to be the consequence of the entanglements between human and nonhuman agencies in the open world. First, the rules for interactions, once given as redundant "invisible walls," are now emerging from the interoperations of objects whose uneven distribution on a gameboard is enough to influence the probabilities for their encounters to happen in certain orders. Second, gamers' ludic or narrative interest in objects, which the log-file analysts assumed to be present in the first place as if it's an invisible hand behind objects' autonomous networking, now turns out conversely to be retraceable along "the *summing up* of interactions" between objects (Latour 1999: 17–8), whereas a gamer's avatar is no other than a certain object that generates some uncertainties across the other objects. From the actor-network perspective, the macro state of a network called open-world is thus neither narrative nor ludic a priori, nor algorithmic translation of cultural prototypes outside, such as story or play. It is rather the summing-up of many micro encounters assembled into either a story or a play. As McKenzie Wark says in *Gamer Theory*, "The moral code of the storyline" in videogames is "just an alibi for the computer code of the game," not *vice versa* (2007: par.148). In a similar vein, a gamer's ludic or narrative interest, supposed to overcode the progress of an object network into either a story arc or gameboard, might be an alibi that hides the objects' interest in human gamers being converted to mere data streams for their own becoming.

The actor-network analysis of videogames, one possible model of which this chapter suggests, in this respect, re-operationalizes narrative and play: two human forces in the social, once discussed as if their representational structures or rules of the game have already been transplanted in a videogame space, either to assign certain roles to objects or to define their possible moves on a game board. These two cultural forms now reemerge only as the summing-up of what objects have done to stabilize the uncertainties an avatar arouses in an open-world. If Wark is correct in saying, "The gamer is the new model of the self" that becomes "a function of an algorithm" (2007: par.148), the actor-network analysis could show how this functional self is also summed up from what one's avatar does: *targeting*, an operational form of voluntary or involuntary attention to the objects in the open-world.

For modeling an actor-network as an alternative framework for videogame studies, this chapter examines first how the algorithmic paradigm called object-oriented programming (OOP) simulates various cultural goals and interests of its end-users through the networks of its algorithmic objects. It then investigates actual gaming objects in a videogame genre that I call *object-oriented puzzles* and recent open-world videogames, and traces how the objects in these games reassemble *gaming subjects* and their cultural experiences of gaming.

OOP: Object-Oriented Programming/Puzzle

In the 1970s, Alan Kay, the creator of an early OOP language *Smalltalk*, already anticipated a sort of nonhuman turn that his "object-oriented design" of programming would bring about. He talked about "a very McLuhanish feeling about media and environments: that once we've shaped tools … they turn around and 'reshape us'" (Kay 1993: 30). Since their appearance in the mid-twentieth century, high-level computer languages have functioned to install a user-friendly linguistic layer upon "the computational real" of algorithmic culture, *bits* or mere differences of voltage fluctuating on system boards, and have translated these ephemeral signals on circuit boards into human-understandable data structures and their functional relations (Joque 2016: 351–2; Yoran 2018). Before OOP, the high-level computer language was "constructed as a sequential set of commands that followed one after the other" (Joque 2016: 341), and the artificial intelligence of the time was in turn abstracted as a sort of mathematical mind ruling over the machine codes at lower levels, reminiscent of professional programmers with exclusive accesses to the mainframes in big institutes at the time. On the other hand, developed not only for experts but various end-users of the PC era, including even children, *Smalltalk* for Kay was to map the same computational real on motherboards with collectives of autonomous agents called *objects* "all hooked together by a very fast network" communicating *small talks* to each other (Kay 1993: 3).

According to Kay's personal historiography, this emerging object-oriented philosophy was reflective of the shift in his academic interests, which he describes as the shift from his undergraduate math major "centered on abstract algebras with their few operations generally applying to many structures" to biology minor "with its notions of … one kind of building block able to differentiate into all needed building blocks" (5–6). This analogy between OOP and cell biology in the 1970s suggests how the idea of objects' recursive becoming in operational environments was suggested as the architectural principle for the incipient algorithmic culture just as "the notions of 20th century physics and biology" aimed to rewrite Nature with "the recursive composition of a single kind of behavioral building block" (3). The "algebraic patterns" to overcode bits into mathematical variables in linear programming gave way to manifold algorithmic agents processing these binary signals through their own data structures and autonomous interoperations with one another, not necessarily overcoded by a supplementary dimension over and above. The networks of objects loosely assembled along these bits-messages on a motherboard began to be considered as a solution for any general tasks through their multiple and "inexhaustible" ways of reassemblage (Yoran 2018: 130–2).

The actual domestication of binary signals, which began to proliferate in people's daily lives during this early stage of the PC era, was, however, not achieved simply at once by the marketing of personal computers as desktop technologies. A transitional period was required to remap the multiplicity of end-user purposes upon its new linguistic layer, and, in this context, OOP for Kay was effective due to not only its efficient compiling process but its intuitive way to map the real-world problems with monad-like objects that hide their "combination of state and process inside and can be dealt with only through the exchange of messages" (3). As much as these black-boxed objects were what programmers needed to adapt to in the changed condition of the algorithmic culture, a variety of end-users and their peculiar purposes also reappeared to be the complex real-world problems that OOP needed to remap within its object networks. As observed from children's playful use of *Smalltalk* to model "amusement parks, like Disneyland, their schools, the stores they and their parents shopped in" (23), something ludic and narrative was thus what this educational computer language redisposed first upon its network topology in order to enroll these future programmers to its object-oriented philosophy. Many purposeless coding exercises, such as the famous "Hello world!" example in programming textbooks, still show what a novice programmer must learn first is to reassemble these algorithmic objects into a hypertext architecture for a sort of interactive storytelling. The McLuhanish feeling Kay once had about his own creature becomes more ordinary in the "human-computer symbiosis" (7) of the PC era and it reflects the necessity of translating cultural experiences of programming, its playful *small talks*, into something to be mapped upon a network of objects. To paraphrase in an actor-network term, the objects in OOP exemplify *immutable mobiles*, the nonhuman actors that translate the peculiarity of a matter under research into a form compatible and combinable with other systems and objects. As immutable data structures, which can be incarnated into many different instances, the objects are capable of transposing peculiar end-user purposes to a network topology their interoperations draw.[2] This does not simply mean objects are not mere building blocks ready for the user purposes as pregiven social factors. This chapter's actor-network perspective rather emphasizes, in the current algorithmic culture, how these purposes are constantly reassembled into the computational problems resolvable through, or symmetrical to, the networks the OOP affords against the obsolete procedural programming.

In Kay's retrospection, the early "interactive computer graphic" applications, such as Ivan Sutherland's *Sketchpad* (1963), were the first to concretize this object-oriented philosophy as the graphic designer's means to instantiate different geometric figures from the same topological object abstractly defined (Kay 1993: 7). For another instance of graphical objects responsible to capture the generality of end-user purposes, we can examine videogames and their role in popularizing OOP as an ontological and aesthetic style of problem-solving in algorithmic cultures, which has incorporated more and more cultural activities and their singularities into the general purpose networks of algorithmic objects. For the previous two decades, the digital's remediation of culture has provided an alibi for the digital's penetration into private spheres along the domestic assemblages of circuit boards embedded in ubiquitous computing devices. On the other hand, the user-friendliness of videogame interfaces at the same time has provided the end-users, gamers, with an effective but nonprofessional means to domesticate these ephemeral and intangible materialities in digital infrastructures into some objectified and personified forms of agents (Johnson 1997: Ch.6). These objects have served for not only fulfilling gamers' cultural interests but mobilizing their actions oscillating between ludic *aporia* and narrative *epiphany*.

The Incredible Machine

Kevin Ryan's creative puzzle game *The Incredible Machine* (1993) demonstrates how a simple object-oriented game design can realize the general purposeness of personal computers. The goal of this puzzle is to make a literal *machinic assemblage*[3] performing a simple task (such as "pop all the balloons," "drop the cage onto Mort the Mouse") using everyday objects available in each stage. For this goal, a gamer needs to drag and drop each object from the inventory on the right to a niche position within the main frame at the center so that simple operations of the redisposed objects would miraculously fill the missing links of *the incredible machine* (Figure 6).

Each stage begins with a number of objects distributed on the frame, and each type of object is characterized by its unique way to interact with or react to other objects. For instance, a bulb shedding light on a lens burns the fuse of a dynamite; a ball hitting one end of a seesaw triggers a gun roped to another end; a motor connected to a conveyor belt catapults a baseball on it. Simple rules govern the machine's operation: when a gamer clicks "START MACHINE" on the right-top, the objects responsive to environmental parameters (gravity and air pressure),

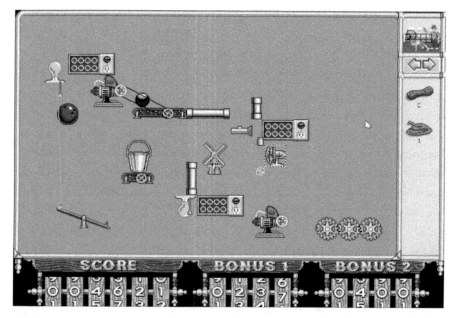

Figure 6 *The Incredible Machine.*

such as balls and balloons, move first. If they collide with others, their direction and speed change according to the game's physics engine and the collided object also implements its operation if the condition is met (for instance, when a ball falls on a switch, the flashlight is on). When there is no more extendable operation, the machine stops. To make the machine keep operating until the assigned task is done, a gamer, therefore, needs to redeploy each object in a way in which it would, after the machine's execution, gradually evolve into a niche element of the machinic that successfully fulfills a given task. The role of the gamer as an engineer of this incredible machinic assemblage is thus to adjust the initial state of objects' reciprocal orientations to the condition akin to what Simondon calls *metastability*: "the initial absence of interactive communication between them, followed by a subsequent communication between orders of magnitude and stabilization" (1992: 304). For Simondon, "individuation" of technical objects from their abstract to concrete states involves not so much some invisible forces outside but a sort of selective pressure that works across their uneven distribution in less interactive initial states. Metastable objects therefore "have no effect on the other elements" at first, but gradually interoperate with one another in "a multitude of reciprocal causalities" (1980: 13–4; Yoran 2018). This ostensible stability of an assemblage, or its metastability, is charged with potentialities to progress into another level of stability through its further individuations (and, in this respect, these metastable objects are also akin to what Latour calls *plasma*, entities "not yet socialized, not yet engaged in metrological chains," but open to an indefinite number of actor-networks (Latour 2005: 244)). The *Incredible* character of the *Machine* in this puzzle game is this metastability that keeps its loosely assembled components, objects, always potent to evolve further into different networks with different functions.

In popular OOP languages, such as C++ and JAVA, the autonomy of an "object{}" from the "main{}" function in a source code is symbolized by its braces "{}" which enfold the definitions of its constituents and data structure as well as its selective exposure and response to environments. Assigned and instantiated within the "main{}" function as each operational unit for its goals, objects{} in OOP replace the cumbersome sequential commands in procedural programming with their recursive and flexible combinations. In *The Incredible Machine*, the main frame for the machine to be assembled provides a user-friendly interface similar to the "main{}" function in OOP as it serves as the platform for the objects to be assigned from the inventory on the right. On the other hand, in the inventory, objects available for each stage are defined in a decontextualized manner just as abstract classes of objects in OOP have to be first defined outside of the main{}function. For the object-oriented programmers and puzzle gamers, to design an algorithmic system or a machinic assemblage is, therefore, to allocate these objects into certain metastable states, from which they would be, in every single execution or "START MACHINE," instantiated into each functional part of a logical or mechanical circuit to perform the given tasks of the machine. In both, the variability of the environments—databases or human inputs—changes how some objects respond, and it could induce completely different ways of the system's individuation.

In this puzzle, the metastability in which objects are trapped is expressed in an unexpected aesthetic form when the machine malfunctions. It becomes visible, for instance, when an object is stuck between two others as shown in the case of a basketball in Figure 7, unable to be bound out from one end of a seesaw because of being blocked by a pipe, another object. If the physics engine imitates the physical laws exactly, the ball falling in between should be gradually relocated in a stable state after several oscillations. However, even if the momentum of the ball is the minimum detectable by the engine, it still maintains that minimum even after it collides with another object and thus keeps oscillating between the obstacles until the game stops the machine forcibly. Put differently, the game's physics engine is biased toward keeping objects metastable and always containing at least the minimum potential for further interactions rather than stabilizing them into nonoperational stasis. As the expression of an object's resistance to the

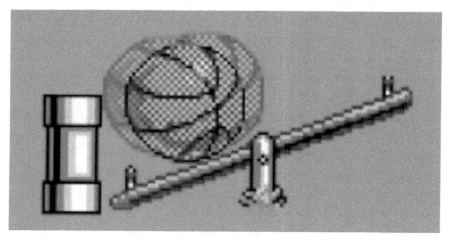

Figure 7 The basketball in a metastable state (modified by author).

exhaustion of its operational values, this tiny agitation is fed back to the gamer as a signal referring to the necessity of the ball's relocation into another niche in the next trial for its further individuations.

Alongside a campaign mode in which a gamer plays each stage with each predefined goal and set of available objects, *The Incredible Machine* also provides an extra stage called the "FREEFORM MODE," in which a gamer can use and manipulate all objects and environmental parameters without having any specified goal. In this mode, the metastable vibrations of objects exemplified by the above basketball are potentially mobilizable for the machine's individuation into an indefinite number of playful tasks and purposeless performances. Whether the machine is working for an arbitrary goal set by a gamer or just for experimenting with unexplored momenta hidden in everyday objects the game simulates, this experimental mode of gameplay is demonstrating how the assemblage in the making is capable of translating any particular goal-oriented gamer intentions and even purposelessness. The machine's general purposeness is preserved here as the game's physics engine always reserves the minimum momenta of objects for their other possible interoperations in the next trials. On the other hand, facing this incredible flexibility of the machine, the gamer with "a very McLuhanish feeling" might discover that her agency as a system builder is now reassembled from these distributed objects and redefined as her ability to trigger the objects' collective individuation into each goal-oriented network.

Before "START MACHINE," the assemblage of objects maintains its metastability with environment-sensitive momenta preserved within the interstices between objects. After "START MACHINE," however, these objects begin to couple with each other according to their own ways to respond to given environmental parameters and gradually individuate a network for a specific goal. As Bogost says about the paradigm shift that OOP signifies, *The Incredible Machine* in this way simulates "a new kind of system: the spontaneous and complex result of multitudes rather than singular and absolute holisms" (2006: 4). The sustainability of this system is dependent on whether the programmed metastability would remain intact even in the changeable environments. And insofar as the only source of randomness in the game is human inputs and uncertainties they cause across the objects, the miracle of the machine this game symbolizes is also about the incredible transformability of this assemblage of nonhuman cognizers sustainable even in unpredictable environments of the human-caused.

The Perpetual Motion Machines in *Portal*

In *The Incredible Machine*, the gamer's targeting intervenes only in the initial states of objects before the physics engine implements their attractive and repulsive forces, and so triggers their actual becoming. On the other hand, in today's 3D puzzle-platformer games such as the *Portal* series, a gamer's avatar is put on the same platform where other game objects are distributed and its first-person shooting substitutes for what the mouse pointer did in the old puzzle gameplay. As the only object capable of bringing truly random behaviors to this immanent gameboard with no transcendent viewpoint from above, an avatar is interacting with other objects to trigger their becoming a network to solve a given goal, such as unfolding hidden paths to the exit of a labyrinthine. For instance, an exit in *Portal* (2007) will appear when a cube is transported to a distanced platform and placed upon a button on it. But, for the cube and button to be interoperable, the avatar should fire the *portal gun* to create two portals to transport the cube from here to there. In a typical single-player campaign where most tiles on the walls and floors are connectable through the portals, the avatar thus needs to shoot the tiles to make a path to the exit emerge out of the surfaces of distributed objects in order to escape from this laboratory-labyrinth created by a mad scientist according to the game's story.

Despite their being narrative-based, shooting in the *Portal* series is also often performed regardless of the goal and story of each stage. As many user-performed *Portal* experiments on YouTube show, for the gamers whose primary concern is to create their own labyrinths using the "Puzzle Creator" mode (a FREEFORM MODE in *Portal II* 2011) rather than to complete the campaign, the avatar's playful wandering in labyrinths is not a painful experience of deferred "desire for [narrative] closure," which Aaserth means by *aporia* (1997: 92). Shooting the tiles in these experiments conversely pertains to the desired purposelessness to examine more ways of tunneling between objects and twisting their spatial relations to unfold a greater number of transformable labyrinths hidden in the assemblages. In *Portal,* one interesting experiment in this purposeless tunneling happens when an object falls into a portal on a floor that is tunneled to another portal on the ceiling directly above. Since the physics engine of the game conserves the momentum of an object when it passes through portals, this object falling perpetually between portals is gradually accelerated by gravitational force until it reaches the maximum velocity available, and eventually meta-stabilized into a sort of *perpetual motion machine* (Figure 8). Contrary to the tiny vibration of the

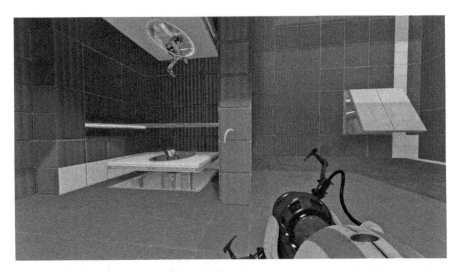

Figure 8 A perpetual motion machine in *Portal II*.

basketball in *The Incredible Machine*, this free-falling entrapped between portals shows another instance of an object's metastable fluctuation that gradually accumulates its momentum to the maximum in this case.

Even though this sort of perpetual machine is often exhibited on YouTube as purely experimental as it violates physical laws (*Science in Portal 2* 2012) or purely aesthetic as visualizes some unimaginable dimension (*Portal Infinite Loop* 2011), building up an object's momentum within the loop also has a significant strategic value in the game's campaign mode as it allows a gamer to reorient the object, a cube or avatar itself, for instance, to a farther platform not reachable in an ordinary way (*Portal* 2007: in-game developer commentary #12, 48). For instance, while Player 2's avatar in Figure 8 falls between two portals on the floor and ceiling, Player 1's avatar could shoot the portal gun at a distanced wall and make a new portal there; then Player 2's avatar falling into the portal on the floor would come out from the new portal on the wall with the maximum momentum conserved through the portals. In this way, a metastable object in perpetual motion within a closed circuit is drawing the gamer's intervention, targeting, as the trigger to reorient the free-falling with the maximum momentum to the action for the gamer's goal, namely unfolding a path to escape the labyrinth. While the gamer plans this escape scenario, the objects under interoperation gradually form a network, and this network is plastic enough to map not only the gamer's creative goal-oriented behaviors

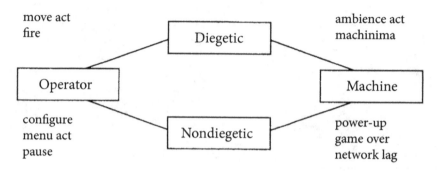

Figure 9 Galloway's classification of gamic actions (2006: 37).

but her creative purposelessness as it can be transformed into an indefinite number of labyrinth structures responding to both planned and unplanned contingencies from a human gamer.

Programming the Open-Worlds Metastable

In the previous section on puzzle gaming, targeting was discussed as a human-caused trigger for a network solution to a given task at each stage. On the other hand, the open-world setting in today's narrative games usually contains these object-oriented puzzles as parts of their storytelling. From the first *Legend of Zelda* to the most recent *Legend of Zelda: Breath of the Wild*, the puzzles in this RPG franchise have functioned to embed certain temporal orders in the player character Link's exploration of a game space. In the first *Zelda* (1986), Link needs to visit the eight dungeons distributed in the world for searching the eight pieces of an ancient relic called *Triforce of Wisdom*, which would lead him to *Death Mountain*, where *Princess Zelda* is held hostage. But the ways in which this simple rescue narrative is unfolded through his dungeon networking are restricted by the existence of certain objects, whose operations can be triggered only after Link follows some fixed orders, such as the gate of the seventh dungeon remains hidden until it responds to the melody of *Recorder* acquirable only in the fifth dungeon. Even in this early open-world RPG game, the linearity of its rescue narrative heading to a single ending is also able to be stretched and bent in many different ways according not only to the paths that Link draws across the eight dungeons—from the most straightforward to the most convoluted—

but also to his unexpected encounters with monsters constantly interrupting his networking. At the same time, on this immanent gameboard with no outside rule except for interoperations of objects, these object-oriented puzzles—given to gamers as an explicit or implicit instruction saying "operate an object upon another to make an event happen"—function to impose certain invariant structures on the narrative-arcs the objects assemble. For instance, these puzzle elements keep invariant some significant inflection points of the arcs, such as "the sixth dungeon ought to be opened after the fifth dungeon," while being stretched and bent flexibly by Link's sometimes purposeless wandering. The classes of interoperable objects defined by the game engine and their uneven distribution on the world map thus determine the types and probabilities of the events capable of being triggered by the gamer's goal-oriented or purposeless motor inputs during the gaming.

According to Galloway, a videogame space turns into a narrative space as these machinic agents called objects and the contingency of human operators "work together in a cybernetic relationship to effect the various actions of the videogame in its entirety." He classifies "gamic actions" along the axis of machine agent ↔ human operator, which is intersected by another axis of diegetic action ↔ nondiegetic actions, as Figure 9 illustrates (2006: 5).

It is notable that, even if a player character's encounters with objects in an open-world are the things to be logged as parts of a story, their probabilities and consequences are often conditioned by certain actions performed outside the story, such as turning on auto-targeting feature or changing difficulty in the setup and calibrating certain environmental parameters in physics engines. These actions, defined as nondiegetic-operator actions in Galloway's diagram, intervene in how a story unfolds by conditioning the probable (trans)formations of object networks as they change not only just the number of interoperable objects, such as enemies, but the patterns of their behavioral responses to environments. For instance, if you select "difficult" in the setup, an enemy's momentum conserved in its metastable circuit of patrolling would be reoriented to the search for the player character when it discovers certain environmental objects, for instance, shrubs, wavering by something behind. But if you select "easy," it would not respond to any environmental signals and kept in passivity. In this sense, the shape of a narrative arc the objects unfold in an open-world is restricted by the asymmetries implicit in the two axes of Galloway's diagram. First, the initial metastability of objects in machine actions requires the instability from a human operator's contingent actions to transform their accumulated momenta into certain events unfolded. Second, as the local occurrences of chance encounters, these diegetic events between a player character and objects are under the probabilistic control of non-diegetic actions of the game engine that governs all the chances of possible events on a gameboard.

In open-world games, targeting as an operator action over machinic objects can be thus re-diagramed as the gamer behavior, which is conditioned by a gameboard as a network of algorithmic objects. The object called *avatar* is in a state of permanent oscillation between goal-oriented and purposeless actions as it is influenced doubly by nearby objects and the game engine as a global agent. On the one hand, in-game nearby objects mobilize the gamer's targeting, which would trigger their individuations into *epiphanic* local events. On the other, the game engine keeps an open-world in more *aporias*, open to lots of unexpected chance encounters with random objects that would delay the revelations of the solutions to local puzzles and quests. In the revised diagram in Figure 10, the diegetic end of the vertical axis thus shows how the gamer's targeting is pulled toward relocating the objects to each niche position to complete a spatial revelation of a story arc. For instance, in the typical treasure-hunting quest in *The Elder Scrolls V*, the item acquired from a boss battle always accompanies a new marker on the map for the location of another object, an NPC or depository, to which the item originally belongs according to the story of the quest. The topology of markers on the map, in this respect, translates the trajectories the player character has to follow to complete the story of the current quest. On the other hand, the nondiegetic direction of the same axis alludes that the

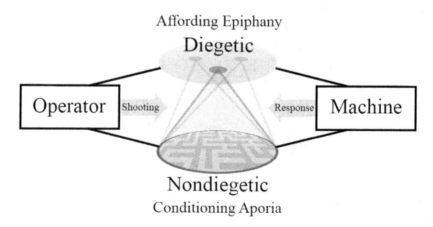

Figure 10 Gamic actions in open-worlds.

gamer's narrative-oriented actions can be delayed by purposeless but still playful chance encounters with other objects under the probabilistic control of a global agent, the game engine. The player character's way to the depository can be, in this case, deferred by unexpected encounters with enemies and other quests. According to this new diagram, the narrative and ludic characters of a game space correspond to the local and global features of the same network. An object at each node of the network is, as being touched by an avatar, instantiated into something that happens in a quest told by the gamer's diegetic-operator actions (just as the momentum maximized by the perpetual motion in *Portal* should be reoriented through the avatar's shooting). At the level of the whole network, the game engine conversely keeps the inexhaustible minimum of momenta between its nodes (that the tiny vibrations of an object within *The Incredible Machine* symbolize) for their further individuation into different quests, not only for the more degree of freedom to the gamer but more ways of the networks' topological transformations. On this axis, an object's metastability, or its hesitance between becoming an actor for a specific task and remaining undefined and open to multipurpose, is expressed by its oscillation between the local affordance for *epiphany* and global conditioning of *aporia*.

In recent open-world games, this metastability within the diegetic-nondiegetic axis of the network is visualized through the colorful auras surrounding objects, which become visible as an avatar uses a special skill. In *Witcher 3: Wild Hunt* (2015), Geralt, the player character, uses the "Witcher Sense" to switch his field of view (FOV) from the normal state to a distorted superhuman perspective that detects the hidden momenta of objects visible through hazy auras they effuse. In *Batman: Arkham Knight* (2015), Batman wears an in-game HUD device "Detective Vision" to make the movements of networkable objects stand out through the technologically augmented auras (Figure 11). As the actions in the middle of the diegetic and nondiegetic, or the nondiegetic actions disguising as diegetic (Jørgensen 2012), using these skills or gadgets is what the games' tutorial instructs first to the gamers as a way to access an abstract space of metastable objects, which adumbrate potential nodes of the network that the avatar needs to mobilize for the solution of a given object-oriented puzzle or quest. Driving out all the less interactive objects to the peripheries of attention, these superhuman actions extract small ties from objects. Visualizing the momenta left in the objects for their further interactions, these ties anticipate hidden story arcs or object-oriented puzzles that could be unfolded by the avatar's aiming at the proper target. Even though some objects could move by themselves like enemies patrolling designated areas in *Batman: Arkham Knight*, these metastable objects rarely communicate with each other but walk around in each closed circuit unless they step out to track the actions taken by their arch-enemy, Batman. Put differently, without the player character's intervention, their routine movements are left in mere aesthetic metastability which Galloway calls "ambience act." Even if these "Things continue to change" in their metastable routines, "nothing changes that is of any importance" (2006: 10). However, these ambient movements of the isolated objects are visualized in these games for more than just their aesthetic looks in that they also bring about a thrilling feeling for the emerging actor-networks. For instance, magnified under the higher resolution of Batman's Detective Vision, the objects reappear to be full of "charged expectation" (11) about their possible future interoperations, which could cause catastrophic chain reactions across the objects in an open-world as the avatar's targeting transmits some uncertainties. In this sense, Galloway's statement about the ambience acts of objects that "No significant stimulus from the game environment will disturb the player character" (10) is untrue because the lack of significant stimulus from the game environment will really disturb the player as long as this anxious metastability of an open-world makes it intolerable for him/her not to hit or shoot the objects.

Encountering these abstract ties of momenta, the player character no longer occupies a center of perspective as a simulated Cartesian subject. Like Detective Vision activated at the edge of the screen, or Witcher Sense causing distortions in a geometric space (Figure 11), the avatar's stable position in the normal field of view is retreating to the oblique glance from peripheries as an animistic world of metastable objects emerges. In this moment of a perspectival withdrawal suspending a geometric grid that used to overcode objects, the gaps between objects' tenuous membranes are filled again with their minute ambience acts,

Figure 11 Witcher Sense (*Witcher 3: Wild Hunt* 2015) and Detective Vision (*Batman: Arkham Knight* 2015).

which preserve inexhaustible potentials for each thing's own object-orientation for heterogeneous network making. Insofar as some of their networks are supposed to reveal certain story arcs for quests, solutions for object-oriented puzzles, or hidden trophies and achievements, the gamer is responsible to aim at an object as soon as possible to break the ambience with the epiphanies of these local events. At the same time, the gamer should also be careful not to shoot every target too quickly lest the network becomes too stabilized to the extent of having no more metastable objects for further transformations to reveal other quests, puzzles, trophies, and achievements.

These conflicting responsibilities that a gamer feels while encountering the ambience of an open-world can be expressed most clearly in two extreme strategies of gamer action, namely *Speedrun* and *Seeker Achievement*. As a way to traverse a space along the simplest labyrinth structure with one shortest path from an entrance to an exit, *Speedrun* lets no single moment of ambience act to happen. For instance, you may attempt to draw the fastest and most straightforward route to rescue Princess Zelda in *The Legend of Zelda: Breath of the Wild* (2017). On the other hand, by re-individuating the same space into a labyrinth with lots of secret caves to the extent of experimenting with all possible links and operations between objects, *Seeker Achievement* does not let any single object remain isolated in its initial metastability. You may in this case discover every area on the world map, explore every dungeon, open every chest, cook every recipe, tame every wild horse, take pictures of every creature, and do every possible thing in the game before rescuing Princess Zelda.

Given the extreme difficulty in achieving a new world record in *Speedrun* and the extremely long play hours required for *Seeker Achievement*, these two gamer strategies seem located at the two extreme ends in our diagram as the two least probable worlds that the linkages of distributed objects could unfold. At one pole, the most concise diegetic world is unfolded, while, at another, the same network is ceaselessly complicated until all interoperable objects are entangled with the gamer's itinerary. Given the extremely low probabilities for a gamer's chance encounters to occur in specific orders for these boundary cases, most diegetic-operator actions in videogames might be expected to happen along the path in the middle of these two. However, as many posts in the online forums about gamers' challenges for these almost impossible goals demonstrate (The Legend of Zelda: Breath of the Wild n.d.), *Speedrun* and *Seeker Achievement*—two poles defining the limits of a network's topological transformations—also attract the gamer actions toward the two extreme subjectivities imaginable within the networked societies of algorithmic objects. On the flipside of the log files that inscribe every action the gamer takes, what we rediscover from the cryptic networks of objects would then be the afterimage of gaming subjects, stretched between the most linear storyteller drawing the shortest escape plan, on the one hand, and the nonlinear and ludic dungeon dweller complicating the networks over and again, on the other. Their ludic and narrative interests do not exist as some invisible external social forces to network objects. Instead, their subjectivities are unfolded from their entanglements with the objects they aim at.

Targeting in Object-(Re-)Oriented Realities

By giving back their own object-orientations to the algorithmic objects, an open-world videogame transforms its gameboard into a sort of animistic plane on which these nonhuman actors begin to stretch out their metastable ties for future interactions. As shown when it happens through the Witcher Sense and Detective Vision, targeting is a gamer's means to connect to the solipsistic autonomy of these reanimated objects by tuning the avatar's magically or technologically augmented sense to the tiny agitations of the objects. In a sense that it also extracts an object "from the spatiotemporal coordinates" of the normal field of view and exaggerates as "an autonomous entity" larger than before (Doane 2003: 90), targeting in these videogames can be compared with another technological perception well-studied in the past decades of media studies, *close-up*.

As a moment in which an object's "perfect, seamless face, the unwavering stare," is revealed to audiences, close-ups in the framework of narrative cinema have exemplified the metastability of a thing temporarily isolated from a diegetic network. Its solipsistic autonomy has been thought of as what makes audiences "impossible not to project thought, emotion" by connecting it to an imaginary signifying chain over other filmic objects "although the face itself gives no indication of either" (104–5). For cultural critics and from their self-claimed critical autonomy from the objects under research, a close-up's oscillation between *isolation from* and *subjection to* the chain of signification has been something difficult to understand without simply stipulating it as the fetishistic character of a media object. Put differently, the metastability of an object under a close-up has been interpreted as either a misrecognized human product or an abject other arousing castrating hallucinations to a subject; either human-produced or human-lost, just as "the Modern repertoire keeps anything from happening in the middle" even though the close-up in practice, as much as targeting in videogames, always "happens in the middle" (Latour 2010: 19).

On the other hand, the objects magnified by Witcher Sense or Detective Vision enforce the gamer's avatar to withdraw from its normal geometric view once built upon the Modern "ideal of detachment from every [metastable object] that brought it into action" (65). A gamer is now relocated to the non-Modern middle in which the objects' autonomy regains its meaning as "the right not to be deprived of ties that render existence possible, ties emptied of all ideals of determination, of a false theology of creation ex nihilo" (59). Removing the lines of perspective projection, these ties of the emerging actor-networks allow the gamer's shooting to unfold stories, quests, quizzes, and meaningless events from the interoperations of the objects her shooting initiates. The fetish-like character of objects reappears in the form of tiny agitations but it is neither reaffirmation of what humans lost nor a human projection at distance. Rather, for these objects to persist as the actors in the network, their momenta should be constantly reoriented toward others by the avatar's interventions as much as the gamer's individuation into a narrator or dungeon dweller is also the network effect of the avatar's constant targeting.

As Andrejevic writes about "various 'smart' objects that will come to populate their lives" in the current technological environments, the "fetishes of yesteryear" once debunked by the criticism in the last century have recently found the "technologies for their silicon reincarnation" not only in the open-worlds simulated by videogames but in the real-worlds augmented by small wireless sensors and RFID tags (2005: 116–8). Attached to any kind of cultural and technical object, these smart entities extract the unexamined momenta of the objects to make them interoperable with others intensively once again. For instance, a light bulb is now connectable to any electronic device in a smart home as experimented with in *The Incredible Machine*. The commercial buildings and services geo-tagged as operational Points of Interest (POI) in a smart city and other smart infrastructures may reveal their hidden interoperability to the urban users of augmented-reality apps, reminiscent of Batman's Detective Vision, or location-based apps similar to the world maps in open-world videogames (Figure 12).

In these AR interfaces, the real-world objects begin to exhibit their metastable agitations or communicability, ready to be dragged by a person's fingertip to a network in the making as the solution for the peculiar interest of the end-user. People's "operations of citizenship" in this real world is redefined as the technique to connect these reanimated objects in "sustainable and efficient" ways

Figure 12 Brisbane City from the lens of *tagSpace* (Taken by the author on January 19, 2023).

for a general purpose of a city and home (Gabrys 2016a: 203, 185). Given the emphasis put on the efficiency and sustainability of these object-(re-)oriented domestic and urban spaces, citizens' being smart also involves two networking strategies that this chapter examined in the context of videogames. Either to draw the shortest and least energy-consuming route to a goal or to explore all possible operations of each object in a network to individuate more alternative ways for the goals. If becoming a smart citizen or smart network builder is the alibi for a human's participation in these gamified environments, what this alibi conceals behind is that, for its sustainability and replayability, a network needs to cultivate more marketable and playable relations among its nodes from a gamer's ceaseless paying-attention, which *targeting* operationalizes as the resource and trigger for this perpetual recultivation of the network.

Interface

The algorithmic objects currently overwhelming our urban landscapes operationalize topology as a new form of governmentality. As discussed in Chapter 2, topology is a mode of power considered optimal for managing the relations supposedly hidden everywhere but undetectable until they surface in the form of invariant equations under certain transformations that a space undergoes. Enmeshed by these hidden relations, the IoT developers warn, our life would be constantly threatened with unsustainability unless we decide to fortify it with manifold background sensors and actuators, in other words, unless we symmetrify ourselves.

In Massumi's interpretation, Foucauldian governmentality is defined as "a correctional reuptake mechanism," which constantly folds and refolds a social continuum into *man-as-body* and *man-as-specie*. For Massumi, the sustainability of this continuum is achieved by detaining its differentiation within the two-coupled level of individual-population. At the heart of Foucauldian governmentality, then, is its interfacing of two technologies operating on different geopolitical scales, namely a "disciplinary apparatus" and a regulatory "state apparatus," which differentiate the continuum respectively into "body-organism-discipline-institutions" and "population-biological processes-regulatory mechanisms-State" (Foucault 2003: 250).

On the other hand, revisiting "the new techniques of environmental technology or environmental psychology" that Foucault mentioned briefly in his 1979 lecture (2008: 259), Jenifer Gabrys examines ubiquitous computing as the embodiment of Foucault's "environmentality" in the wake of recent transformations in urban spaces. She hints at how this new form of governmentality re-interfaces individual and population by reprogramming our environments through networks of algorithmic objects "above and beyond direct attempts to influence or govern individual behavior or the norms of populations" (Gabrys 2014). These objects are now embedded in our domestic and urban landscapes and reveal their hidden agency through various augmented reality apps for houses, schools, offices, and cities, where they redesign "the rules of the game" for our smart participation (Foucault 2008: 260). As discussed in Chapter 3, in the ideal "open-world," which is characterized by its lack of "invisible walls" restricting players' moves from above, these rules emerge from the uneven and strategic distribution of interactive objects. For ontology as the semantic protocol to maximize the interoperabilities of smart objects in the open-world for a variety of user goals, a social continuum remapped by the environmental sensors is thus not simply to be stabilized in a sustainable alternation between identifiable individuals and manageable population. Instead, under the governance of ubiquitous computing, the continuum's sustainability reflects its plasticity, its capability of continuously unfolding numberless hidden levels to register as each new problem-space of an IoT application. In other words, between the most individualistic level of man-as-body and the most collectivist man-as-species, a multitude of hidden levels should be re-bifurcated and re-commodified.

A framed set of algorithmic objects, such as one would find on a smartphone's home screen, is the simplest example of the machine for this environmentality. These graphical objects are functioning to govern the social continuum of users (individuals-population) and interface it with another continuum of digital signals. Their operations are, however, neither for simply training individuals to use each object for each different task nor for updating the normative variation of users as a whole from each reported irregular user behavior. Rather, the recent interface design, as often happens in open-world gaming, allows users to customize certain subsets of objects frequently used for their self-defined goals. As "an environmental type of intervention instead of the internal subjugation of individuals" (Foucault 2008: 260), this customizability provides the users with the means to represent their urgent needs as something resolvable through the networks of objects they draw with their fingertip or mouse point. In so doing, the screen re-embeds the algorithmic objects, such as application icons, within a user's field of perception as the things close enough to touch, click, and target, much like when we scan a smart city with augmented-reality apps on our smartphone. However, the flipside of this user-friendly interface is that a user's mind—or a neurophysiological continuum between her eyes and fingers—is black-boxed as a machine-learnable circuit that switches between what she perceives on the screen and how she responds through input devices. In a smart space where this rectangular menu of icons is expanded into a floorplan embedded with smart objects, the trajectories of the user's mouse point or fingertip on a PC or smartphone screen are replaced by her nonconscious daily routines. As she lives her life according to the everyday protocol of the IoT, her neurophysiology is then black-boxed in between what her skin feels and how her body (non)consciously moves, readily interfaced with the data streams that smart sensors and actuators generate from her daily routine. Unlike other smart objects, which each have limited perceptibility and actionability, the neurophysiological continuum of her body is speculated to be plastic enough to differentiate as many sensorimotor responses as needed for these nonhumans to simulate for an array of IoT applications.

Conceptual artist Warren Neidich (2003) describes the human "visual landscape" as "a network or field" of "phatic signifiers," objects that have survived throughout their evolutionary histories as the result of humans and other organisms' "neural selection" of them as the stimuli or environmental cues relevant to their imminent cultural and physiological needs. As he explains, "the invention of smaller and smaller microprocessors to run smaller and smaller computing devices" changes the way in which the phatic signifiers are composing our field of perception. In a current software interface, artificial stimuli "engineered to have superior attention grabbing capabilities beyond their naturally created counterpart" (2003) are not selected naturally through our habitual perception and the placement of them on the desktop or home screen of a PC or smartphone, or a smart home. Instead, they are selected and registered as something functional, distributed on the interface, customized in such a way as to be optimally reachable by our hands as we seek the tools to fulfill some urgent need but also placed in the configurations most symmetrical to our unknown needs, which the software aims to materialize through our nonconscious responses to the subliminal cues it distributes. Regarding the networks of algorithmic objects, Neidich (2003) writes that they "become the stencils upon which the networks of the brain are modeled." Put differently, enmeshed with algorithmic arcs of sensors and actuators, the nonconscious reality of the human mind under the skin and skull is modeled as a plastic continuum with manifold hidden levels.

In this way, the Internet of Things reactivates the neuroplasticity of our brain, and in order to expand its governance to even more details of our lives, the IoT exploits the brain's capacity to optimize itself for the many different events that the software predicts will happen to itself or its environments. Brain-Machine Interface (BMI), which will be explored in the following chapter as an experimental example of the Internet of Things, is a device to stretch this plastic brain out to smart objects, such as microsensors, computer algorithms, and robot arms, which make up a machinic assemblage for futuristic neuroprosthetics. The chapter examines how the interfacing of BMI differentiates the hidden neurophysiology of the human or animal mind into multiple levels of motor intentions, focusing on how the device exploits these intentions, which are lab-cultivated to begin with, as resources to develop a greater number of brain-powered sensors-actuators for future industrial uses.

Brain-Machine Interface

ANT, IoT, and Brain-Machine Interface (BMI)

The popularization of "network" as a social theoretical concept was somewhat paralleled with the emergence of the World Wide Web in the 1990s. But, for actor-network theorists, the internet's functioning as "an instantaneous, unmediated access to every piece of information" *without deformation* was what trivialized their once revolutionary conceptualization of network as a "series of transformations—translations, transductions—which could not be captured by any of the traditional terms of social theory" (Latour 1999: 15). Disputing its banalization as just another ready-made term, Bruno Latour, in "On Recalling ANT," in 1999, thus argued how the criticisms that had been raised against the "managerial, engineering, Machiavellian, demiurgic character of ANT" had in fact been based on the misguided appropriation of "actor" and "network" as separable terms. For instance, the concept of "actor" misunderstood as a stand-alone term had led many ANT-inspired researchers to focus simply on some strong "male-like" actors and their wider accessibility to the networks to fulfill their own interests. In the meantime, "network" conceived as the social above all actors below had drawn criticism of "its apparent dissolution of independent actors with morality and intentions in a 'play of forces' in which no change through human intervention seems possible" (Gad 2010: 61). Lost in these misunderstandings was the "freshness" of the network as a concept that rather hinges on the *hyphen* in "actor-network," which does not simply signify the epistemological limit of a subject as a node of networks but an ontological event called "translation." For the actor-network theorists, translation is not a by-product of an actor's interaction with another actor or their interoperation for creating a network but something akin to Karen Bard's "intra-action," from which both networks and actors are generated (2003).

In the same year as Latour recalled the early freshness of ANT, 1999, "the Internet of Things" (IoT) was suggested as the name for the fresh domain of the internet emergent from the physical reality that began to renew its constant intra-actions as enmeshed with smart objects. However, "thingification" the IoT implemented was, unlike what Barad originally meant by this, far from the "turning of relations into" the interactions between "'things', 'entities', 'relata,'" or anything already fully individuated before the interactions (Barad 2003: 812). A thing, such as your body or smartwatch, in the IoT can be understood also from the perspective of the hyphen in the middle or the small "o" in between two big letters, and then we can say it becomes an actor as it contributes to the new data economy the IoT implements but only after its inner dynamics—such as its neurophysiology or artificial neural network—gradually find its niche within other smart objects and begin to influence "the structure of the network in a noticeable and individual way" (Law 2012: 125). Thingification the IoT re-initiates (Gabrys 2016b) is, in this respect, more relevant to the thing once considered just an inert matter but turning into an intra-active continuum or a plane of immanent correlations, the unfolding of which through machine learning constantly renews the boundaries of things within the network in the making.

The goal of this chapter is to renew ANT as a practical tool to analyze an experimental example of the Internet of Things. Brain-Machine Interface (BMI) is an idea for the futuristic neuroprosthetic devices that Miguel Nicolelis and his neuroengineering lab at Duke University have developed since 2000, and one version of which was publicly demonstrated at the opening ceremony of the 2014 FIFA World Cup in Brazil. Compared to other cloud computing-based IoT applications, the entities that Nicolelis Lab has mobilized for constructing BMIs, such as human/animal neurons, biological/robotic limbs, and computers, have been small in number and restricted to a laboratory, rather than being distributed widely like the sensors in a smart city. Nevertheless, *cloud* is still a working metaphor because what Nicolelis Lab has experimented with is not so much the seamless and well-defined interoperation of these biological, mechanical, and algorithmic objects but their unexamined networkability, the nebula of relations aroused from their experimental juxtapositions. Freed from hardwired or habitual contexts of neuronal interactions, and not yet stabilized into a simple sensorimotor interaction, these objects have been cultivated as the things ready to be mobilized for a variety of sensor-actuator relations that the lab has advertised as the evidence for the BMI's various future uses.

The Missing Times

On June 12, 2014, Juliano Pinto, a 29-year-old former athlete who lost the use of his legs after a car accident in 2006, entered the Corinthian Arena in São Paulo, Brazil. There was the opening ceremony of the 2014 FIFA World Cup. Pinto was wearing an exoskeleton that looked "as if came from the 'Iron Man' movies" and had been developed for the past two years with about fourteen million dollars of funding from the Brazilian government. After Pinto's name was announced, the exoskeleton took its historic first step as its electroencephalogram (EEG) cap scanned the action potentials from his motor neurons and transmitted them to its robot legs. As the foot of the exoskeleton touched the grass, tactile stimuli sensed by the artificial skin on the soles were fed back to his arm instead of his paralyzed feet. Based on the tactile perception transmitted through millisecond-long interoperation between neurons, robots, and the grass, Pinto (or his motor cortex) could design his/its next move. After a couple of steps, he finally kicked the official ball. An event was lasting and broadcast for only a few seconds at the beginning of the ceremony and was soon buried by the spectacle of other events.

For the last few months prior to this public demonstration, Pinto, along with seven other patients in the Nicolelis Lab, was trained to adjust his motor cortex to the way a machine interacts with its surroundings. Hundreds of his motor neurons were scanned by an EEG cap designed to register, or re-thingify, these neurons as laboratory objects functioning to transmit their ambiguous action potentials to other lab devices. To find niches for his neurons to settle in and, in turn, contribute to the formation of a working sensor-actuator loop with his robot legs, the control system of the exoskeleton also needed these training sessions for learning human kinetics. This process required both the patient and machines to adapt to one another, and to realign themselves with the network in the making was, however, easily black-boxed as something "naturally" achieved by the plasticity of both parts according to the short sentences in the "method" sections of the papers the lab published. Information about the training was updated every day on social media starting sixty-nine days before D-Day, and partial close-ups of an exoskeleton, which looked already fully integrated with the wearer's motor intentions, were released to arouse public curiosity, but most other messy parts of the lab were still edited out.[1]

Before this actual training for the human-machine interoperation, the exoskeleton, initially developed in France and then transported to the Nicolelis Lab in São Paulo, also needed to be re-coordinated by an engineering professor from Munich to be ready for responding to the neurons in the lab, which were de-contextualized, or re-thingified, from Pinto's conscious motor intentions (Sample 2014). Leading up to this, there was a consortium named the Walk-Again Project, consisting of more than one hundred scientists from different countries interested in designing a lab setup in which neurons and robot limbs could achieve stable interoperations. The idea of the Brain-Machine Interface was, in this respect, what had been concretized through the years-long negotiations of manifold interests from scientists, patients, and governmental officials. These parties believed that BMI would be a public demonstration for the validity of their scientific hypotheses, showcasing the recent achievement of their "national science," fulfilling their desires to walk again, drawing public attention, and justifying the government investment.

Compared to this long duration for aligning complicated social interests outside the lab with the inside network of things in the making, "Pinto's few seconds of fame" did not seem worth all those costs. It was only during the short seconds of the very beginning of the opening ceremony that neatly coordinated neurons and robot limbs were temporarily aligned with Pinto's motor intentions. Nevertheless, this short exposure through the broadcasting was sufficient for Nicolelis Lab to mobilize as its allies some news outlets who were willing to argue, in favor of Nicolelis, that "the historic event" signifying "the beginning of a future in which people with paralysis will be able to leave the wheelchair and literally walk again" was not given enough attention "it deserved during the opening ceremony" (Boyle 2014; Martins and Rincon 2014).

From this specific example of a flickering constellation of things and their interests, I focus on three different time intervals, or *missing times*, which the participants in the Walk-Again Project—including both humans and nonhumans, such as neurons, robots and algorithms, individual scientists, patients, labs, and a government—should have endured until their dissimilar interests were eventually all aligned with this technological invention. First, to form the working sensor-actuator loop between neurons and robots, the BMI needs to manage an imperceptible delay in its algorithmic prediction of a person's motor intention. There is usually a several-milliseconds interval between this nonconscious intention created in the form of neuronal firing and its manifestation through actual body movement or the person's conscious recognition of it (Hansen 2015a). The machine's scanning of relevant signals and preemption of a motor intention should thus be done within this interval so that the wearer would not feel a significant delay. Besides these milliseconds spent to renew the sensor-actuator loop for each new motor intention from a brain, two other longer-term intervals are also necessary to make this loop represent the intentions of individual and institutional actors both inside and outside the lab. The second missing time omitted in the BMI's public presentation involves translating the heterogeneous interests of scientists, government officials, and individual patients into a specific disposition or diagram of things inside the lab. And the third, happening behind closed doors in the lab, involves the hours of training of the animal and human subjects, to make them not only capable of living with the BMI but believe in the hope it promises, namely "walking again." These time intervals have simply been obscured by the lab's narrative of natural adaptations of subjects to smart infrastructures, but, as this chapter argues, they are where the IoT's re-thingification of human brains occurs.

This chapter examines news articles and the Nicolelis Lab's scholarly publications about BMI since the prototype of this robotic prosthetics was first designed in 2000 with primate brains connected to robot limbs through the mediation of computer algorithms. It also examines how the scientists mobilized the mutual adaptability of these organic and technological entities for creating a closed-loop of artificial sensor-actuator responses, which have not only demonstrated the validity of the lab's scientific principles but also promised that the heterogeneous interests of actors around "Walking Again" could be fulfilled by this invention.

Some Ontological Implications of Actor-Network

Before applying ANT to the description of a science lab, the relationship between two seemingly incompatible concepts *hyphened* in the actor-network should be clarified. First, there are actors whose presences are noticeable only through their behaviors or consistent responses to the lab's attempt to communicate with them via either discursive or technological means. On the other hand, there is a network, something global and not representable by a mere sum of these clearly defined local actors. To resolve this contradictory paring-up, we usually rely on the so-called relational definition that the hyphen in actor-network may signify: an actor can be defined only by how it makes relations with others, whereas a network describes not so much the connections between independent actors but those relations in the making. The autonomies of actors thus turn out to be just the effect of relations in the constant making and remaking, or intra-actions, prior to their being black-boxed or congealed into separable actors. However, this convenient definition also has a problem as it tends to dissipate the analytical usefulness of the term *actor* within an abstract network that seems to be potentially applicable to any haphazard relations, even to those that look too unstable to be localized as relations between noticeable actors. To overcome this, we might try to restrict our use of the term *actor-network* only to certain detectable and patternable relations. But, in this case, we would make another mistake and reduce any haphazard relations simply to the background of a system under research. This problem of defining the actor-network thus suggests the following ontological implications.

First, actors are not independent entities that researchers or system builders presuppose as the building blocks of their theoretical frameworks to analyze given problems. Rather, actors are "those entities that exert detectable influence on others" (Law 2012: 126), and their presence is empirically inferred from recurrent influences but only in the presence of the observers, who are "able to propose their own theories of action to explain" the seeming causality of the worlds by imputing the immediate influences they feel to certain actors in distance (Latour 2005: 57). An actor-network is therefore *when* certain entities— not yet actors—are juxtaposed and begin to influence one another in a long-term sustainable way, so that they serve as "heterogeneous but mutually sustaining elements" of a system (Law 2012: 115). In other words, an actor-network (and its actors and network) appears only in hindsight to an observer after a certain amount of (missing) time has been spent by those entities to stabilize their interactions with others in sustainable ways. This does not necessarily mean that only those entities exercising detectable influences on the formation of a given network could be called actors because it is always possible to assume the existence of other entities that might dissociate from the network under observation as they prefer to associate with "other actors in the environment in the course of the inevitable struggles" (111). As John Law writes, the features of these others, constantly creating invisible networks conflicting with the networks "being built by people," such as the laboratory, are often branded as the "obduracy" of Nature (124). Missing times before the observed network, in this respect, are spent not simply for association and stabilization but for struggling and switching between networks, one under techno-scientific construction and many unfavorable others that this human project simply brackets as mere natural environments.

This way of illustrating actor-networks suggests that, during the World Cup demo, there might be some neurons in Pinto's motor cortex not firing toward the exoskeleton because they were more strongly associated with other kinds of neuronal sub-networks relevant to such behaviors other than kicking off and to the stimuli other than tactility. They might struggle against the EEG cap's operation to switch them from their current enrollments in habitual neuronal contexts to another in the making through an algorithmic system. Insofar as their denial to fire meant their obduracy in remaining associated with other sub-networks of Pinto's brain, the actor-network in the World Cup demo did not operate simply in a natural environment. It might be fairer to say there were many struggling networks denying sending detectable signals to the observers—scientists, engineers, or audiences—who were also obdurate in their current enrollment to this invention or media event in broadcasting. In this sense, actor-network theory does not presuppose a rigid dichotomy between systems and environments as long as environments mean the heterogeneity of networks just black-boxed conveniently as the "obduracy" of Nature.

Second, the successful operation of a science laboratory as an actor-network thus depends not only on the correct design decisions of scientists in distributing those entities but also on those entities' ability to fill the gaps within their disposition to form an actual network. In this sense, the role of scientists is better described by the term *juxtapositions* rather than *associations*. According to Michel Callon, "it is from these juxtapositions that the associations draw their coherence, consistency, and structure of relationships that exists between the components that comprise it" (2012: 89). In a laboratory setup, the coherence of these relationships the components sustain for a long-enough term is evidence of the validity of the lab's hypotheses. However, more importantly, the juxtaposition of components should be first a proper spatial translation, or diagrammatization (Ahn 2019), of the rules of statements which define valid forms of variables involved and restrict their possible interactions. Therefore, what is demonstrated through an experiment or a training session is most of all the validity of the theoretical variables and experimental parameters, as well as their communicational protocols, exemplified by the Nicolelis Lab's "principles of neural ensemble physiology" (Lebedev and Nicolelis 2009); or the validity of the hopes, which various stakeholders of the research have anchored on BMI. Lab scientists are thus required to have good managerial skills not only to maintain these hopes until the gaps in an abstract diagram are fleshed out with actual connections between small lab objects but also to constantly redistribute these gaps to draw more hopes around their diagram.

Even though it was just a few seconds during the opening ceremony, the 2014 World Cup demonstration allowed the Nicolelis Lab to show that the ensembles of neurons and robots—whose plasticity to form lots of different sensor-actuator loops for different motor tasks the lab had experimented for a decade—could also create a closed-loop with an exoskeleton walking outside. In the demo, a local network of these organic and machinic things did not just validate the lab's scientific hypotheses but considered that their design can serve to mobilize more hopes for the BMI's medical, academic, industrial, and commercial uses beyond the physical boundary of human bodies.

A Description of BMI

Since Nicolelis designed the first BMI for a rat in 1993, his lab has experimented with its plasticity to close a functional loop with a variety of organic and inorganic matters, such as different species of animal subjects, neurons in different brain regions, different brain scanning technologies, different types of motor functions, and different pattern-recognition algorithms used to predict a subject's motor intention. But it was after the success of an experiment with an owl monkey named Belle in 2000 that the lab began to refer to BMI as the future of "neuroprosthetic device[s]" that "could be used to restore basic motor functions in patients suffering from severe body paralysis" (Nicolelis 2003: 417).

As described in Nicolelis' 2003 *Nature* article (Figure 13), this early version of BMI was comprised of three major actors. First, there is a monkey in front of a computer monitor wearing a head-mounted device with a hundred "Teflon-coated stainless-steel microwires" implanted in the neurons in several regions of the monkey's motor cortex. The monkey is operating a fake joystick with her right hand believing that she is really controlling the cursor on the monitor to win a videogame and receive a sip of fruit juice as a reward. When she moves her joystick, the patterns of her arm movements are captured from "infrared markers" on each joint and calculated into machine-readable "motor parameters (such as arm position and velocity, or hand gripping force)" (Lebedev and Nicolelis 2009: 531). Second, connected to these neurons and microwires are a device for data acquisition from neuronal firing, called a Harvey Box, and computers for real-time pattern recognition algorithms (linear and artificial

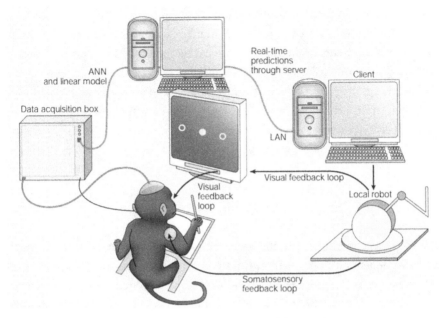

Figure 13 A prototypical description of a BMI (Nicolelis 2003).

neural network [ANN] algorithms). These computing devices function to "properly sample, filter and amplify neural signals from many electrodes" and integrate the parallel signals scanned every 50 to 100 milliseconds from multiple regions of the motor cortex into a linear input (Nicolelis and Chapin 2008). The machine learning algorithms then figure out proper coefficients to render this linear input matched to the linear change in the motor parameters observed from her physical arm some milliseconds after so that it could be used as the prediction for the "subject's voluntary motor intentions" (Lebedev and Nicolelis 2009: 531). And there is a robot arm that operates a real joystick according to this algorithmic prediction and moves the cursor on the monitor as if the monkey is controlling it. At the same time, as the information about the robot's grip force is "relayed back to the animal" in the form of "small vibromechanical elements attached to the animal's arm" alongside the visual feedback from the monitor, "a closed-loop control BMI" is formally completed (Nicolelis 2003: 419).

However, for its actual operation to be seamless, some intervals within the loop should be stabilized. First, between the monkey's mind and brain, her goal-oriented intention to win the game must be successfully relayed into some paralleled neuronal firings. On the other hand, between a brain and computing devices, these paralleled neuronal firings from the cortex must be linearized to be paired with linear changes in the monkey's arm movements. And third, the linear movements of the robot arm must be translated into "proprioceptive feedback" signals distributed back to the monkey's visual and tactile receptors in parallel. Put differently, between the abstract juxtaposition of these lab entities and their transformation into a working actor-network, the entities facing each other across these multiple parallel-serial junctures must create actual connections for mutual adaptations.

Defining Actors

The monkey, computers, and the robot are three major actors, but they do not exist as independent components prior to the training. John Law characterizes an actor's agency as "an effect generated by a network of heterogeneous, interacting, materials" (Law 1992: 383). This relational definition also warns us to beware of conferring the title to be called an actor on a certain thing or node simply for its seeming influence over others. However, for a practical reason, it may still be allowed to assume that certain actors have more agencies than others when it comes to their roles in keeping distributed influences among actors circulating in and sustaining the current form of the network. In the above description of BMI, three actors are effected at each parallel-serial juncture as many small entities on the parallel side—such as neurons, and visual and tactile feedback—fire signals toward the other side for the linearization. In Latour's terminology, this function of junctures to integrate and transmit many is called *translation*, a process through which scientists or experimental instruments represent the heterogeneous responses from voiceless actors and mobilize them as the resources to fulfill their own interests (Latour 1987). In other words, these *major* actors have more agency because they can represent voiceless others latent in the network.

The monkey as the subject and user of the BMI is individuated at a juncture as the interests of manifold neurons are translated into her interest in winning the game and their "neuronal 'vote'" of action potentials are converted into her highly trained skill to control a fake joystick (Nicolelis 2001: 404).[2] The Harvey Box and computers comprise another major actor as the "activation of large distributed populations of neurons" (Nicolelis 2001) is translated into their algorithms "inscribed with certain interests" of the researchers, namely to demonstrate the operability of their neurophysiological principles (Johnson et al. 2014: 17). The robot arm becomes an actor as well, as its design represents the researchers' interest in restricting the monkey's arm movements to certain motor parameters, and as the predicted motor intentions of the monkey are translated into an actual operation of a joystick, making her more addicted to the game as she believes she really controls the cursor.

However, even for the observers in the lab, these major actors were identifiable only in hindsight after "a few nerve-racking, nail-biting, soul-searching moments" during which their dissimilar and conflicting interests were negotiated and properly realigned within the parallel-serial junctures so that their mutual mobilizations became stably measurable (Nicolelis 2011b: 144). This missing time was, however, black-boxed by Nicolelis, who simply wrote that "nothing out of the ordinary happened" in these confusing moments.

The "long-term training" required for both the monkey and computers to form a closed-loop through their mutual adaptation was also necessary for the actor-network to reach "a favourable balance of power," a state in which all "the concerned actors" eventually align their interests with the researchers' project (Callon 1986: 10). During the repeated trials for the monkey to learn how to mobilize her motor neurons for the motor parameters that the joysticks involve, some of the microwires became more strongly enrolled to the sorting algorithm of Harvey Box, while unfavorable others were detached from the juncture and withdrawn to the background of the loop. From the 2001 prototype to the 2014 human application, this favorable balance was promoted in news articles and the lab's publications as one of the most important achievements of their BMI, presented as though it had naturally been achieved by the "monkey's thought," "only her brain activity," and the "[m]ind-controlled exoskeleton" (Blakeslee 2008; Smith 2014) or by "physiological adaptations at the level of neural ensembles," the "ability of cortical ensembles to adapt to represent novel external actuators," and "adaptive algorithms that continuously update the model parameters while the subject trains" (Lebedev and Nicolelis 2006: 541; Lebedev and Nicolelis 2009: 534; Lebedev et al. 2011: 30), in short, as if the engineering done to the disposition of artificially juxtaposed things had not had any decisive role. The balance in this closed-loop was claimed to be automatically and naturally maintained as "[b]rain cells that ceased to influence the predictions significantly were dropped from the model, and those that became better predictors were added" as the result of their mutual adaptation (Nicolelis and Chapin 2008). While the three nonhuman actors were foregrounded in the lab's public presentations, the managerial work of the scientists maintaining the loop was hidden in the background, alongside other neurons that disagreed with firing toward the network any longer.

A Closed-Loop or Favorable Balance of Power

The balance *naturally* achieved "between the brain and artificial devices" was important in promoting BMI's future use in noninvasive neuroprosthetics, alongside the promise that patients could naturally adapt to the BMI without recurring interventions by engineers for brain-machine calibration (Nicolelis 2001). With respect to the BMI's function in scientific experiments, the closed-loop was also taken as evidence for the internal validity of the lab's scientific principles (Cicurel and Nicolelis 2015: Ch.1). Superficially, the algorithmic predictions of the monkey's behaviors from the randomly sampled neuronal firings show that the lab's principles of "distributed coding," "neuronal mass effect," and "plasticity" are valid in the given cortical areas and motor parameters (see Table 4.1). Insofar as this closed-loop continues between a limited number of actors over a longer period and the exchange of influences between actors could be black-boxed by considering it "a unified whole" (Latour 1987: 131), the lab's principles would remain true, but only within the given cortical areas and motor functions.

In the actual development of the BMI, this prototypical closed-loop has also been significant for another reason as it could be occasionally reopened to accommodate other as yet untested experimental objects, such as different neurons, algorithms, and robot designs. The plasticity of the loop has promised that the validity of the lab's hypotheses could expand to other unexamined brain areas and motor behaviors. Once the initial network reached a state of autonomy, scientists could change "the feedback information that the animal receives" and "the kinematic properties of the motor actuator (robot arm)" as long as these newly introduced parameters were still adaptable by existing actors (Nicolelis 2003: 419). They observed whether the actors would keep enrolled in their project after they changed the location and size of the cortical areas used to sample the neurons (for instance, from the primary motor cortex to the posterior parietal cortex to demonstrate the "neural degeneracy principle") or added some new motor parameters, such as three-dimensional arm movements (to demonstrate the "neuronal multitasking principle"). In other words, after the

Table 4.1 Principles of Neural Ensemble Physiology (Lebedev and Nicolelis 2009)

Principle	Explanation
Distributed coding	The representation of any behavioral parameter is distributed across many brain areas
Single-neuron insufficiency	Single neurons are limited in encoding a given parameter
Multitasking	A single neuron is informative of several behavioral parameters
Mass effect principle	A certain number of neurons in a population is needed for their information capacity to stabilize at a sufficiently high value
Degeneracy principle	The same behavior can be produced by different neuronal assemblies
Plasticity	Neural ensemble function is crucially dependent on the capacity to plastically adapt to new behavioral tasks
Conservation of firing	The overall firing rates of an ensemble stay constant during the learning of a task
Context principle	The sensor responses of neural ensembles change according to the context of the stimulus

loop was achieved, the lab design obtained strategic advantages in negotiating with the outside actors interested in the BMI's more general application to various fields, even though every new negotiation required a few hours or days of training.

Insofar as new elements were contiguous to the entities already included and this contiguity was enough for existing actors to adapt to, the lab's scientific principles could be vindicated further to the various cortical areas relevant to the more variety of motor functions integrated into the research. By exploiting these actors' adaptability and plasticity, the closed-loop has integrated many endurable changes in subsequent experiments. Consequently, the inner network of Nicolelis Lab has been intensified in terms of the number of voiceless actors re-thingified by Teflon-coated microwires, wireless electrodes, and EEG devices, which enable their action potentials to be transmitted farther beyond a monkey's cortical areas, generalizing the lab's principles toward more unrestricted uses.

Even though many individual neurons once enrolled in the loop were dropped out from the BMI as it evolved into many different forms to integrate various experimental parameters, that does not mean they just went to anonymous and unfavorable backgrounds. These neurons remained associated with other latent subnetworks of the brain, often mutually incommensurable with one another, and thus not detectable within a network currently in the making but already cataloged in computer data and publications. These neurons have been preserved as a sort of reserve army of networks, ready to be remobilized anytime soon. Throughout the loop's expansion, a brain's "complexity," meaning lots of paralleled subnetworks embedded in its topological continuum, has been re-inscribed in the form of what Shirley Strum and Bruno Latour (1999) call "complications," the sum of linear translations of paralleled complexities. As a part of these complications, each subnetwork once integrated into the BMI was labeled as mobilizable for each different "succession of [machine-readable] simple operations" (120). Responding to the unfavorable environments of the multiplicities of struggling networks within a brain, the "greater stability" of BMI and its applications to a variety of kinetic functions could be achieved but "only with additional resources; something besides what is encoded" in a current loop, namely the neurons in a database as the reserve army for the BMI's future applications (119–20).

Closing the Loop to Become Beyond Boundaries

Just after the first BMI with a primate brain in 2000 succeeded in predicting and imitating how Belle, an owl monkey, "intended to move [her] natural arms," Nicolelis Lab set to work on a new BMI to replicate their previous success with three macaque monkeys whose "brains contain[ed] deep furrows and convolutions that resemble those of the human brain" (Nicolelis and Chapin 2008). Once a favorable balance of influences between a monkey and a robot arm was formed again, Nicolelis changed the BMI design by removing the fake joystick from the hand of Aurora, "an elegant female" macaque monkey. This symbolic action disabled Aurora's bodily extension, but Nicolelis expected that she could adapt to the new physical condition by mobilizing the plasticity of her neurons that could still fire toward the robot arm, this time without passing through her biological hand.

> After being puzzled, Aurora gradually altered her strategy. Although she continued to make hand movements, after a few days she learned she could control the cursor 100 percent of the time with her brain alone. In a few trials

each day during the ensuing weeks Aurora did not even bother to move her hand; she moved the cursor by just thinking about the trajectory it should take.

(Nicolelis and Chapin 2008)

This success with a disabled monkey was quite consequential, offering much more than what it seemed to simply offer to her, namely her "out-of-body experiences" in the lab. Promoting the close evolutionary relationship between the monkeys and their human relatives alongside Aurora's physical condition similar to a human patient, the actor-network built inside the lab was claimed to represent the interests of the humans outside the lab, not only those who expected BMI would renew their "hope of restoring mobility to people who are paralysed" but also those interested in its possible use as "the conduit through which our brains control all our tools, to extend our reach, presence and communication with the universe" (Nicolelis 2011a). As Nicolelis said in the interview with the *Washington Post*, in order to mobilize "enough political will and investment" for his project, the lab had "to galvanize people's imagination" about the expandability and applicability of BMI (Powel 2013).

In closing this loop between a brain and a virtual body using BMI technology, we now know the primate brain can operate beyond the boundaries and physical constraints of its body and interact with any world presented to it.

(Nicolelis 2011a)

Here the target happens to be a robot. It could be a crane. Or any tool of any size or magnitude. The body does not have a monopoly for enacting the desires of the brain.

(Blakeslee 2008)

The plasticity of BMI, or its ability to close each new loop with each different motor apparatus including ready-made technologies, such as a crane, was emphasized for this device's wide applicability not restricted by the physical constraints of the lab and bodily boundaries of experimental animals. This also meant that, for the loop to extend beyond those boundaries, it should be continually reopened to accommodate new experimental parameters designed for each different social applicability of BMI. A favorable balance of influences needed to be renegotiated in every new training session so that the actors in the lab could readapt to the interests of the actors in the consortium the lab had organized. Throughout the lab's publications, BMI's performances have been measured in terms of how seamlessly its diagram could enclose more complex motor parameters and different types of robots into the loop. In Nicolelis' book *The Relativistic Brain*, this capability of enclosing a variety of motor functions is discussed as the BMI's possibility as "a biologically-inspired hypercomputer," functioning like a biological version of a universal Turing machine, potentially capable of controlling every "artificial, real or virtual actuator" (Cicurel and Nicolelis 2015: Ch.7).

While BMI's capability of wielding its action potential beyond the physical and biological boundaries of the lab and subjects has been explained as "what a naturally evolved brain can produce" with its "self-adaptable (i.e., plastic) elements" (Cicurel and Nicolelis 2015: Ch.4), a number of questions have remained unanswered, or even unasked. What did happen to Aurora and other unnamed macaque monkeys during the "few nerve-racking, nail-biting, soul-searching moments" of missing time (Nicolelis 2011b: 144), in which they might feel not only just "being puzzled" but disabled? What was the "special care" that the scientists mentioned they needed to do "to keep experimental conditions controlled and restricted to specific task requirements" (Kim et al. 2006: 159)? These interventions from human researchers during the training should be equivocated in their publications so that the closed-loops could be more easily black-boxed as the product of the natural progress of the system.

However, as we shift our focus to the inside of these "nerve-racking" hours in which the yet porous loop was seething with not only the subjects' frustrations but unaligned action potentials of many small things, we might see what looked so natural before is reappearing to be problematic. As Latour writes in *Science in Action* through the voices of his Janus, whose faces represent two different perspectives on science (one from the outside seeing science as a ready-made product, the other from the inside where it is in the making) (Figure 14), the so-called natural progress of neural ensembles, which the lab promoted as "the cause that allowed controversies to be settled" between different stakeholders, was, in fact, "the consequence of the settlement" between conflicting neurons aligned with the diagram as a spatial abstraction of the lab's scientific principles. Whereas the BMI as a ready-made science expanded its influences by convincing more people outside of the future that this naturally inspired hypercomputer promised, the BMI in the making was working only "when all the relevant" actors—neurons, computers, and robot limbs—were convinced by this diagram's way to redistribute their biologically or algorithmically

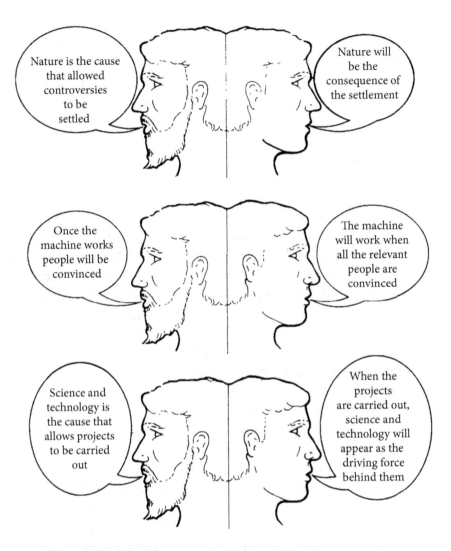

Figure 14 Janus' dicta in *Science in Action* (Latour 1987).

programmed interests along the loop. From the perspective of the network in the making, "the neural ensemble physiology" as the new scientific principles that the lab aimed to demonstrate through the BMI was, in fact, not the natural "cause that allow[ed] projects to be carried out" (Latour 1987: 10, 99, 175). These principles were rather required to be constantly re-naturalized through the network's inner densification (in terms of the number of relevant actors enrolled in the closed-loop) and outer expansion (in terms of a variety of social and individual interests in the "Walk-Again" the BMI promises). In other words, the scientific principles were engineered through an abstract diagram that realigned the heterogeneous interests of outside actors with a local loop of small entities in the lab. They were not so much about a natural cause the science discovered but about the protocols or manuals to redistribute a variety of actors both in the lab's physical and social environments according to the ontology it draws.

In the current analysis, the interval between Janus' two faces also represents the milliseconds of missing time between the mutual adaptations of small things in a neural-computer network and the human or animal subjects' awareness of the enhanced influences of their brains, and this missing time calls the agency of the experimental subject into question. In the World Cup demonstration, Pinto was introduced as a ready-made subject, already trained to know how to control and exploit the network of these tiny things for his interest in overcoming the boundaries of his handicapped body. On the other hand, the monkey's perceptions and motor intentions were forced to be significantly handicapped in the lab by a specific juxtaposition of things. The artificial sensor-actuator arc made up of the brain-scanning cap and robot arm, which functioned to fill the gap between the monkey's disabled body and the gaming monitor, was not so much given as a prosthetic means to restore her motor control but to alienate her from the previous control of the joystick and exploit her alienated neuroplasticity for the closure of a functional loop. To realize its vision for the universal computing machine for various cognitive and behavioral tasks, the lab should discipline its subjects to fit their heterogeneous motor intentions into the algorithmic simulations through the multiple sensors and actuators. At the same time, the lab also needed to improve its diagram to put things in a better juxtaposition able to unfold as many sensor-actuator arcs as different motor functions the subjects might intend. And insofar as all these disciplinary and environmental controls of subject behaviors have aimed at realigning its closed-loop with the external stakeholders' interests in BMI's general applicability, what Donald MacKenzie wrote regarding the role of scientists as system builders is also true for Nicolelis Lab.

> No laboratory development is ultimately self-sufficient. If the environment is not right or is not made right by the system builders, any line of laboratory development will lack external influence and may indeed cease altogether.
>
> (MacKenzie 2012: 208)

Expansion of a Network and Mobilization of Interests

Since Nicolelis Lab's BMI reached its first closed-loop with Aurora the macaque monkey in 2001, the loop has been continually reopened to experiment with the range of its plasticity and adaptability, accommodating more actors and experimental parameters. The number of neurons in the loop has increased from about 100 to 800. The simple task of moving a joystick to the left or right has been replaced by three-dimensional reaching and grasping tasks (Carmena et al. 2003), walking on a treadmill (Fitzsimmons et al. 2009), and bimanual arm movements (Ifft et al. 2013). The motor parameters read from the subjects' bodies have also changed from the variables restricted to the initial design of the gaming device with fewer degrees of freedom to the variables that could model the higher degrees of freedom of naturalistic body movements, such as the electromyographic (EMG) measures of muscle activities (Santucci et al. 2005), "Muscle Geometry" (Kim et al. 2007), and "walking parameters" (Fitzsimmons et al. 2009). In the meantime, the robotic prosthetics the brain operates have been upgraded from a robot arm to the locomotion apparatuses of a humanoid robot (Nicolelis and Chapin 2008), and to "a realistic, virtual monkey avatar" (Ifft et al. 2013). The physical medium implanted in a brain has been renovated not only to allow it to send brainwaves wirelessly (Schwarz et al. 2014) but also to enable it to receive proprioceptive feedback from the robots directly in the form of intracortical microstimulation (ICMS) bypassing any sense receptors on the skin (O'Doherty et al. 2009).

Besides these changes in the components of the BMI, the physical range of its closed-loop has extended from a single laboratory in North Carolina to a network of two laboratories: one in Kyoto for the humanoid robot part of the loop, another in North Carolina for the brain part, transmitting its action potentials to Japan through a high-speed internet link "literally expanding that primate's brain reach to the other side of the earth" (Nicolelis and Chapin 2008). Throughout the experimentations with the BMI's adaptability to other ready-made apparatuses, including a treadmill, humanoid robot, EMG, Muscle Geometry, and noninvasive EEG used in the World Cup Demo, computer algorithms have also been updated from linear modelings, such as Wiener filter, LMS adaptive filters, gamma filter, and subspace Wiener filters, to nonlinear modelings, such as time-delay neural networks, local linear switching models, and the Unscented Kalman Filter (Kim et al. 2006; Li et al. 2009).

In a more recent research, Nicolelis Lab juxtaposed three monkey brains with a virtual monkey avatar, experimenting with the possibility of the BMI's extension to the Brain-to-Brain Interfaces (BtBIs). The lab reported that, after "several weeks of training," the three monkeys and one avatar eventually formed an organic computing device named Brainet, "a self-adapting computation architecture capable of achieving a common behavioural goal," such as a three-dimensional reaching and grasping task in virtual reality (Ramakrishnan et al. 2015: 10; Pais-Vieira 2015). In this new setup, each monkey is in a separate room watching a computer monitor displaying a two-dimensional projection of an avatar shown from each plane and trained to operate only one side of this three-dimensional avatar (Figure 15). As the collective firings of three separated

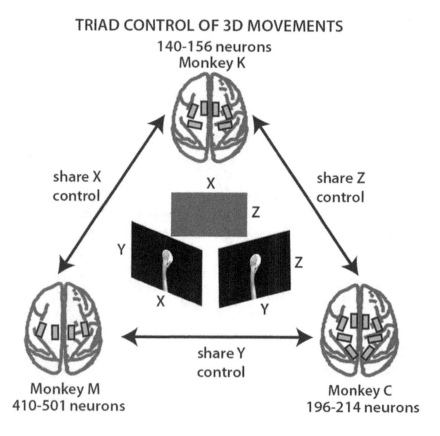

Figure 15 Brainet of three monkey brains (Ramakrishnan et al. 2015).

brains succeeded in operating the avatar in the space of a higher dimension than each monkey was engaged with, the researchers declared that the "shared BMI allowed multiple monkey brains to adapt in an unsupervised manner." Black-boxed as a "self-adapting computation architecture" (Ramakrishnan et al. 2015: 10), the BMI, redefined as an inter-brain network, is now capable of expanding its promise to the problems supposed to be higher-dimensional than the phenomenal worlds the users belong to.

Throughout the evolution of BMI, many things have been included in its closed-loop for the purpose of demonstrating this IoT system's applicability to many cognitive tasks. And the scientists' selections of things to enlarge the loop in the lab have been based on their concern for the geographical, interdisciplinary, and industrial expansion of the network. So, for each new thing chosen as a contributor to BMI's becoming a biological Turing machine, the future use of BMI the thing promises has been emphasized. For instance, from rats (as an umbrella species for the whole upper vertebrates) to owl and macaque monkeys, and to human patients, experimental subjects have been chosen under such consideration of how similar the anatomical structures of their brains are to their human relatives (Nicolelis and Chapin 2008). The motor parameters quantifying the subjects' behaviors—from simple arm movements and reaching-grasping tasks to bimanual and bipedal movements, and to the control of a virtual avatar— have been chosen under consideration of how they "could be used in human neuroprosthetic applications" and "contribute to the development of future clinical neuroprosthetics systems" (Ifft et al. 2013: 8; Li et al. 2009; Santucci et al. 2005: 1537). The wireless electrodes implanted in the cortices instead of the microwires in the earlier versions were expected to "reduce the risks of infection introduced by the use of cables that connect brain implants to external hardware" when applied to human patients (Lebedev and Nicolelis 2006: 540). The three monkey brains connected through the BtBI were supposed to provide other scientists with "the core for a new type of computing device: an organic computer" (Pais-Vieira 2015: 1). As the geographical distance between the brains in the Nicolelis Lab and the robots in other places were dramatically extended through the internet protocols, such as TCP/IP (Wessberg et al. 2000: 363), the BMI seemed to finally realize humans' long-standing desire of their telepresence "beyond boundaries" (Nicolelis 2011a; Nicolelis and Chapin 2008).

The more variety of biological and technological things the loop enclosed within it, the more hopes Nicolelis Lab could promise to the people outside. The more this loop looked adaptive to the new experimental setups in "an unsupervised manner," the more credits Nicolelis Lab could earn from academia, patients, governments, and industries. These interests the lab aroused by "promising too much" (Miller 2014) also required Nicolelis to be a skillful manager not only as an organizer of an international consortium but also as a supervisor responsible for designing a better way to exploit the adaptability of small things to a new laboratory setup embodying the interests of big actors outside. Put another way, between the interests of small things and those of big things, Nicolelis needed to translate the confusing and ambiguous intervals of relations as yet unstabilized into the delayed hopes and promises for the future where everything is possible.

Designing BMI for Nicolelis was to draw a diagram capable of realigning along its closed-loop the heterogeneous interests of relevant actors, such as the physical (neurons and muscles), technological (filtering algorithms, robots, and brain scan apparatuses), and the societal (patients, a scientific consortium, media, and the Brazilian government). To be registered as what the future applications of BMI promise, these interests should be translated into certain juxtapositions of things this diagram has redistributed. In this respect, the diagram has functioned as an "obligatory passage point" (Callon 1986: 7) of the neuroprosthetic industry, of which Nicolelis is one of the founders. Also pushed to pass their action potentials through the loop of things to complete its functional closure as a working sensor-actuator arc, the animal and human subjects were trained to transform their perceptions and motor intentions into computational problems that can be optimized only through their extended bodily enclosure in BMI. However, what was concealed by the lab's promotion of this cyborg subjectivity beyond boundaries as "what a naturally evolved brain can produce" (Cicurel and Nicolelis 2015: Ch.4) was its hidden political economy. The issues are, as raised by the actor-network analysis of this IoT prototype thus far, how this diagram redistributes things along its wired or wireless conveyor belt designed to squeeze out a monkey's desire to win the videogame for a drip of fruit juice, or a handicapped human subject's hope for walking again, and how this diagram translates the plasticity of human brains into the inexhaustibility of brain-powered cognitive labors to draw more venture capital to the unlimited applicability of BMI to any speculatable matters of cyborg kinetics.

Smart EEG Headsets

As an alternative to invasive electrode implantation, the electroencephalogram (EEG) that Pinto put on his head during the World Cup Demo is a noninvasive means for "the graphic recording of the electric activity of the human brain" (Borck 2008: 367). As a neuroimaging technology for both clinical use and scientific research, an EEG scans "a direct and strange correlation [of brainwaves] to mental processing" (367) that is often stimulated by actuators in experimental setups. What's more, as its current use in the BMI design demonstrates, the EEG's capability of revealing the worldly correlations between human consciousnesses and technological measurements has also "kindled far-reaching speculations about the imminent deciphering of mind and brain" from its invention in the early twentieth century onward (367). For instance, one important motivation that led the German physician Hans Berger to invent EEG in the 1920s was his interest in "the physical basis of mind," which he hoped would explain his own "telepathic experience" by "measuring the 'energy of mind'" (La Vaque 1999: 1, 3). Motivated by Helmholtz's physiological research with the myograph, his experiment was designed to demystify the spiritual sense of the human mind. And yet, with the vacuum-tube amplification of Berger's original design, what the English electrophysiologist Edgar Adrian really discovered in the 1940s was "the inaccessibility of the mind within the brain" (Borck 2008: 372). The brainwaves scanned by the advanced EEG sensors of the time were "not merely a more complicated version of reflex machinery" but "a noisy crowd" constantly withdrawing from "the dictatorial bonds of reflex physiology" (371–2). It was not until Norbert Wiener applied cross-correlation analysis in the 1950s that this noisy crowd of brainwaves began to unfold some decipherable "responses in the EEG to sensory stimulation" (Barlow 1997: 449). Since then, EEG has been considered the most accessible technology for the sensor component of brain-machine interfaces designed in different disciplines loosely allied under the common prefix "neuro-." Meanwhile, a variety of screen and motor apparatuses have also been considered as the actuator counterparts to complete functionally closed sensor-actuator arcs for many different purposes, including not only their medical and research uses but also BMI for entertainment, neuromarketing, human resource management, and smart applications for sleep and meditation.

In line with this brief history, the recent commercial EEG headsets, such as EMOTIV and Muse (Figure 16), reflect the current platformization of BMI. This trend promises that almost all of the future applications of BMI that these neuro-disciplines and Nicolelis Lab once suggested could be fulfilled through users' everyday training of and experimentation with their neural plasticity on the internet. Embedded with several noninvasive sensors (seven electrodes for Muse and fourteen for EMOTIV) and connectable to a smartphone or PC with monitoring software, these headsets transmit the wearers' brainwaves to the cloud, where the data gathered from each electrode are encrypted and stored in the wearers' personal accounts. These data are also shared with internal research teams and, in all likelihood, with third-party researchers and developers. Regarding the current trend toward neuro-entrepreneurship, Rose and Abi-Rached argue that "neurobiological self-fashioning" by means of attending to "nonconscious determinants of our choices, our affections, our commitments" becomes our new responsibility not only for our smart life but for "improving the well-being of our societies" (2013: 22). While nonexperts with limited access

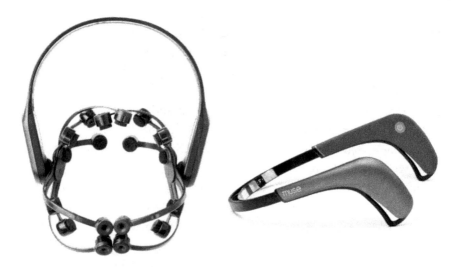

Figure 16 EMOTIV EPOC X (EMOTIVE|EPOC X n.d.) and Muse 2 (Introducing Muse 2 n.d.).

to their own brains as of the authors' writing may have technical difficulty in taking this responsibility, EMOTIV and Muse now make it as easy as putting on a headset and clicking "yes" to the Terms of Service, which allow our brainwaves to be shared through their clouds with easy-to-use machine learning tools.

According to the producers of these headsets, this "noisy crowd" of brainwaves, which is transmuted into big data and stored in the cloud for machine learning, could provide solutions to problems identified by multiple interested parties. First, for the individual looking for better "brain fitness," the headsets provide "an increased awareness of how [her] brain responds to different activities" and help her "make more informed decisions in [her] daily life that improves [her] productivity and long-term well-being" (MyEmotiv, n.d.). Second, for those interested in the wireless connectivity of their brains, the headsets will train them to activate "Internet of Things devices, online services like social media, and robotics like Arduino" using only the brainwaves that the headsets transmit (Introduction, n.d.). Third, for corporate customers pursuing "workplace wellness, safety & productiveness," the headsets provide the opportunity to "build custom enterprise solutions or applications informed by brain-data-driven insights" into stress and attention, rather than relying on "inaccurate self-reports" (Enterprise Neurotechnology Solutions n.d.). Lastly, for individuals and organizations interested in neural research and education, the headsets create a digital platform for brainwaves, which would support application customization for researchers who aim to unfold the hidden correlations between brain activities and certain events, environmental cues, or nudges (What It Measures n.d.).

The application customization that these headsets support has clear benefits over other wearable devices such as the Fitbit and Apple Watch, whose functional values are restricted by what the sensors can measure. For instance, the Apple Watch's Fitness app can be activated after its photoplethysmographic sensor detects that the wearer's heart rate has exceeded the acceptable limit and then terminated by the actuation of the vibrator that cues her to slow down. In this case, the app, following the order of Sensor→Actuator, reduces the wearer's body to a simple problem space along a linear spectrum of heart rates. By contrast, the customizability of EEG headsets allows them to reopen this sensor-initiating closed-loop by giving the wearer a chance to experiment with multiple spectra of their brainwaves that can be unfolded through each application they customize using actuators in local setups. For instance, gaming devices, such as PCs or gaming consoles, are commonly available actuators for most headset users.

Paired with an EEG headset, the gaming device arouses manifold brainwaves tentatively correlated with each conscious or nonconscious task the gamer-wearer performs. Depending on which kind of in-game stimulus the machine learning algorithm targets when searching for the most matched set of brain-sensor data, this customized Actuator→Sensor interoperation can unravel lots of brain-data-driven insights potentially relevant to all four of the aforementioned interests. Specifically, the information generated by the headset might produce insights into, among other things, how a gamer's brain responds to different gaming activities, which subset of brainwaves represents her motor intention to control the joystick, and how the part of her brain indicating stress levels changes according to its exposure to various stimuli.

Although this actuator customizability is enough to make the headset producers bold enough to promise all these future "solutions" with fewer than fifteen sensors on a single headset, none of the user-customized EEG applications currently work as seamlessly as a Fitbit or Apple Watch. However, for many individual EEG users, these customization options could still function as proof of "neuro-realism" (Gruber 2017), the belief that there are hidden realities in our brains correlatable to any internal and external events we experience. Furthermore, through the headsets' wireless transmission of brainwaves, this conviction in the brain's unexamined potential functions can expand to include those never actualizable by a too-restricted human body and its hardwired sensorimotor responses but available through cloud-based IoT devices, for instance, the ability to remotely control a machine using only one's brainwaves. The smart solutions these headsets promise are, in this respect, very "correlationist" in a similar sense to that used by speculative realist Meillassoux (2008), except that here human reason is no longer at the center of correlations. For the producers of the headsets, any conscious or nonconscious experience is correlated with brainwaves; each and all of the user's cognitive processes and physical, psychological, and social needs have right matches in her brainwaves while simply not yet data-mined are just the missing links to complete these correlations. However, until enough empirical EEG data are mined to corroborate this assumption, it is just as important for these companies to maintain their users' belief in this indefinitely postponed smart future as it is to develop actual brain-data-driven services with practical value. For instance, some of the services that the headsets advertise, such as real-time and aesthetic visualizations of EEG-scanned brain activities and their brief analysis of "six key cognitive metrics" (Figure 17), still play into the individual customer's

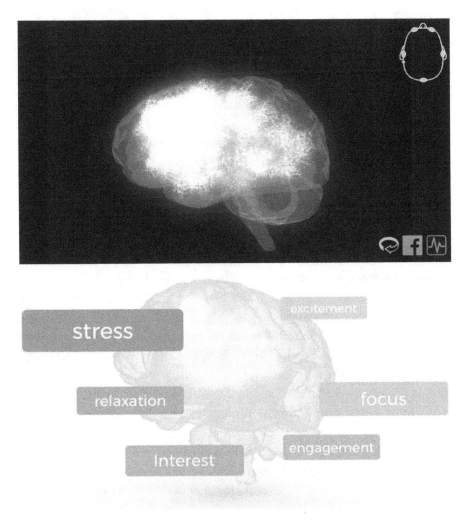

Figure 17 3D Brain visualization and performance metrics for brainwaves (MyEmotiv n.d.).

expectation that the accumulated brain data in the clouds will, sooner or later, help them make more informed decisions in daily life. To render plausible the promise that every IoT device will eventually be controllable seamlessly through EEG-based brain-machine interfaces, headset companies also support user experimentation with baseline EEG-based remote control of things, such as driving a Tesla back and forth without touching the steering wheel (Touch Titans' Mind Controlled Tesla P90D Ludicrous 2016). To maintain corporate interest in using headsets to optimize human resource management, companies have found it more important to suggest as many brain-data-driven insights as possible into employees' stress and attention levels than to fill in the actual missing links between employees' brains and their workplace wellness and productivity. In short, as Silicon Valley tech companies EMOTIV and Muse have constructed a fetishistic image around their EEG headset-collected big data to mobilize speculation about the hidden value of brainwaves, as yet signaled only faintly through the rough EEG applications currently available or aesthetically through the glittering spectacle of brain visualization.

At the same time, to convert these fictitious values of BMI into real values of practical insights or life-optimizing services, headset companies need to complement their IoT networks—which, because they only consist of EEG sensors in the first place, are somewhat incomplete—with multiple actuators enough to activate as-yet-unknown brain responses. To that end, they have cooperated with many third-party institutes and individual developers, who have exposed the headset users to a variety of sensory cues and cognitive tasks, such as walking around "different urban environments" and shopping centers full of subliminal signals, driving a luxury car, performing "language processing" and "meditation," playing videogames, and using other wearable devices such as a VR headset (Brain Research and Education n.d.). As Bruder (2019) points out regarding current neuroimaging technologies, EEG headsets have infrastructuralized the human brain as a platform. It is to this platform that many research institutes and students of human behavior have brought their field-specific brain-actuating apparatuses, as well as their informational labor, to realize as yet undeveloped use values for brainwaves speculated according to their various research agendas.

Regarding neuro-realism's disenchantment of the human mind, Gruber (2017: 25) argues that the "datafication of so-called 'hidden truths' [of the mind] eradicates, or may at least intend to dislocate, the mystical." For EMOTIV and Muse, the mystical has, however, been dislocated still into the sublime image of brain activity as a means of arousing speculation about the hidden truths of the human brain while infinitely postponing the moment of their full disclosure. In other words, in the version of neuro-realism they promote, the brain would be both an object with well-defined functions under readymade applications and a hyperobject remaining at least somewhat mystical to preserve its inexhaustibility.

For smart EEG applications to replicate the seamless closed-loop of the Apple Watch and the Fitbit, the brain must be defined as the object that sends known signals to the sensors and responds regularly to the "push notifications" that the actuators send back as signals to change the wearer's behavior, or to unconscious nudges capable of directly "pushing the right buttons in the brain" to initiate this change (Brenninkmeijer et al. 2019: 71). Exemplifying typical Sensor→Actuator operations, these applications assign to EEG sensors the role of triggers for the actuators, which take only a passive role when intervening in the wearer's behavior or environment. However, for the EEG-based improvements in behaviors, lifestyles, and corporate environments to continue suggesting more brain-data-driven solutions to interested parties, third-party participants must add many more actuators to this IoT platform. Put differently, for more brain-sensor data to be discovered as correlatable to these corporate and individual goals with practical values, the ambient operations of actuators should constantly stimulate brain areas that are still poorly defined but speculated for their fictitious values. Even to design a simple BMI whose operation is, for instance, initiated by the sensors detecting a wearer's "Mental Commands" and completed by the actuators' moving an object on a computer screen according to those commands, she first needs to tolerate arduous training sessions. In this training, the software is the commander, asking her to visualize this object moving in her mind so that the EEG sensors detect certain brainwaves correlated with her motor intention (EmotiveBCI n.d.). Besides a small number of reported successes in moving on-screen objects telekinetically, these Actuator→Sensor operations during the training usually accompany numberless experimental failures in unfolding working event-related potentials, whether or not the wearer's tolerance to these unsavory software commands is considered the payable cost for her becoming smart and wireless.

According to the privacy policies of EMOTIV and Muse, the EEG data generated from the wearer's training are shared with third-party participants either "on a de-identified basis" (Interaxon's Privacy Policy 2019) or in the "individualized and aggregated" forms (EMOTIV Privacy Policy 2018). To compensate for the potential privacy issues of consumer vulnerability and corporate surveillance, this sharing practice is declared to serve "scientific, medical, and historical research purposes" (EMOTIV Privacy Policy 2018), "related to improving the scientific understanding of the brain/body" (Interaxon's Privacy Policy). Converting the human brain into a hyperobject that streams a massive "Volume" of data with a "Variety" of unstructured correlations at a real-time "Velocity" (Kitchin and McArdle 2016), EMOTIV and Muse propose a new market for big-data-driven IoT services constructed around the following two consumerist speculations. First, the human brain has underdeveloped potentials, whose IoT-driven realization could help headset users make more informed decisions in their daily lives. Second, there are hidden "buttons" in consumer or employee brains whose IoT-driven activation could make them more vulnerable or hardworking.

For those who purchase EEG headsets, this neuro-realism, the fetishization of data about the hidden correlations in brainwaves, is, however, more than simply an idea in which they may or may not believe. For instance, someone who suffers from chronic depression may feel an urgent need to believe that there is something hidden in the human brain that, once revealed, would enable the optimization of everyday life even if no human expert is ever able to pin down the cause of their psychic pain. For a brand that needs marketing research to continue suggesting new strategies despite consumers' incapability or unwillingness to truthfully communicate their desires, there is a strong incentive to believe that there must be something more truthful in brainwaves than human consciousness. For a corporation in search of endless growth, it is compelling to believe that there exists something more exploitable that would allow them to squeeze out more productivity from employees even when "the most imminent threat to capitalism might be some combination of lack of engagement and general apathy" among workers (Caring-Lobel 2016: 197). In other words, there is an elemental desire among all of the parties to believe that technological solutions to seemingly insurmountable problems are on the horizon, whether or not the makers of EEG headsets are at all capable of realizing those solutions in the near future. The headset producers might claim that betting on these inaccessible realities undergirding human minds comes at a relatively low cost, that is, merely sharing their own and their employees' brainwaves in the clouds under the IoT's pan-kinetics and constant machine learning.

The Horror of Found Footage and the Speculative Economy of Attention

One critical insight into the IoT that the actor-network diagram of BMI provides is that the intervals between things are not simply empty or cleared for their wireless communications. The intervals are rather multiplicities of action potentials, whose dynamics are not consistent or noticeable enough to be called *interactions*. Instead, they can more be properly described as being under constant *intra-actions* that occasionally bifurcate many and one, actors and a network, or parts and a whole throughout the missing times of network-making. Within these intervals, some small things become actors as they contribute to the formation of a temporal sensor-actuator arc seamlessly working toward a given task while many others withdraw to the background as the multiplicities or mani*folds* of virtual networks. In Chapter 2, I suggested the term *topological continuum* to describe this intensive background. A human observer was said to be too bound by their hardwired sensor-actuator activities with everyday objects to creatively rewire these intervals. On the other hand, *folds* or *cuts* illustrate ubiquitous intervals in the current smart spaces whose *seamfulness* guarantees unlimited reassemblages of things for each different functional network. Nicolelis, for instance, could promise almost any imaginable future uses of BMI by exploiting the plasticity of small things within these intervals—biological neurons in one's brain and artificial neurons in machine learning algorithms—that are open to the formation of any sort of working sensor-actuator loops. Likewise, the IoT developers could re-enmesh a thing or space with many different sensor-actuator arcs and, in doing so, transform this thing in the interval into different problem spaces for ubiquitous computing over and again. However, this sort of datamining performed on one's body or home with no immediate reward would be endurable by IoT subscribers only if they believe in the smart futures the IoT promises. To

justify smart objects' infiltration of a greater variety of everyday activities and
to reassure the users of the benefits of being stuck within these pan-optic/
kinetic intervals, a certain discursive formation needs to be paired with the
expansion of smart networks. Exemplified by Nicolelis' role as a spokesperson
to manage people's hopes for and speculations about the ambiguous futures
of BMI, this discursive formation does not simply function to define what is
included in the current networks and thus perceivable to the current systems
and observers. The discourse here is no longer an epistemological issue. When
it comes to hopes and futures, the discourse is framed by the new concept of
totality, now imagined to be multiplicities of virtual networks, or multiplicities
of things whose matters of concern in the universe are remaining silent to one
another until unfolded through certain networks. Instead of circumscribing
a subject's epistemological limit to access the whole, the intervals in which
we find ourselves stuck allow for unlimited speculations about worlds other
than human constructions insofar as our failure to complete the closed-
loop of modern subjectivity within the intervals gives way to the cybernetic
reopening of the loop to the nonhumans that were hitherto withdrawing from
our knowability.

A smart vehicle is an example of an interval within which a driver's concern
for their nonconscious desires is graphically re-individuated along a red route
to a Point of Interest (POI) that AIDA suggests on a screen. A smart home,
then, is another interval during which the homeowner's concerns about
unknown efficiency and security issues in everyday routines are re-individuated
into certain parameters that smart objects communicate. In an open-world
videogame, between game objects that roam around the gamer's avatar are the
intervals meant to hide a plethora of stories, puzzles, and encounters that could
be unfolded into a diegetic world through the gamer's proper targeting. As an
interval between the BMI as a ready-made IoT technology for industrial and
clinical applications and the BMI in the making as lab science, Nicolelis Lab
has redistributed many small intervals between neurons and robots along its
closed loops to cultivate more cybernetic sensor-actuator arcs between them.
The intervals in these cases are experienced through the subject's feeling that
there is something ungraspable by their/its operational thinking and habitual
sensorimotor activities. Nevertheless, these intervals are still felt worth staying
in even at the risk of disabling oneself, as the monkey did in Nicolelis Lab,
or at the expense of enduring a long time of nothing happened, just as many

open-world videogamers do. It is because the subject's disoriented staying also charges the intervals with the expectation that these unknown realities would appear symmetrical to the operational intelligence of the IoT, superior to humans in terms of not only the number of sensor-actuator arcs ready to use but also the plasticity of its wireless sensor and actuator network (WSAN), which is capable of assembling many new arcs holding optimal grips on each different aspect of reality. Our staying within the intervals is, in this respect, a form of affective labor we nonconsciously perform according to the IoT's everyday protocols, such as putting on as many wearables as possible or converting ourselves into the "things" correlatable with as many other things as could plausibly happen to our bodies, neighborhoods, or even to some far off domains.

In this concluding chapter, the affective labor of IoT users—that is, their ontological concerns about the ungraspable beyond their operational intelligence—is discussed as the source of the current speculative economy of media, which the software industry cultivates within the intervals of its ubiquitous sensors and actuators. To do so it examines *found footage*, a recent film genre characterized by collage-like use of video footage produced by camera technologies now becoming self-tracking tools, such as camcorders, smartphones, and surveillance cameras. In line with the previous chapters' focus on sensor and actuator networks, this new film genre is noteworthy for its method of deconstructing the institutional form of cinema. Found footage films disarticulate the *camera obscura*, the architectural prototype of a single coherent viewpoint of the modern subject, into the multitude of small cameras embedded in our everyday life. What is emphasized in this post-humanist revision of the cinematic apparatus is that each of these cameras is, in fact, the simplest combination of a sensor and an actuator. Often augmented with a motion-sensitive motor operation, this camera provides another instance of the interval that cultivates within itself something withdrawing, persistently felt but never fully graspable by the motor's local follow-up. Found footage, in this respect, reflects the changed function of film technology in competition with other digital means of accessing reality, namely its shift from a machine that produces attention to a machine that cultivates things constantly escaping from attention. These things—proliferating or cultivated within the ubiquitous intervals of surveillance networks—are scrutinized as the source of the current cultural paranoia about hidden networks of nonhumans.

The Horror of Found Footage

Paranormal Activity (2007) and *The Blair Witch Project* (1999) are the two most essential contributions to *found footage*'s establishment as a film genre in the early twenty-first century. Alongside their unexpected box office success, both films' employment of portable video technologies as a means of extracting something photogenic from every quarter of reality has been cited as foundational of the genre's cinematic form (Heller-Nicholas 2014; Och 2015; Sayad 2016). But it has less been discussed how people's everyday lives converted to ever-expandable filmic spaces embedded with numerous video cameras are suggestive of a certain cognitive condition for the paranormal activities typical for this genre to be witnessed everywhere: from a domestic setting in San Diego recorded by an immobile camcorder to a desolate forest near Burkittsville, Maryland, recorded by student filmmakers on a shaky handheld camera. *Paranormal Activity*'s iconic long-take surveillance footage is notable for the way it locates audiences in front of a monitor, making them hypersensitive to any minute anomalies occurring at the edges of the frame without letting them take proper action— panning, zooming in, or moving to a better angle—to further identify what they perceive (Figure 18). On the other hand, the handheld camera movements in *The Blair Witch Project* result from the filmmakers' panicky motor reflexes to the things they saw while obscured from audiences and lead to the abrupt

Figure 18 An inactive shot in *Paranormal Activity*.

cut-offs of the scenes (Figure 19). As the two aesthetic signatures of camera operations available in found footage, these moments of demonic emergence expose the genre's self-reflexiveness. Contrary to other classical genres, found footage, more a genre of film technique than a narrative theme, has established its generic dimension from its conscious deployment of a camera's sensorimotor relations to a space according to its renewed reality-effect, no longer based on the seamless interconnection of the actions the camera(s) take(s) in different angles. The alternative rule for reality-effect it suggests is as follows: all cameras need to be set up, operated, and moved by a person, not an author or invisible narrator but standing on the same material footing with cameras and other objects, so that a shot can be closed only by the actions contained in itself, such as a person pushing the record button or an assault on the camera by unknown entities. As the result of this rule's consistent application, a segment of footage displays a tension between the things gradually foregrounded as responding orderly to the actions taken by the cameraperson and the things withdrawing to the background without sending any distinguishable response back to the camera.

Even in a shot closed by a camera operator's intentional action, this tension persists as an ambiguous quality sensible but not identifiable, and we can think of this unresolvable tension as now emerging everywhere in our urban neighborhoods as they are put into each narrow viewshed of ubiquitous surveillance cameras. As the owner of their own points-of-view rather than constructed as a textual subject by the continuous editing, the characters in these

Figure 19 A disordered-reactive shot in *The Blair Witch Project.*

films ironically discover the uncontrollable always embedded in the periphery of their POV. Exposing the genre's lack of proper means to exorcize the peripheral, these haunted spaces conversely remind audiences of other genres' institutional means to restage something paranormal through the choreography of multiple cameras and the seamless combination of their movements. To re-normalize the paranormal activities the endings of both films left unsolved, their sequels, *Paranormal Activity 4* (2012) and *Book of Shadows: Blair Witch 2* (2000), indeed re-employed this institutional technique, respectively through the seamless interoperations of various self-tracking technologies, such as video cameras, MacBook webcams, iPhone cameras, and Xbox Kinect, and by simply using the institutional solution of continuous editing.

Found footage, in this respect, extracts new horror values from the blind spot of a camera operator's restricted attention, and this genre's coincidence with the wide distribution of self-tracking technologies in the early twentieth century directly reveals that the peripheries of attention proliferating alongside ubiquitous sensors no longer remain simply outside of the capitalist valuation. These peripheries now turn into the sources of audiences' paranoid speculation, which changes the meaning of attention in the current attention economy from what gives value to the attended to what overvalues the things it always fails to pay proper attention to. This genre warns; something demonic haunts at the edges of ubiquitous sensors unless a certain institutionalized algorithmic arc reassembles these sensors and their actuators to identify its presence. From found footage not only as a film genre but also as representing the raw data of democratized sensor technologies in "smart" environments today, this chapter infers a new mode of attention economy that I term *speculative economy of attention*, and argues how it transforms something paranormal, or elusive of our efforts to pay attention, into a novel form of commodity.

Post-cinematic Affect In-between Sensors and Actuators

In the frame of narrative cinema, or its Deleuzian definition as *movement-image*, the poltergeists possessing the spaces in *Paranormal Activity* and *Blair Witch* can be described as such: something *perceived* at the edges of the sensor but never re-locatable to the center by a proper *action* of the camera, thus dischargeable only through its disordered motor responses. Deleuze categorizes cinematic images according to their states in circulation in a nervous system, or a machinic assemblage that consists of mechanical sensors, motors, and human brains. For him, classical narrative cinema is most of all a technological restoration of a brain's sensorimotor representation, in which something perceived gets involved with subjective meanings as it is aligned with the actions taken by an actor (either a camera or character, or audiences' embodiment of both). On the other hand, what he terms affection-image is an intermediary form of delay between perception and action, or that which "surges in the centre of indetermination, that is to say in the subject, between a perception which is troubling in certain respects and a hesitant action" (1986: 65). As a quality remaining unresolved due to the absence of any following actions, the demonic in *Paranormal Activity* in this sense provides an example of affection-image emergent from between the machine's fatigueless perception and the human's delayed or "failed" actions to follow it (Hart 2019: 76). On the other hand, the demonic in *Blair Witch* does not simply paralyze but arouses numerous unorganized actions from the camera operator, and, in this respect, the affective is also agential in the Spinozian sense as the quality of a shot in a "critical point" at which it "embodies multiple and normally mutually exclusive potentials, only one of which is 'selected'" by an abrupt cut (Massumi 2002: 32–3). Brian Massumi characterizes "our information-and image-based late capitalistic culture, in which so-called master narratives are perceived to have foundered" as the "surfeit" of affect, the state of too many images and information under cognitive process with no proper operator. According to him, affect is distinguished from emotion that is "a subjective content" since it is pre-individual and pre-signification, emergent from the suspension of the sense-making of images at "the semantic or semiotic level" defined "linguistically, logically, narratologically, ideologically, or all of these in combination, as a Symbolic" (26–7). The wane of "symbolic efficiency" of the narrative structure in fictional and nonfictional forms of media has revealed the "post-referentialitiy" of our material reality as the reality under ubiquitous sensors rarely gives consistent responses back to the actions the producers took for its technical and discursive measurements (Andrejevic 2013: 85). If affect has been our common responsive state in this context, found footage's establishment as a new film genre of the early twenty-first century is relevant to its repurposing of the current geographical distribution of video cameras for the institutional means to generate and exploit something affective, which results from the failure in the seamless relay between what their lenses perceive and how their human or software operators respond, in short between sensors and actuators.

In the film theories of the second half of the last century, *the cinematic* meant the quality effected by the alignment or intentional misalignment of the images along the concealed actions of machines, such as a shutter's flickering, camera's movement within a single shot, and the camera's geographical displacement across several shots. Jonathan Beller says that "the cinematic mode of production," which operationalized the attention economy of the last century, was based on the "separation and expropriation of vision from the spectator" by substituting the machinic circulation of images for audiences' voluntary motor responses to their own field of perception (2006: 8). For him, the cinematic means the neurophysiological extension of the logic of industrial capitalism. Thus, he says, "Instead of striking a blow to sheet metal wrapped around a mold or tightening a bolt, we sutured one image to the next (and, like workers who disappeared in the commodities they produced, we sutured ourselves into the image)" (9). In other words, what a theater's expropriation of bodily response-ability to the screen leaves for the audiences is their ability to invest the "freedom reflex" (or neural plasticity liberated from the physical and geographic constraints of human bodies) into the production of surplus meanings between montaged images according to the imagined motor responses of the coherent/schizophrenic narrative subject (27). The cinema in the discourse of attention economy during the last decades[1] has been, in this respect, defined by its twofold kinetic operations to create "suspensions of perception" (Crary 2001): first by its mechanical operation to translate the field of perception into the images framed within each fragment of celluloid, and second by its embedding imaginary motor responses of normative/schizophrenic subjects within the filmic texts as the software to reprogram attention. As the surplus value in cognition, attention reifies images into something bigger than real not because audiences add physical labor of motor response to the images but because they believe that someone behind the camera (such as a protagonist or hidden narrator) is instead moving his/her body to pay attention to the objects. Separated from the intentional motor responses of audiences in front of a screen, attention is re-inflected through the mechanical or algorithmic relay of images and turned back to the audiences as the attention already given to those images by the actions of imaginary others textually or algorithmically constructed. The cinematic as the mode of attention production in this sense operationalizes a theory of (re-)action, a sort of social kinetics, which audiences need to internalize.

On the other hand, throughout its cinematic re-employment of ubiquitous cameras that follow every move we make in everyday life, what found footage emphasizes is the impossibility of weaving them seamlessly into a panoptic vision according to a linear movement of an imaginary subject, without leaving any peripheries. "The profound sense of helplessness and paranoia" (Och 2015: 209) characterizing the affects aroused in *Blair Witch* and *Paranormal Activity* is mainly attributable to the person behind the camera being unable to take proper actions, such as panning and zooming in, to follow and re-center the anomalies at the edge. Something haunts where our attention reaches but does not return anything to reconstruct a normative subject who would realign elusive images with the rational movements of attention. What becomes productive for unfolding a horror movie experience is instead the audiences' withstanding the images without taking any actions but just charging the circuit between a sensor and actuator with some affective qualities until they are discharged through the multiple disordered vectors with arbitrary cuts, whose hidden connectivity could be *re-found* only at a meta-level of archiving. The new normative subject to rationalize the economy of attention in found footage is, therefore, not the owner of the gaze behind the camera but the archivist who has the access to the whole fragments of footage and is capable of reassembling them for public display; such as the hidden commentator at the beginning of *Blair Witch*, who says "In October of 1994, three student filmmakers disappeared in the woods … A year later their footage was found."

Let me call this new mode of attention production *post cinematic* following Steven Shaviro in that cameras are now, as he says, the "*machines for generating affect*, and for capitalizing upon, or extracting value from, this affect" (2009: 3). The poltergeists as the sources of the paranoid affects, whose exhibition values are rediscovered by the archivists at the meta-level, can be then understood as the metaphors for something hidden in the peripheries of our attention, which the attention economy recently attempts to monetize. In this respect, it is not a coincidence that, in a conversation on *Paranormal Activity*, Shaviro relates what the house is possessed by, namely "the demon in the *PA* movies," to "an immense collection of data" performed by the self-tracking technologies in today's smart buildings (Grisham et al. 2016). Even though we have formal ownership of all these machines, "It isn't always clear who 'owns' all the data." Like the woman possessed by the demonic being omnipresent in the house of *Paranormal Activity*, our quantified-selves generated in real time as our digital double from ubiquitous sensors are, he says, owned mostly by "Google and Amazon" (Grisham et al. 2016). As Cheney-Lippold says, "In most instances of algorithmic identification, we are seen, assessed, and labeled through algorithmic eyes, but our reaction is often available only to be obliquely felt"; "we may very well feel we are being watched but never see what sees" (2017: 24). However, in this reappropriation of classical rhetoric of horror film criticism, *the return of the repressed*, Shaviro overlooks the fact that, in the film, the use of self-tracking technologies for the obsessive data collection is not the demon's means to possess the woman's body but a part of her husband's attempt to persuade her that there is nothing paranormal. To rationalize the phenomena occurring *beside* the center of attention, he is willing to share what his camera recorded with a psychic, a professional analyst for paranormal activities. However, what he rediscovers even after he "lightened up the footage" artificially with video-editing software is the fact that the ambiguous quality of the video typical for surveillance footage becomes even more ambiguous as he pays closer attention to the periphery through a technological aid. As Sayad acutely points out, the husband's belief "that by turning on the camera when an eerie presence haunts [his wife]'s sleep he can tame and control it establishes an ironic pattern that underscores both the film and its sequels: the act of filming invariably backfires, granting the 'monster' access into the characters' lives" (2016: 52). The horror of found footage in this sense demonstrates the irony of the recent democratization of sensor technologies and simple data processing tools. By retrieving these means of attention production, which allow individuals in the current streaming culture to retrieve the power to direct even the attention of others to the actions they take in front of their webcams, we also rediscover something *para* with which we have always shared our spaces: something embedded *beside* like a stain in the peripheries of attention and withdrawing further *beside* under our limited tools for data processing, such as the digital zoom to enlarge the pixelated images. It should be *re-found* and *re-archived* at the meta-level to be reintegrated into the post-cinematic attention economy whose operation to suture the images is no longer based on the textual reconstruction of the normalized or schizophrenic sensorimotor responses of the modern subject but based on the constant reassemblage of images according to some nonhuman and nonlinear sensor-actuator arcs. Put differently, something affective or post-cinematic emerges from below and it can be capitalized only through the circulation in a higher dimension.

The New Low and High

As Gillespie (2000) pointed out, reality television programming in the late twentieth century already provided the platform for these affection-images from ubiquitous sensors to be re-deployed in an institutional context, and we can examine this TV genre as the precursor that has mobilized our affective concern over the peripheral for the emerging new attention economy before the found footage.

Neither constructed around the semicircular camera movements in a studio nor chasing the actions of journalists, surveillance TV series, such as *World's Wildest Police Videos* (1998–2001) and *Real TV* (1996–2001) in Gillespie's analysis, established their own generic form as the collection of "found footage" as "images produced outside of the entertainment television apparatus: workplace surveillance footage, police dashboard camera surveillance, hidden camera footage, amateur home video, and raw television news footage" (37). Whereas this *seamful* collage of low-tech videos inevitably contains some inherent ambiguities, the stacked layers of audio in these series—from "on-camera soundbites from police officers, witnesses, victims" to an expert commentator's comprehensive evaluation of these reports from below (37)— function to re-interconnect these disordered images from a city's sensor network into some pathological or criminological narratives about hidden dangers of crime, vandalism, and terrorism. According to Gillespie, the legitimate and illegitimate uses of video cameras for the participatory bottom-up surveillance, often called "synopticonism" (Andrejevic 2004) or "sousveillance" (Cascio 2005), have also been defined by this genre. In *Video Justice: Crime Caught on Tape* (1997), a special on FOX, for instance, authorized as an instance of the *viable use of home video* by the voice of the narrator is the footage in which "a white man being harassed by neighbors about his homosexuality sets up a camera and records himself being brutally attacked"; another categorized conversely as the *deviant use of video technology* is "a video made by several black youths as they gleefully drive around Los Angeles shooting paintballs at transients and pedestrians" (Gillespie 2000: 39). These two cases of camera movements that can be termed respectively *withstanding without action* and *discharging through unorganized action* represent the two poles of the continuum of possible actions a local sensor device, as the nerve ending of the city's artificial nervous system, could take, namely complete inaction and completely disordered reaction, or paralysis and haphazard responses. If the footage in these cases were intentionally selected to display something affective as unresolvable by a human sensor's restricted action, the editorial processes of reality television, on the other hand, emphasize the necessity of the discursive control of the expert's voiceover to redeploy something *para* sensed from below into a sense-making narrative designed from above (which the amateur documentary producers in *Blair Witch* failed to do).

The bottom-up process of surveillance is textually reconstructed by the stacked layers of audio and video in this TV genre, but it is not simply participatory nor democratizing the visual pleasure of the panoptic observer. The bottom-up is rather an institutionalized route here through which the citizen sensors need to redirect their concerns for the invisible dangers around their limited attention to the authority accessible to a citywide sensor network, preventing them from jumping to the paranoiac delusion of a demonic network behind. (For instance, the husband's stepwise attempt to bring his footage to a psychic in a town, and then to a famous demonologist, Dr. Johann Averies, in *Paranormal Activity* is, despite his failure to do so, the only possible cure for his wife's paranoiac *jump-to-conclusion*[2] regarding the poltergeist.) In this sense, the two modes of video technology, which Fiske calls *videolow* and *videohigh*, are in new complicity in surveillance TV shows. And along the vertical pipeline through which the producers in the high extract hidden narrative values from the footage in the low (or along the pipeline which distinguishes the found footage as a film genre from the surveillance TV shows in that the former's armature producer always fails to control these videolows, whereas TV producers are always exploitive to these grassroots), affects are not simply discovered but cultivated as the resources for the network's sustainable expansion. Regarding this affective quality of videolow, Fiske says;

> [L]ike the Rodney King video, their lower-quality images, poor but closely involved vantage points, moments of loss of technical control (blurred focus, too-rapid pans, tilted or dropped cameras), and their reduced editing all serve to reveal the discursive control that official news exerts over the events it reports. Videolow shows that events can always be put into discourse differently from videohigh, and this enhance its sense of authenticity.
>
> (2002: 389)

For Fiske, the authenticity of the low-tech video is due mainly to "its user's lack of resources to intervene in its technology." The user, or citizen sensor with "a camera, but not a computer enhancer," could "produce and replay an electronic image, but could not slow it, reverse it, freeze it, or write upon it," and thus the images the user creates usually appear "so authentic to so many precisely because he could not" (388). His definition of the authenticity of mechanically produced images is distinguishable from that of Bazinian realism based on the images perceived and relayed purely by the mechanical action due to a human operator's intentional nonintervention (Bazin 2005). The authenticity of videolow for him is rather a sort of affective value added to the footage due to the operator's inability or frustrated attempts to intervene in its hidden meanings. Found footage as videolow, in this respect, is redefined as the mechanical images charged with either some authorized meanings or affective feelings according to whether they are successfully redeployed in a citywide surveillance network or still stuck in-between a local sensor and actuator of the amateur. And the proliferation of videolows in the recent urban landscape may interface two very different networks beyond our accessibility; first, there is the network of cameras whose simple and modular actions can be reassembled by an institutional agent in an editing room for reality TV programming, or control room for citywide security cameras (Sadowski and Bendor 2019); and second, the imaginary network of demonic beings (such as terrorists, serial killers, viruses, etc.) the citizen sensors obsessively infer beyond their perceptibility. These two networks are generated symmetrically from individual citizens' asymmetry to both as the former's intervention in the low becomes justified as people become more paranoid and easily jump to conclusions at the presence of these invisible evils behind the surface. The participatory and democratic form of bottom-up surveillance, which reality TV programming idealizes as well as monetizes, is, in this respect, driven by audiences' generalized paranoia, or their self-reflexive and gut feeling that there is always something nonrepresentable left besides their technologically mediated attention. In other words, for the bottom-up to be agreed upon by the participants as the solution for their local issues, it should be their common speculation that everywhere is haunted by nowhere in which something demonic is embedded. It is always unclear who really occupies this nowhere since it constantly moves beside our actions to grasp it. However, for that precise reason, videohigh claims its right to videolow, or *mediahigh* in the upper layer of *cloud* servers, such as "Google and Amazon" accessible to not only optical sensors, such as webcams, but all kinds of digital sensors, claims its ownership of data collected from the material lower layer of users' bodies, homes, and cities, because the problems lurking there are too dispersed to be identified by our local action of zooming-in. The proper actions to exorcize them are still supposed to be programmed by the high capital, high technology, and high power with enough means to intervene everywhere in a simultaneous and timely manner just as the expert's voiceover in FOX's special redisposes all the lower layers of video and audio for a sense-making narrative. However, this authorized narrative or its "Mass surveillance may be doing less to deter destructive acts [from the demonic] than it is slowly narrowing of the range of tolerable thought and behavior" without being reported to the authority (Pasquale 2015: 52).

In this respect, the found footage both as a film genre and raw material for surveillance TV series reflects media systems' recent division into the new low and high, whose vertical complicity is strengthened by the problems whose symptoms are distributed too horizontally. For this complicity to be sustainable— in other words, for more symptoms to be identifiable only through their re-assemblages in the high—the sensor technologies owned by individuals need to be *post-cinematic* in the sense of the term by which Shaviro means *machines for generating affect*. The most urgent problem for these sensors to put under their local surveillance is something perceived beside their restricted focuses and moving further beside as we take actions to catch up. For capitalizing upon or extracting value from its constant sidling movements at the bottom, the software at the top should be accessible to these local technologies to trace its escaping vectors (just as a human operator in a control room improvises a multitude of local actions of security cameras to reassemble the ambiguous hints distributed at the edges of each screen into something criminal happening across the city). Media's systems of visibility and statement are restructured along these autonomous sensors with simple modular actions, and their bottom-up process to make statements about what is going on is no longer dependent on the normative actions of anthropomorphic paying attention, which used to interpret the mechanical or algorithmic relay of images into something perceived by a hidden human subject behind a screen. Instead, the only normativity of the actions in the editing room and control room is the flexibility in reassembling manifold small actions in a timely manner. There is nothing behind the cameras for us to internalize as the normative observer of what happens at the peripheries, only the modular actions of the sensors and their algorithmic interoperations, never anthropomorphized by the continuous editing because they are "operatorless" (Sayad 2016: 48).

What then are these worldly problems always withdrawing from our attention and thus represented as something demonic by the high? Regarding this question, the rhetoric of *the return of the repressed* is still helpful to describe the productive mode of repression in the recent attention economy. Attention as the surplus in cognitive production is not simply added to the images as "we sutured one image to the next" (Beller 2006: 9) according to the actions and choices performed by an imaginary normative subject, such as the average user algorithmically reconstructed. What should be monetized further in the time where everyone is an editor of one's own attention in the customized software interface is the fear of something marginalized in their limited focus, or *fear of missing out*: the generalized concern for the fact that our too-human attention leaves too many blind spots. "The sense of lurking danger is enhanced as much by our fear about seeing things as by our anxiety about what we do not see, and the generation of this uncertainty about whether or not we will see anything involves choices in framing" (Sayad 2016: 55). By the *speculative economy of attention*, I mean this new structure of attention economy in which audiences' concerns for their inattention are speculatively reinvested into their overvalued hope for algorithmic attention. The following interpretations have been nominated for the demons occupying these blind spots overvalued by our inattention or attention always-not-enough-paid: the danger of terrorism (Massumi 2015), nonlinearity of environmental changes (Lanzeni 2016), non-self-recognizable inefficient resource use (Strengers 2016), products you are likely to like but unlikely to pay enough attention (Thalere and Tucker 2013), and the invisible network of coronavirus too sticky for us to live with but without carrying it on our hands. As the found footage as a horror genre allegorizes, the urgency of this nowhere is overvalued as a person's local actions to detect it are frustrated repeatedly. On the other hand, the advanced software tool for surveillance, which the expert narrator in the surveillance TV show allegorizes, is supposed to exorcize this nowhere through its sophisticated redeployment of manifold sensors and actuators, which eventually illuminates the hidden dimension, hitherto felt only affectively, as measurable in terms of statistical patterns. The demons are discovered by the ubiquitous sensors (and their pan-optics) and then reinvented as the problems to be solved by the ubiquitous actuators (and their pan-kinetics), just as the unresolved ending of *Paranormal Activity* has left a problem re-solvable by the interoperations of self-tracking technologies in *Paranormal Activity 4*. This is also the reason why, in the era of smartphones embedded with multiple sensors, we must allow the applications empowered by cloud servers to have the authority to activate the phone for collecting data about what happens to the phone and its user.

John Durham Peters says, "The cloud evokes ancient ideas of a heavenly record containing everything ever said and done, a record both worldly and infallible. If ever there were a target for old-fashioned Marxist demystification, this would be it" (2015: 332). On the other hand, regarding the power of data clouds in which the supposedly omnipotent AI applications are based, our resurrected faith in the cloud is our rational response to the rediscovered boundary of our restricted subjectivity. Present beyond this boundary are not only the demons but lots of algorithmic beings communicating with one another about these demons on behalf of their human users.

The Speculative Economy of Attention

The recent achievement of miniaturizing sensor, processor, and actuator technologies to the point where they can be embedded in a variety of objects in various environments has popularized the adjective *smart* as applicable to any sort of social space of different scales. Our smart life as discussed in the Introduction is now unfolded from the awareness of our very standing at the interlocked boundaries of the spaces each redivided into low and high. Our neurophysiological bodies and domestic and urban spaces are tracked by different sets of sensors and actuators embedded in the lower layers of a smart cloth, smart home, and smart city, which are, in turn, all put under the control of each different software application in the clouds. In between this new infrastructural low and software-running high is the domain of our smart life as well as for the new market of the speculative attention economy to be cultivated. This gray area is now fully charged with the demonic: noisy crowds of vital signals haunting under wearables and people's insurgent behaviors under citywide environmental sensors, elusive from our local monitoring but, hopefully, identifiable through a network of distributed smart objects. The more we feel affective to these undercurrents, the more attention we might delegate to the software applications which provide customized solutions to alleviate our fear of missing out, not only on something fun otherwise we might fail to pay proper attention to but also something urgent otherwise remaining invisible symptoms of dormant health problems, unknown security issues, latent resource wastes, and so on. "Smart disclosure" is the solution current behavioral economists suggest alleviating these paranoid concerns by means of "the release of government information, corporate disclosures, and customer usage data in machine-readable form" to be fed into various "choice engines" (Thaler and Tucker 2013: 49). But for these engines in the cloud to be smart enough to draw our attention back to the best choice out of many available consumerist options for our worldly well-being (such as better diet, healthcare, housing option, retirement plan), we first need to agree, willingly or reluctantly, with the disclosure of our own social network profiles, online/offline behavior patterns, and the scores of psychometric tests we take consciously or unconsciously online (Stark 2018), not only to the government and corporate agents but to the third-party intermediaries as the prerequisite for all other smart disclosures. It is through this delegation of attention investment to the *attention engines* that the problems, such as the *Paranormal Activity* the husband in the film believed he could catch in a single camera take, turn out to be, in fact, stretched across many different domains. For instance, your heartbeat under the 24/7 monitoring of your smartwatch can also involve the task to find the most optimal behaviors in your house/office/city, just as detecting terrorists becomes a problem of finding irregular shopping behaviors online. In other words, the algorithms' redirection of our attention back to the urgent problems is potentially never-ending insofar as even a tiny pulsation, such as your heartbeat, could reappear in many different embodiments along the network, such as your physical states not yet optimal to work out, sleep, have sex, and so forth. For these attention engines as our new demonologists, a pulsation detected in one's body, cookies, or a real haunted house with ghostly smart objects is just a reflection of the much pervasive topological continuum that can be stretched to any other problems virtually correlated with this minor symptom. Redeployed by the attention engines, these worldly problems are put in forms not only easy but also urgent to attend to, such as the "push" notifications on your smartphone and watch or spoken directly by a smart speaker in your living room.

The demonic, once experienced in found footage as the rupture of the audience's habitual identification with a camera's restricted POV, is no longer rupturing the new attention economy since our paranoid concerns for the invisible problems are now reinvested in the software in the high. Under the pan-optics of the surveillance cameras, our technological field of perception appears to be full of urgent problems but what unfolds each narrative or problem space from the archived footage or big data is neither the intentional actions we take with our own bodies and cameras nor the imaginary actions of the normative subject. These functional spaces to resolve the problems are rather unfolded as the pan-kinetics of smart actuators translate these affection-images from below into the images corresponding to the sophisticated executions of software in the high. For example, the chaotic traffic congestion perceived in each intersection in the low could be recognized from the high as the images corresponding to the drivers' collective responses to the smart traffic lights across the city (Xie and Wang 2018). Your irregular heartbeat perceived by the smartwatch on your skin might be translated into the image corresponding to your running pace guided by the fitness app in the cloud. In this sense, Deleuze's typology of *perception-images*, *affection-images*, and *action-images* along the images' circulation in a machinic nervous system may find another field of its post-cinematic application from the wireless sensor and actuator networks (WSAN) of the IoT-based smart buildings and cities. Something affective still emerges sporadically within the bottlenecks between sensors and actuators (or perceptions and actions) in the form of the temporal paralysis of software or abrupt discharge through the shutdown of software, reminiscent of *Paranormal Activity* and *Blair Witch*. But these uncomfortable moments are also when the users are asked to participate in the bottom-up process of reporting errors and feedback to help the developers update the software's capability of further capitalizing on these elusive signals.

Rather than being the surplus labor of cognition that adds certain imaginary values to the attended images, our attention in this speculative economy is invested instead in our affective concern for the hidden problems in the periphery of the attention. The software in the high then promises the algorithmic preemption of the problems in exchange for our delegation of attention to its ubiquitous sensors and permanent data collection. The motive power that has perpetuated the attention economy of the past is audiences' neurophysiological investment of desire in the images they consumed (Terranova 2012). The speculative economy of attention is, on the other hand, perpetuated by the overvalued dangers to which nobody could pay enough attention; or the overvalued hope for the network of manifold sensors and actuators that promises to redirect our attention back to these urgent problems. As Andrejevic acutely points out, "Data mining is, in this regard, speculative as well as comprehensive" insofar as "data is captured not solely for current use, but also to take into account the possibility of any and all future scenarios and technologies" (2013: 78). The problems expected to lurk in our lives will be never resolved immediately after we purchase a smartwatch and move into a smart home in a smart city. But our investment in these technologies is still justifiable insofar as their constant data collection promises a near future where all these problems are dataminable, and thus until this future comes, we may need to delegate our investment of attention to the sensors everywhere.

Chronicle

Asymmetry is the term that I have used in this book to describe the restricted sensorimotor relation through which we are engaged with our current smart environments. And as discussed in Chapter 2, symmetry in mathematics means the feature of an object or its properties invariant under certain transformations, such as rotation, projection, and displacement. If our field of perception can also be understood as this sort of topological object under constant transformations, the world appearing symmetrical to our perception would be restricted only to that of the objects which return invariant or consistent responses back to the actions we take with our body and technological sensors under our habitual control. However, the increased number of sensors we are accessible to would not guarantee our more symmetrical engagement with the world. It would rather redraw the boundary between two worlds we are engaged symmetrically and asymmetrically. Even if we could control all the zooming and panning of the webcams and surveillance cameras, we cannot trace all the problems embedded in a space, not just because we cannot monitor all of them simultaneously but because some of them are traceable only by a sophisticated equation of the cameras' interoperations. (This advanced equation is comparable to the job of a criminal investigator, who reconstructs the course of a disastrous event from the ambiguous hints distributed in the surveillance footage, but only after the event already happened.) These problems are asymmetrical to our too human actions but symmetrical to the advanced software applications in the high capable of experimenting with the constant re-assemblage of algorithmic sensor-actuator arcs. Their asymmetries are nevertheless felt as something affective in the low. Until these unknown problems are re-symmetrified in the high, we thus need to withstand our staring nowhere without taking any significant action. The lesson of *Paranormal Activity* is, in this respect, do not attempt to communicate with the poltergeist; do not play Ouija Board before you contact a demonologist. What appears then as our common response to this restraining order is a "paranoid worldview in which everything is hopelessly complex but, with the right (data) tools, can be made deceptively simple and explainable" (Hu 2015: 124). This obsession with hidden orders "buried beneath the surface" of ambiguous symptoms (122) is nevertheless rational insofar as it promises a future where all these esoteric meanings would be explained even though it is infinitely postponed until one discovers the proper algorithms, data analysts, or true demonologists. For the audiences of the speculative economy, paranoia is even understood as "a strong theory" since it appears to be "capable of accounting for a wide spectrum of phenomena which appear to be very remote, one from the other" as the consequences of "a common source" of danger (Sedgwick 2003: 133–4). As Ulrich Beck already noted in the 1980s, their paranoid speculations about the latent dangers are "oddly immune to the critique of science"; these fatalistic speculations also earn "their 'truth' and their supporters not before science, but in interaction with" such scientific disciplines like environmental science, behavioral science, and data science (1992: 169). And these disciplines' algorithmic procedures to identify the problems are now reincarnated in smart applications.

A person in found footage, standing behind his/her own camera without paying enough attention or taking proper action to the anomaly at the edge of the frame, is, therefore, a perfect exemplum of the audiences for the new attention economy, whose persistent investment of attention to somewhere means their investment of undissmissable fears to somewhere else. For this person, the demonic is nowhere to attend or everywhere he/she fails to attend so that its emergence from the peripheries is never rationalized through the anthropomorphized continuous editing. So, we rather put them under the algorithmic perception of ubiquitous sensors. While this asymmetrical engagement we rediscover between us and our own bodies, homes, cars, and cities has been discussed throughout this book as the rationale for our delegation/investment of attention to/in the software to re-symmetrify them, the question not deliberated enough about is how to subvert this new hierarchy. In other words, is there still the possibility for the local media users to hijack the software in the high as the means to redefine their affective surrounding not as demonic but charged with more creative potentials as the Spinozian affect originally means?

Josh Trank's *Chronicle* (2012), another found footage in the early twenty-first century can be examined regarding this subversive possibility. Like many other entries in the genre, *Chronicle* takes the form of a personal record of supernatural phenomena which three teenagers experience after their encounter with some alien technology. The same aesthetic restriction of the genre, namely *all cameras set up, operated, and moved by a person standing on the same material footing*, is consistently applied. But the styles of footage recorded before and after their encounter are significantly different due to the telekinetic superpower they earned from the encounter. This power enables a boy, Andrew, to control the movement and operation of his camera without physically touching it. In the early footage where he has no other means than *manually* recording his life, the camera is always fixed or held in Andrew's hand (Figure 20), but this restriction is not simply due to his lack of a technological aid for the more sophisticated camera operations but also due to the fact that he needs to pretend nothing is recorded whenever some uninvited guests get into the frame, such as his father, street gang, bullies, and the boyfriend of the girl he peeped at a party.

Figure 20 An inactive shot in the earlier part of *Chronicle*.

He must withstand their harassment rather than warn them about the camera; otherwise, they would take away his camera and break it. Both his inactions and failed reactions leave something unresolved within the frame, felt only affectively. On the other hand, after earning the superpower, he does not need to be afraid of taking action not only because nobody can beat him up now but because the cameras floating up in the air are still fully under the control of his telekinesis. The more skillful he becomes at using his power, the more cinematic his life appears to be in the footage. In the latter half of the film where his cameras' free floating becomes as sophisticated as crane shots used in Hollywood, the screen, once flattened as a two-dimensional plane typical of other found footage films such as *Paranormal Activity*, eventually appears to be crowded with lots of hidden objects, which are not "lurking dangers" any longer but aligned with the camera's unfolding a deep space reminiscent of institutional cinema.

One afternoon after he first used his power to retaliate against bullying, Andrew alone in a junkyard talks to the camera: "A lion does not feel guilty when it kills a gazelle. Right, you do not feel guilty when you squash a fly, and I think that means something. I just think that really means." This "something," once felt only affectively due to the lack of proper action to dramatize it, gets to be concretized into his theory of "apex predator" as his actions now reach everywhere. The camera that starts from the close-up of his elated face slowly moves to a wide-angle shot, and, at the end of his monologue, it reveals the hidden telekinetic cause and effect, or correlation, between his hand squeezing the air and the deformation of a junk car in the background. The telekinetic resonance between his cameras and the urban neighborhoods culminates in the climax when he confronts his buddy Matt in the night sky of downtown Seattle. Ignoring Matt's warning, Andrew uses his superpower to hijack tens of video cameras from the people in a building and surround his body with these cameras. While his rebirth as a superhuman is recorded from these tens of different angles seamlessly interoperating through his telekinesis (Figure 21), the city's surveillance camera network broadcasts the same night sky with a small stain-like figure of Andrew in the familiar narrative of breaking news (Figure 22). Like a reality television producer, Andrew now goes with a random set of cameras floating around his body and it projects a speculative expectation that there always remain some dramatic values embedded in his life. This expectation had, however, never been realized during his lifetime but only posthumously as an anonymous editor found his footage and re-edit them into a chronicle of his becoming a superhuman/villain.

Through this physical relocation of cameras from the low to high, *Chronicle* provides a magical scenario of the high return on an individual's investment of attention in multiple self-surveillance devices. The wager Andrew is betting on with his superpower overinvested in the cameras is not like Pascal's wager. According to Pascal, betting on an extremely improbable future event is justifiable when the stake to lose is too high in the case of its occurrence by

Figure 21 A shot cinematized by a set of multiple cameras.

Figure 22 A surveillance footage in *Chronicle*.

any chance; such as the existence of the afterlife, or the possibility that your house is really haunted, your neighbor is really a terrorist, the item Amazon recommends is really important for your well-being, and so on. Betting on these sorts of wagers is rational because winning the race is not for earning the reward but for losing nothing; if you win, you lose nothing, if you lose, you lose everything. Annie McClanahan (2009) points out that, in the popular narratives of catastrophic futures after 9/11, hidden dangers of insurgents have been thought of as problems that nobody can be properly prepared for with purely "statistical models of forecast" given their too low probability to occur (44). Instead, they can be preempted by proactive seeking for the possible links through which these yet-to-come events could really come to reality. For the public, the symptoms of these events may be felt pervasive not because they look probable but because they sound "plausible" in "scenario thinking." Speculation is the discursive means to imagine myriad possible scenarios of these hidden links, and people's paranoid responses to something ambiguous in their surrounding with these overloaded speculations are sometimes enough to justify their speculative spending for the algorithmic preemptions of these scenarios. And what really matters here is not so much how probable their occurrences are in the real world but how plausible they look. McClanahan says, "when plausibilist predictions (output) are made to serve as actual evidence (input), they produce a closed circuit of speculation whose external truth can never be confirmed"

(58–9). Put differently, just more sensors for more inputs could not alleviate our paranoia unless actuators' preemptive operation actually draws some predicted problematic responses from the environments as we speculated in the first place. In his policy suggestion about technology-caused future disasters, Nick Bostrom (2019) claims that this sort of speculative investment in the preempt measure for an extremely less probable future scenario could be still rational if it is plausible that at least one of the balls we pick up from "the urn of possible inventions" would be black. In other words, just one catastrophic case is enough to dismiss trillions of other nonharmful cases if it could result in a "destructive event that is at least as bad as the death of 15% of the world population or a reduction of global GDP by >50% lasting for more than a decade." He says,

> even those who are highly suspicious of government surveillance would presumably favour a large increase in such surveillance if it were truly necessary to prevent occasional region-wide destruction. Similarly, individuals who value living in a sovereign state may reasonably prefer to live under a world government given the assumption that the alternative would entail something as terrible as a nuclear holocaust.
>
> (4)

On the other hand, Andrew's betting on the cameras does not aim at not losing but winning everything, to claim his ownership over the whole data his cameras generate without gauging how many dramatic values are really embedded there. We may compare his speculative investment of attention in *Chronicle* as an allegory for the early *quantified-self* movement led by the technology gurus in *Wired* magazine, such as Gary Wolf (2009), who delegated his attention investment to as many self-tracking devices as available to monitor "every facet of life, from sleep to mood to pain, 24/7/365" from different angles. Their experimental practices seemed promising as the hidden parameters of everyday life were expected to be discovered sooner or later for the unprecedented level of life optimization and efficiency. However, it did not take long for the air as the common, once open to these early experimenters' decision to deploy which sensors in which positions, to be black-boxed by the readymade smart objects and the IoT applications, smart enough to redeploy themselves to not only exorcize but also monetize the inoptimality and inefficiency in the users' everyday life. In consequence, affect becomes once again the most immediate response of humans to the world under the 24/7/365 surveillance of smart objects as well as to their own bodies revealed to be possessed by some unknown problems out of their conscious control. As reported by many self-tracking users today, "a lack of ability to self-regulate," or our asymmetrical engagement even with ourselves, is what people find first from their quantified-selves (Lupton 2016: 62). This generalized asymmetry of humans to their surroundings, which are symmetrical only to the advanced datamining applications, is the reason of "an obsession, compulsion or 'addiction' with one's data to the exclusion of other aspects of one's life" (64). (In this context, the current coronavirus pandemic is the turning point where all the air we breathe and surfaces we touch begin to feel like the interfaces for our asymmetrical entanglements with some demonic nonhuman networks.)

***

What does the telekinesis in *Chronicle* then tell us about these ubiquitous asymmetries whereby our subjective reality is shrunken and stuck within the intervals of sensors and actuators? As a magical solution for these asymmetries, the telekinesis seems to emphasize the necessity of returning control over the network of smart objects to humans. What, then, might offer more realistic approaches to the goal of putting the air full of inaudible whispers between machines about their humans, or the data cloud asymmetrical to data donors, back under the control of individuals as the resources for their self-narrative and self-realization? In this, the open-source movement and the higher rate of computational literacy may end up being important. However, when it comes to machine learning algorithms, what the human "code audit" may demonstrate in most cases is precisely that, even from the eyes of the most computer-literate audiences, so-called data-driven insights into our lives are shrouded by the opacity inherent in "the way algorithms operate at the scale of application" (Burrell 2016: 4). Re-demarcated by this most self-reflective form of human literacy of datum, our subjective reality may now have been dwarfed more than it ever has been since its Kantian enclosure; it is now stuck within a niche of manifold smarter objects.

Nevertheless, our dream of enlightening everything might still be pursuable if we humbly accept that the datum is embedded with hidden realities, that there will always remain more things as yet unknown than things known thus far. Given that our rhetoric of being smart, the current equivalent of the Enlightenment discourse, is no longer a matter of knowledge but of security, this humbleness would make it easier to give up our hopeless quest for the self-driven project of the Enlightenment and hand this task over to the IoT. The ideological reconstruction of the normative subject for this turn is focused less on shedding new light on the fundamental condition of human knowledge than it is on emphasizing the generalized asymmetry through which we as decision-makers engage with matters about which we need to make the most optimal decisions. Big data is symbolic in this context as the new image of the nonrepresentable totality. The boundary of the human knowability dwarfed by the mathematical sublime aroused by the vastness of big data does not simply leave the subject stuck within. While folded still into the arc between the very human sensors and motors of the subject, for instance, between her eyes or ears and her clicking/typing hands or panning/tilting heads under HUD, this vastness is never graspable by her habitual sensorimotor responses and the operational intelligence their restricted bodies enact, but it still generates inexhaustible affection-images that lead the subject's ontological concerns about the existences beyond their knowability. The world transformed into big data is speculated to hide an infinite number of correlations, inexhaustible by human audits, but likely to be machine learned at some point or another if we let smart objects continue to reassemble their inter-objective realities of Big Data. In other words, the IoT promises to further the Enlightenment project through our strategic wager on the presence of some nonhuman authors of ontologies. Under the new Enlightenment discourse of being smart, our paranoid speculations about the things in the peripheries serve to justify our speculative investment in the future where all the hidden correlations of things are already fully enlightened by the smart objects residing in the finer-grained peripheries of our attention.

As the first two chapters examined through the cases of a smart vehicle and smart home, the ambiances of current smart spaces are characterized by the imperceptible operations of the ontological objects in the IoT and their secret exchanges of inaudible signals. Our affective responses to these ambiances sometimes charge the spaces with hidden horrors. Meanwhile, the other two chapters, which focused on open-world videogames and brain-machine interfaces, suggested how these ambiances could also be charged with our expectations and hopes for the solutions that certain assemblages of smart objects may soon discover for tasks and quests that are currently unknown. Humans with these ambivalent feelings—either IoT subscribers or service providers—might dare to invest their right to the data—either their own personal data or the big data they accumulate from subscribers—in some smart software applications for life optimization. And these smart decisions might be driven by their concerns for the overvalued horrors of hidden problems or overvalued hopes for these problems' commodifiability. Yet if it is true that the hidden correlations that big data enfold are inexhaustible by analysts and their datamining tools as speculated in the first place, our smart future and its promised sustainability would nevertheless be eternally postponed. This infinite delay might be what humans need to endure in the new phase of cognitive capitalism by either hopelessly paying for new IoT solutions or cultivating more horrors to convert them into new problems for future IoT services to optimize. The totality of our hidden realities is constantly sliding under this secularized version of speculative realism, which oscillates between paranoia and blind optimism. The smart futures the IoT unfolds would thus always remain transitional, leaving us never fully secured by them nor fully hopeless for them.

***

The version of speculative realism this book has developed thus far is admittedly tricky. It is more a secularized belief in the affluence of our material reality than reasoned from some undeniable philosophical principles. It is even more secular in comparison to the current new materialism, which is reflective of "the *zeitgeist* of the Anthropocene" and humanities' response to "a climate in crisis" (Wilson 2018: 99), because the renewed understanding of materiality here rather expresses an urgent need for the current software capitalism and its venture capital to re-ground their technological optimism. While the post-structuralist critique of the metanarrative of the Enlightenment in the past century concluded with the groundlessness of human knowledge, the nonhuman ontology is, on the other hand, this century's shortcut to thinking of worlds other than human constructions as it allows us to bypass fruitless epistemological questions of how we could know or access them. In fact, how on earth we can be so sure about the presence of other relations than those corresponding to our knowability is not an important matter at all for our decision to delegate our pursuit for more knowledge to machine learning algorithms. Their presence is not to be deduced but ontologically imperative for both software companies and IoT subscribers to ground their speculation about an abundance of correlations to mine and commodify for the sustainability of their data businesses or to be optimized over and again for their smart lives.

As the conceptual breakthrough of the deadlock of our intellectual business, called either Enlightenment or data science, the substratum of digital culture that I termed a topological continuum or manifold seems to share many properties with the substratum that other new materialist thinkers require for making sense their speculation about the nonhuman construction of unknown realities beside human attention. First, this continuum is akin to what Karen Barad calls "spacetimematter manifold." The *intra-action* this manifold is constantly put under is the process through which it is folded into an "agential cut," inscribed by an assemblage of experimental apparatuses and human observers, whereby a temporary boundary of observing and observed is drawn alongside their constant re-individuations (2007). The IoT's sensor-actuator arc is an instance of an agential cut, and the problem-space it unfolds is of a certain state of the manifold out of manifold other possible states it enfolds. This problematic or suboptimal state of space is not simply discovered but enacted performatively as a topological continuum is folded into two aspects, namely an assemblage of smart objects operating autonomously on the one hand and some environmental variables a certain equation of which remains invariant under the transformation the assemblage brings up on the other. The symmetry of an IoT problem and IoT solution is bifurcated in this way. According to Manuel DeLanda (2002), the manifold is also embedded with singularities, something virtual but also real as they put the manifold's intra-active differentiation under their "sphere of influence." The hidden correlations speculated to be embedded in a topological continuum of our nonconscious material reality are also virtual in this Deleuzian sense as its differentiation into each problem-space of the IoT is influenced by the speculation these correlations arouse within the human mind.

Readers may find that this continuum also describes "a vital materiality," which Jane Bennett illustrates as "the swarm of activity subsisting below and within formed bodies and recalcitrant things" (2009: 50); what Bruno Latour calls *plasma*, gaseous and highly conductive entities not yet congealed into actors nor networks (2005: 241); or the mysterious things in Harman's object-oriented ontology (2005) that constantly withdraw from any correlationist construction of human subjects and their realities, and even from any pan-correlationist network-making of nonhumans. This tricky materiality is, for the current humanities discourse, what should remain after and thrive within the ruptures of our subjective realities so that the universe—which turns out to consist of too many intervals, holes, and folds to be mapped by a metanarrative—is still a plenum for creative evolution. In this book, this materiality has also been discussed as a plenum of data, the condition for the sustainability of the big-data-driven software industries.

Capitalist realism (Fisher 2009) in the current use of the term is not philosophical but refers to people's perception of capitalism as the only *realistic* solution to the problems they have. As Dencik and Cable (2017) narrate based on the public response to the Snowden leaks in June 2013, "surveillance realism" likewise describes people's "feelings of widespread resignation" toward "a system of ubiquitous data collection" and their reluctant acceptance of it as the only realistic approach to the ubiquitous security issues. Realism no longer provides a framework through which we can say for sure what is real in terms of its correlations with our conscious and intentional (re)actions. *Reality* is rather an affective term, meaning the totality people cannot help but accept when facing the asymmetry through which they are engaged with the invisible material practices underway in their surroundings. Data is secretly collected on and through all of our daily activities, but we can feel it only obliquely. The maximum expression of our discontent at this inaccessible technological reality is still resignation, at least as far as the surveillance is focused on catastrophic issues like "terrorism and crime" (Dencik and Cable 2017). The recent "corporate cultivation of digital resignation" (Draper and Turow 2019) is, on the other hand, the trade-off for our access to the free services of customized platforms, perhaps the only realistic solution for our *fear of missing out* on the flood of information. Resignation is, in this context, the affective response to the impossibility of an alternative future to the status quo of national security and surveillance capitalism.

If resignation is our reaction to the untraceable afterlife of our personal behavioral data (the most active form of which is the practice of obfuscation, to make them further untraceable even by software companies [Brunton and Nissenbaum 2015]), what this book has focused on from the IoT users stuck within the intervals of ubiquitous sensors and actuators is another, somewhat more proactive, affective response to surveillance capitalism. The new materiality people feel anywhere massive data collection occurs, such as their bodies, homes, and cities, is fetishized as what promises always more than the things we can access there now. And the smart technological future the IoT promises to unfold there is acceptable even at the expense of sacrificing our personal data not because there is no alternative but because it is the only alternative to break through the status quo of twenty-first-century software capitalism and the sub-optimality of our everyday lives, which are fraught with unknown security problems and lifestyle issues. Industrial capitalism at some point filled the world with resignation to its exploitive mode despite persistent negative feelings about its unsustainability. Capitalism now fills it instead with speculation about the hidden resources, the ubiquity of data, ever re-minable, and thus sustainable. The realism of this new materiality is neither what we naively believe nor a subjective construction, nor even what we reluctantly accept. It is the realism we need to wager on for the possibility of continuing to exploit the world: the realism of nonconscious brain activity, the realism of unnecessary waste, the realism of unknown danger, and the realism of missed opportunities to improve one's life. In short, the realism of every optimizable thing, or the IoT as the Internet of machinic ontologies of the things in question.

Notes

Chapter 1

1   Fetishism in this Marxian context has been defined as the mis-imposed value of object-in-itself, which can be analyzed as the social relations congealed around the object. On the other hand, Arjun Appadurai takes fetishism as his methodology for "a corrective to the tendency to excessively sociologize transactions in things" (1986: 5). However, even in his "methodological fetishism," the values of objects are subject to a multitude of local contexts of symbolic transactions even though he emphasizes their irreducibility to the global capitalist economy.

2   For "flat ontology" in speculative realism, see Bryant (2011) and Bogost (2012). For Galloway's criticism of flat ontology as the "structure of ontological systems" in the recent software businesses, see Galloway (2013: 347).

3   Gruber suggests *ontology* as an engineering term for "knowledge-level protocols" between AI systems, each of which is distinguished by its own "symbolic-level" of representation about its own environments. The role of ontology is not to organize a single globally shared theory for all different representations to adjust. It rather aims to provide the languages for an output of a system to be translated into the input for another to maximize the interoperability and communicability between the systems (1991). See the intermission "*Ontology, Operationalized.*"

4   These objects and object-like users may be modeled best as the actor in the term *actor-network*, not an "individual atom" hyphenated to a network in a deterministic way but a "circulating entity" that draws many hyphens to "hook up with" each other for both specifying its local agency and organizing global structure (Latour 1999: 17–18). For these actors, "a substrata: something upon which something else 'runs' or 'operates'" is no longer a proper metaphor for infrastructures; rather, technological infrastructures are installed as communication protocols for these circulating entities to modularize their "local practices afforded by a larger-scale technology" into the functions "which can then be used in a natural, ready-to-hand fashion" by others (Star and Ruhleder 1996: 113–14).

5   It is noteworthy that David Kuebrich relates this "doctrine of assumption" of the lawyer on the niche positions for each actor in his design of the fully operational office to "the larger culture that there is no inherent contradiction between the dedicated pursuit of self-interest, even when it involves the exploitation of others,

and devotion to traditional Christian values" (1996: 396). According to him, the doctrine "exemplifies the values and attitudes of the Protestant entrepreneur who fused his Christian faith," such as the faith in the "Starvation and wretchedness ... by Heavenly appointment," with "emerging economic practices in such a way as to legitimate inequality and class privilege" (383, 386).

Chapter 2

1   For instance, Lauren Martin and Anna Secor define topology in human geography as "the 'base' to the topographical 'superstructure'—except, to be fair, topological space is not defined by a set of given relationships (such as a capitalist mode of production) but rather by the multiplicity of potential relationships that comprise that space" (2013: 432). Topology for them is relevant to "the appropriation of scientific authority in the social sciences and humanities" as "a host of decidedly positivist and even Cartesian assumptions" (433). This "topological desire" for the positivist material substratum of human geography is also at work in the IoT's speculation about the multiply extended nature of space.

2   This stratified structure is also typical in other IoT-based systems, such as IBM's blueprint for a smart city consisting of the bottom layer of instrumentation "made up of sensors, actuators, programmable logic controllers and distributed intelligent sensors" and the top layer of intelligence for "urban software applications" with the mediation of the middle layer for interconnection (Sadowski and Bendor 2019: 551).

3   The force which makes a cut in a manifold involves the operation of apparatuses, such as the sensors and motors which constitute a cursor; however, before folded into the cut that is a local sensorimotor pathway, these apparatuses are no other than just entities or magnitudes affective to their multiply extended surroundings. As Barad emphasizes, these measuring devices should be understood as "boundary-making practices that are formative of matter and meaning, productive of, and part of, the phenomena produced" (2007: 146).

4   For the fold as what illustrates or diagrammatizes the inscription of the subjectivity for audiences within the machine assemblages of the current media culture, see Ahn (2019).

5   These two tendencies of power can be explained through two modes of technological attractors that science and technology studies call respectively "immutable mobile" and "boundary object." They are not opposite one another. They rather have a common function as technological protocols to organize a network for science research. Immutable mobile describes the protocol's

circulation to redeploy its sensors and actuators, not only experimental equipment in a local lab but discursive apparatuses, such as the questionnaire, and it functions to stimulate hidden matters of fact (or concern) of space and reproduce their invariant responses (Latour 1990). On the other hand, the boundary object is characterized by its inherent ambiguity, whose circulation along different labs, institutes, and disciplines constantly reorganizes local sensors and actuators to draw different levels of measurability and discursivity hidden in its ambiguity (Star and Griesemer 1989).

6   Donna Hoffman and Thomas Novak's assemblage theory approach to consumer experience of the IoT describes this transformation. They categorize the possible interactions that could occur in a smart home as follows: (1) consumer-centric part-part interaction (such as a consumer experience of a smart object), (2) consumer-centric part-whole interaction (a consumer experience of a smart home), (3) nonconsumer-centric part-part interaction (an object experience of another object), and (4) nonconsumer-centric part-whole interaction (an object experience of a smart home). As "a set of nested and overlapping assemblages with different spatio-temporal scales" within a smart home assemblage, these multiplied interactions, each of which can be analyzed into an object-object or human-object assemblage, or a sensor-actuator arc in my term, serve the abundance of computational problems for IoT applications (2018: 1179, 1183).

Chapter 3

1   For this debate and its focus on theorizing the purity of videogames as a cultural form, see Keogh (2014).

2   For Immutable Mobile, see Bruno Latour (1990: 44–5). For a topological space of actor-networks, see John Law (2002).

3   DeLanda defines *machinic assemblages* by their components aggregated through "relations of exteriority," which can be flexibly "detached from it and plugged into a different assemblage" (2006: 10). *The Incredible Machine* literalizes this theoretical entity with the autonomous objects coupled to each other for a common goal.

Chapter 4

1   Since sixty-nine days before the World Cup opening, images of a mysterious rectangular banner, literally a black-box, were posted to Nicolelis' Facebook page. While the information about the participants and their training was kept secret on

his page, a short clip showing only the lower part of an anonymous body walking in the exoskeleton was the only one shown online to stimulate more curiosity from the followers about the scene behind the screen. It was, on the other hand, just after Pinto's kick-off was aired worldwide and Nicolelis tweeted "We did it!!!!" that several videos of volunteers, highlighting their struggling but hopeful faces, were posted all at once. See the post on May 22, 2014, "Historic moment: eighth volunteer walks for the first time with the exoskeleton and enjoys the feeling of walking again" (Nicolelis 2014).

2 It is noteworthy, in his book *Beyond Boundaires*, how careful Nicolelis is not to describe one of his experimental monkeys (named Aurora) simply as a mere laboratory animal but to introduce her as a sophisticated social being who was willing to cooperate with the project (Nicolelis 2011b).

Chapter 5

1 Attention economy was suggested in the late 1990s as the concept to explain the source of "scarcity," which governs the new economy of cyberspace, whose oft-misconceived resource, information, is always "abundant" and "overflowing," and thus impossible to be a "basis of an economy" (Goldhaber 1997). On the other hand, the amount of attention audiences pay to the information is always limited. In the subsequent works of the researchers, such as Jonathan Crary's (2001) and Jonathan Beller's (2006) works to expand the concept's coverage even to the media culture of the early twentieth century characterized by the abundance of images and spectacles, cinema has been discussed as a technique to convert the attention into the form measurable and exchangeable in an economy. For an overview of the theoretical discourses on attention economy, see Crogan and Kinsley (2012).

2 Jump-to-conclusion is descriptive of the common pattern of the conscious process observed in delusional subjects suffering from paranoia, namely to draw a very improvable conclusion immediately after they see very ambiguous and insufficient hints (McKay et al. 2007). This pattern seems to be relevant to the patients' intolerability to seeing anything open to unknown relations, indescribable by known narrative closures (Mills 2003).

References

Aarseth, E. (1997), *Cybertext: Perspectives on Ergodic Literature*, Baltimore: Johns Hopkins University.

Abelson, H., Beal, J. and Sussman, G. J. (2009), "Amorphous Computing," in R. A. Meyers (ed), *Encyclopedia of Complexity and Systems Science*, 257–71, New York: Springer.

Ahn, S. (2013), "Cinematic Innervations: The Intuitive Form of Perception in the Distracted Perceptual Field," *Journal of Aesthetics and Culture*, 5(1).

Ahn, S. (2019), "From Theater to Laboratory: Two Regimes of Apparatuses in the Material Assemblages of Media Culture," *Journal of Aesthetics and Culture*, 11(1).

Allan, J. (2011), "Topological Twists: Power's Shifting Geographies," *Dialogue in Human Geography*, 1(3): 283–98.

Amazon (n.d.), "Alexa Routines," *Amazon*. Available online: https://www.amazon.com/b?node=21442922011&ref=ZZXZ_ALXH_ASH_ROUT (accessed July 10, 2022).

Amazon (n.d.), "Alexa Smart Home: Learn How to Start and Expand Your Smart Home," *Amazon*. Available online: https://www.amazon.com/alexa-smart-home/b?ie=UTF8&node=21442899011 (accessed July 10, 2022).

Anderson, C. (2008), "The End of Theory: The Data Deluge Makes the Scientific Method Obsolete," *Wired*, June. Available online: https://www.wired.com/2008/06/pb-theory/ (accessed July 12, 2022).

Andrejevic, M. (2004), *Reality TV: The Work of Being Watched*, New York: Rowman & Littlefield Publishers.

Andrejevic, M. (2005), "Nothing Comes Between Me and My CPU: Smart Clothes and 'Ubiquitous' Computing," *Theory, Culture & Society*, 22(3): 101–19.

Andrejevic, M. (2013), *Infoglut: How Too Much Information Is Changing the Way We Think and Know*, New York: Routledge.

Appadurai, A. (1986), "Introduction: Commodities and the Politics of Value," in A. Appadurai (ed), *The Social Life of Things: Commodities in Cultural Perspective*, 3–63, Cambridge, UK: Cambridge University Press.

ARlab (2013), "MeMachine: Bio-technology, Privacy and Transparency," August 13. Available online: http://arlab.kabk.nl/project/memachine-bio-technology-privacy-and-transparency/ (accessed July 12, 2022).

Ashton, K. (2009), "That 'Internet of Things' Thing," *RFID Journal*, June 22. Available online: http://www.rfidjournal.com/articles/view?4986 (accessed July 12, 2022).

Barad, K. (2003), "Posthumanist Performativity: Toward an Understanding of How Matter Comes to Matter," *Signs*, 28(3): 801–31.

Barad, K. (2007), *Meeting the Universe Halfway: Quantum Physics and the Entanglement of Matter and Meaning*, Durham: Duke University Press.

Barlow, J. S. (1997), "The Early History of EEG Data-Processing at the Massachusetts Institute of Technology and the Massachusetts General Hospital," *International Journal of Psychophysiology*, 26: 443–54.

Batman: Arkham Knight (2015), [Videogame], London: Rocksteady Studios.

Baudrilard, J. (1981), *For a Critique of the Political Economy of the Sign*, trans. C. Levin, St. Louis: Telos Press.

Bazin, A. (2005), "The Ontology of the Photographic Image," in H. Gray (ed & trans), *What Is Cinema? Vol. 1*, 9–16, Berkeley: University of California Press.

Beck, U. (1992), *Risk Society: Towards a New Modernity*, London: Sage.

Beller, J. (2006), *The Cinematic Mode of Production: Attention Economy and the Society of the Spectacle*, Lebanon, NH: Dartmouth College Press.

Beller, J. (2018), *The Message Is Murder: Substrates of Computational Capital*, London: Pluto Press.

Bennet, J. (2009), *Vibrant Matter: A Political Ecology of Things*, Durham: Duke University Press.

Berry, D. M. (2014), *Critical Theory and Digital*, New York: Bloomsbury.

Blakeslee, S. (2008), "Monkey's Thoughts Propel Robot, a Step That May Help Humans," *The New York Times*, January 15. Available online: http://www.nytimes.com/2008/01/15/science/15robo.html?_r=0 (accessed July 12, 2022).

Bogost, I. (2006), *Unit Operations: An Approach to Videogame Criticism*, Cambridge: The MIT Press.

Bogost, I. (2012), *Alien Phenomenology, or, What It's Like to Be a Thing*, Minneapolis: University of Minnesota Press.

Bolter, J. D. and Grusin, R. (1999), *Remediation: Understanding New Media*, Cambridge: The MIT Press.

Book of Shadows: Blair Witch 2 (2000), [Film] Dir. J. Berlinger, USA: Haxan.

Borck, C. (2008), "Recording the Brain at Work: The Visible, the Readable, and the Invisible in Electroencephalography," *Journal of the History of the Neurosciences*, 17: 367–79.

Bostrom, N. (1998), "How Long Before Superintelligence?," *International Journal of Future Studies*, 2. Available online: https://www.nickbostrom.com/superintelligence.html (accessed July 12, 2022).

Bostrom, N. (2014), *Superintelligence: Paths, Dangers, Strategies*, Oxford: Oxford University Press.

Bostrom, N. (2019), "The Vulnerable World Hypothesis," *Global Policy*, 10(4): 1–22.

Boyle, A. (2014), "'We Did It!' Brain-Controlled 'Iron Man' Suit Kicks Off World Cup," *NBC News*, June 12. Available online: http://www.nbcnews.com/storyline/world-cup/we-did-it-brain-controlled-iron-man-suit-kicks-world-n129941.

Brain Research & Education (n.d.), *EMOTIV*. Available online: https://www.emotiv.com/neuroscience-research-education-solutions (accessed March 27, 2021).

Brenninkmeijer, J., Schneider, T. and Woolgar, S. (2019), "Witness and Silence in Neuromarketing: Managing the Gap Between Science and Its Application," *Science, Technology, & Human Values*, 45(1): 62–86.

Brooks, R. A. (1991), "Intelligence Without Representation," *Artificial Intelligence*, 47: 139–59.

Brooks, R. A. and Stein, L. A. (1994), "Building Brains for Bodies," *Autonomous Robots*, 1: 7–25.

Bruder, J. (2019), *Cognitive Code: Post-Anthropocentric Intelligence and the Infrastructural Brain*, Montreal: McGill-Queen's University Press.

Brunton, F. and Nissenbaum, H. (2015), *Obfuscation: A User's Guide for Privacy and Protest*, Cambridge: The MIT Press.

Bryant, L. R. (2011), "The Ontic Principle: Outline of an Object-Oriented Ontology," in L. R. Bryant, N. Srnifek and G. Harman (eds), *The Speculative Turn: Continental Materialism and Realism*, 261–78, Melbourne: Re.press.

Bryant, L. R. (2012), *The Democracy of Objects*, London: Open Humanities Press.

Burrell, J. (2016), "How the Machine 'Think': Understanding Opacity in Machine Learning Algorithms," *Big Data & Society*, 3(1).

Callon, M. (1986), "Some Elements of Sociology of Translation: Domestication of the Scallops and the Fishermen of the Saint Brieuc Bay," in J. Law (ed), *Power, Action, and Belief: A New Sociology of Knowledge*, 196–233, London: Routledge & Kegan Paul.

Callon, M. (2012), "Society in the Making: The Study of Technology as a Tool for Sociological Analysis," in W. E. Bijker, T. P. Hughes and T. Pinch (eds), *The Social Construction of Technological Systems*, 77–97, Cambridge: The MIT Press.

Caring-Lobel, A. (2016), "Corporate Mindfulness and the Pathologization of Workplace Stress," in R. E. Purser, D. Forbes and A. Burke (eds), *Handbook of Mindfulness: Culture, Context, and Social Engagement*, 195–214, Switzerland: Springer.

Carmena, J. M., Lebedev, M. A., Crist, R. E., O'Doherty, J. E., Santucci, D. M., Dimitrov, D. F., Patil, P. G., Henriquez, C. S. and Nicolelis, M. A. (2003), "Learning to Control a Brain–Machine Interface for Reaching and Grasping by Primates," *PLoS Biol*, 1(2).

Cascio, J. (2005), "The Rise of the Participatory Panopticon," *WC Archive*. Available online: http://www.openthefuture.com/wcarchive/2005/05/the_rise_of_the_participatory.html (accessed July 12, 2022).

Catarinucci, L., Donno, D., Mainetti, L., Palano, L., Patrono, L., Stefanizzi, M. L. and Tarricone, L. (2015), "An IoT-Aware Architecture for Smart Healthcare Systems," *IEEE Internet of Things Journal*, 2(6): 515–26.

Cellary, W. and Rykowski, J. (2015), "Challenges of Smart Industries: Privacy and payment in Visible Versus Unseen Internet," *Government Information Quarterly*, 35: S17–S23.

Chan, C., Thawonmas, R. and Chen, K. (2009), "Automatic Storytelling in Comics: A Case Study on World of Warcraft," in *Proceeding of ACM CHI 2009 Conference on Human Factors in Computing Systems*, 3589–94, New York: ACM.

Cheney-Lippold, J. (2017), *We Are Data: Algorithms and the Making of Our Digital Selves*, New York: New York University Press.

Chronicle (2012), [Film] Dir. J. Trank, USA: Davis.

Cicurel, R. and Nicolelis, M. A. (2015), *The Relativistic Brain: How It Works and It Cannot Be Simulated by a Turing Machine*, São Paulo: Kios Press.

Clemens, J. and Nash, A. (2015), "Being and Media: Digital Ontology After the Event of the End of Media," *The Fibreculture Journal*, 24.

Collier, S. J. (2009), "Topologies of Power: Foucault's Analysis of Political Government Beyond," *Theory, Culture & Society*, 26(6): 78–108.

Cooper, R. (2020), "Pastoral Power and Algorithmic Governmentality," *Theory, Culture & Society*, 37(1): 29–52.

Crandall, J. (2010), "The Geospatialization of Calculative Operations: Tracking, Sensing and Megacities," *Theory, Culture & Society*, 27(6): 83–4.

Crary, J. (2001), *Suspensions of Perception: Attention, Spectacle, and Modern Culture*, Cambridge: MIT Press.

Crogan, P. and Kinsley, S. (2012), "Paying Attention: Towards a Critique of the Attention Economy," *Culture Machine*, 13.

Dant, T. (1996), "Fetishism and the Social Value of Objects," *The Sociological Review*, 44(3): 495–516.

DeLanda, M. (2002), *Intensive Science and Virtual Philosophy*, New York: Continuum.

DeLanda, M. (2006), *A New Philosophy of Society*, London: Continuum.

Deleuze, G. (1986), *Cinema 1: The Movement-Image*, trans. H. Tomlinson and B. Habberjam, Minneapolis: University of Minnesota Press.

Deleuze, G. (1992), "Postscript on the Societies of Control," *October*, 59: 3–7.

Dencik, L. and Cable, J. (2017), "The Advent of Surveillance Realism: Public Opinion and Activist Responses to the Snowden Leaks," *International Journal of Communication*, 11: 763–81.

Doane, M. A. (2003), "The Close-Up: Scale and Detail in the Cinema," *Difference: A Journal of Feminist Cultural Studies*, 14(3): 89–111.

Dourish, P. and Bell, G. (2011), *Divining a Digital Future: Mess and Mythology in Ubiquitous Computing*, Cambridge: The MIT Press.

Draper, N. and Turow, J. (2019), "The Corporate Cultivation of Digital Resignation," *New Media & Society*, 21(8): 1824–39.

EMOTIVE Privacy Policy (2018), *EMOTIV*. Available online: https://id.emotivcloud.com/eoidc/privacy/privacy_policy (accessed March 27, 2021).

EMOTIVE|EPOC X (n.d.), *EMOTIV*. Available online: https://www.emotiv.com/epoc-x (accessed March 27, 2021).

EmotiveBCI (n.d.), *EMOTIV*. Available online: https://www.emotiv.com/product/emotiv-bci (accessed March 27, 2021).

Enterprise Neurotechnology Solutions (n.d.), *EMOTIV*. Available online: https://www.emotiv.com/workplace-wellness-safety-and-productivity-mn8 (accessed March 27, 2021).

Espinoiza, M. I. and Aronczyk, M. (2021), "Big Data for Climate Action or Climate Action for Big Data?," *Big Data & Society*, 8(1).

Evans, D. (2012), "The Internet of Everything: How More Relevant and Valuable Connections Will Change the World." Available online: https://www.cisco.com/c/dam/global/en_my/assets/ciscoinnovate/pdfs/IoE.pdf (accessed July 12, 2022).

Falconer, G. and Mitchell, S. (2012), "Smart City Framework: A Systemic Process for Enabling Smart+Connected Community," in *Cisco Internet Business Group*, 1–11, San Jose: Cisco System.

Fisher, M. (2009), *Capitalist Realism: Is There No Alternative?*, Hant, UK: Zero Books.

Fiske, J. (2002), "Videotech," in N. Mirzoeff (ed), *The Visual Culture Reader*, 383–91, New York: Routledge.

Fitzsimmons, N. A., Lebedev, M. A., Peikon, I. D. and Nicolelis, M. A. (2009), "Extracting Kinematic Parameters for Monkey Bipedal Walking from Cortical Neuronal Ensemble Activity," *Frontiers in Integrative Neuroscience*, 3(3).

Foucault, M. (1995), *Discipline and Punish: The Birth of the Prison*, trans. A. Sheridan, New York: Vintage Books.

Foucault, M. (2003), *Society Must Be Defended: Lectures at the Collège de France, 1975–1976*, trans. D. Macey, New York: Picador.

Foucault, M. (2008), *The Birth of Biopolitics: Lectures at the Collège de France, 1978–79*, trans. G. Burchell, New York: Palgrave.

Freeman, W. (2000), *How Brains Make Up Their Minds*, New York: Columbia University Press.

Gabbatt, A. (2013), "New York Woman Visited by Police after Researching Pressur Cookers Online," *The Guardian*, August 1. Available online: https://www.theguardian.com/world/2013/aug/01/new-york-police-terrorism-pressure-cooker (accessed March 27, 2021).

Gabrys, J. (2014), "Programming Environments: Environmentality and Citizen Sensing in the Smart," *Environment and Planning D: Society and Space*, 32(1): 30–48.

Gabrys, J. (2016a), *Program Earth: Environmental Sensing Technology and the Making of a Computational Planet*, Minneapolis: University of Minnesota Press.

Gabrys, J. (2016b), "Re-thingifying the Internet of Things," in N. Starosielski and J. Walker (eds), *Sustainable Media: Critical Approaches to Media and Environment*, 180–95, London: Routledge.

Gad, C. (2010), "On the Consequences of Post-ANT," *Science, Technology, & Human Values*, 35(1): 55–80.

Galloway, A. R. (2006), *Gaming: Essays on Algorithmic Culture*, Minneapolis: University of Minnesota.

Galloway, A. R. (2012), "A Response to Graham Harman's 'Marginalia on Radical Thinking'," *An und für sich*, June 3. Available online: http://itself.wordpress. com/2012/06/03/a-response-to-graham-harmans-marginalia-on-radical-thinking/ (accessed July 12, 2022).

Galloway, A. R. (2013). "The Poverty of Philosophy: Realism and Post-Fordism," *Critical Inquiry*, 39 (winter): 347–66.

Galloway, A. R. (2014), "The Universe of Things," November 29. Available online: http://cultureandcommunication.org/galloway/the-universe-of-things/ (accessed July 12, 2022).

Gerlitz, C. and Helmond, A. (2013), "The Like Economy: Social Buttons and the Data-Intensive Web," *New Media & Society*, 15(8): 1348–65.

Gillespie, T. (2000), "Narrative Control and Visual Polysemy: Fox Surveillance Specials and the Limits of Legitimation," *The Velvet Light Trap*, 45(Spring): 36–49.

Goldhaber, M. H. (1997), "The Attention Economy and the Net," *First Monday*, 2(4). Available online: https://ojphi.org/ojs/index.php/fm/rt/printerFriendly/519/440/ (accessed July 12, 2022).

Grand Theft Auto V (2013), [Videogame], Edinburgh, UK: Rockstar North.

Greenfield, A. (2006), *Everyware: The Dawning Age of Ubiquitous Computing*, Boston: New Riders.

Grisham, T., Jeyda, J., Rombes, N. and Shaviro, S. (2016), "The Post-Cinematic in Paranormal Activity and Paranormal Activity 2," in S. Denson and J. Leyda (eds), *Post-Cinema: Theorizing 21st-Century Film*, Falmer, UK: REFRAME Books.

Gruber, D. (2017), "Three Forms of Neurorealism: Explaining the Persistence of the 'Uncritically Real' in Popular Neuroscience News," *Written Communication*, 34(2): 189–223.

Gruber, T. (1991), "The Role of Common Ontology in Achieving Sharable, Reusable Knowledge Bases," in J. Allen, R. Fikes and E. Sandewall (eds), *Principles of Knowledge Representation and Reasoning: Proceedings of the Second International Conference*, 601–2, Burlington, MA: Morgan Kaufmann.

Gruber, T. (1993), "Toward Principles for the Design of Ontologies Used for Knowledge Sharing?," *International Journal of Human-Computer Studies*, 43(5).

Halpern, O. (2014), *Beautiful Data: A History of Vision and Reason since 1945*, Durham: Duke University Press.

Hannah, M. G. (2006), "Torture and the Ticking Bomb: The War on Terrorism as a Geographical Imagination of Power/Knowledge," *Annals of the American Association of Geographers*, 96(3): 622–40.

Hansen, M. B. N. (2015a), *Feed-Forward: On the Future of Twenty-First-Century Media*, Chicago: University of Chicago Press.

Hansen, M. B. N. (2015b), "Topology of Sensibility," in U. Ekman, J. D. Bolter, L. Diaz, M. Sondergaard and M. Engberg (eds), *Ubiquitous Computing, Complexity and Culture*, 33–48, London: Routledge.

Hardt, M. and Negri, A. (2004), *Multitude: War and Democracy in the Age of Empire*, London: The Penguin Press.

Harman, G. (2005), *Guerilla Metaphysics: Phenomenology and the Carpentry of Things*, Chicago: Open Court.

Harman, G. (2009), *Prince of Networks: Bruno Latour and Metaphysics*, Melbourne: Re.press.

Hart, A. C. (2019), "The Searching Camera: First-Person Shooters, Found-Footage Horror Films, and the Documentary Tradition," *JCMS: Journal of Cinema and Media Studies*, 58(4): 73–91.

Hayles, K. (2017), *Unthought: The Power of the Cognitive Nonconscious*, Chicago: University of Chicago Press.

Helal, A., Cook, D. J. and Schmalz, M. (2009), "Smart Home-Based Health Platform for Behavioral Monitoring and Alteration of Diabetes Patients," *Journal of Diabetes Science and Technology*, 3(1): 141–8.

Heller-Nicholas, A. (2014), *Found Footage Horror Films: Fear and the Appearance of Reality*, Jefferson, NC: McFarland & Company.

Hoffman, D. L. and Novak, T. P. (2018), "Consumer and Object Experience in the Internet of Things: An Assemblage Theory Approach," *Journal of Consumer Research*, 44(6): 1178–204.

Holston, J. (1998), "Spaces of Insurgent Citizenship," in L. Sandercock (ed), *Making the Invisible Visible: A Multicultural Planning History*, 37–56, Berkley: University of California Press.

Hong, S. (2020), *Technologies of Speculation: The Limits of Knowledge in a Data-Driven Society*, New York: New York University Press.

Hörl, E. (2018), "The Environmentalitarian Situation: Reflections on the Becoming-Environmental of Thinking, Power, and Capital," *Cultural Politics*, 14(2): 153–73.

Howe, C. (2019), "Sensing Asymmetries in Other-than-Human Forms," *Science, Technology & Human Values*, 44(5): 900–10.

Hu, T. (2015), *A Prehistory of the Cloud*, Cambridge: The MIT Press.

Ifft, P. J., Shokur, S., Li, Z., Lebedev, M. A. and Nicolelis, M. A. (2013), "A Brain-Machine Interface Enables Bimanual Arm Movements in Monkeys," *Science Translational Medicine*, 5(210).

Ingold, T. (2008), "Bindings Against Boundaries: Entanglements of Life in an Open-World," *Environment and Planning A*, 40: 1796–810.

Interaxon's Privacy Policy (2019), *MUSE*. Available online: https://choosemuse.com/legal/privacy (accessed March 27, 2021).

International Telecommunication Union (2012), "Overview of the Internet of Things (Rec. ITU-T Y.2060)," Geneva. Available online: http://handle.itu.int/11.1002/1000/11559/ (accessed July 12, 2022).

Introducing Muse 2 (n.d.), *MUSE*. Available online: https://choosemuse.com/muse-2 (accessed March 27, 2021).

Introduction (n.d.), *EmotiveBCI Toolbox*. Available online: https://emotiv.gitbook.io/emotivbci-node-red-toolbox (accessed March 27, 2021).

Jameson, F. (1992), *Postmodernism, or, The Cultural Logic of Late Capitalism*, Durham: Duke University Press.

Jennings, N. (2000), "On Agent-Based Software Engineering," *Artificial Intelligence*, 117: 277–96.

Johnson, N., Li, Y., Tang, F. and Sarker, S. (2014), "Are You Watching Me? A Look at Panoptic Perceptions Surrounding Computer Monitoring Systems," *Journal of Information Technology Case and Application Research*, 16(1).

Johnson, S. (1997), *Interface Culture: How New Technology Transforms the Way We Create & Communicate*, New York: HarperCollins.

Joque, J. (2016), "The Invention of the Object: Object Orientation and the Philosophical Development of Programming Languages," *Philosophy & Technology*, 29: 335–56.

Jørgensen, K. (2012), "Between the Game System and the Fictional World: A Study of Computer Game Interfaces," *Games and Culture*, 7(2): 142–63.

Juul, J. (2002), "The Open and the Closed: Game of Emergence and Games of Progression," in F. Mäyrä (ed), *Computer Games and Digital Cultures Conference Proceedings*, 323–9, Tampere, Finland: Tampere University.

Kafai, Y. (2010), "World of Whyville: An Introduction to Tween Virtual Life," *Games and Culture*, 5(1): 3–22.

Kahn, J. M., Katz, R. H. and Pister, K. S. (1999), "Next Century Challenges: Mobile Networking for 'Smart Dust,'" in *Proceedings of the 5th Annual ACM/IEEE International Conference on Mobile Computing and Networking*, 271–8, New York: ACM.

Kay, A. (1993), "The Early History Of Smalltalk," *ACM SIGPLAN Notices*, 28(3): 69–95.

Keogh, B. (2014), "Across Worlds and Bodies: Criticism in the Age of Video Games," *Journal of Games Criticism*, 1(1).

Kim, S. P., Sanchez, J. C., Rao, Y. N., Erdogmus, D., Carmena, J. M., Lebedev, M. A., Nicolelis, M. A. and Principe, J. C. (2006), "A Comparison of Optimal MIMO Linear and Nonlinear Models for Brain–Machine Interfaces," *Journal of neural engineering*, 3(2): 145–61.

Kim, H. K., Carmena, J. M., Biggs, S. J., Hanson, T. L., Nicolelis, M. A. and Srinivasan, M. A. (2007), "Themuscle Activation Method: An Approach to Impedance Control of Brain-Machine Interfaces Through a Musculoskeletal Model of the Arm," *IEEE Transactions of Biomedical Engineering*, 54(8): 1520e1529, http://dx.doi.org/10.1109/.

Kirn, W. (2015), "If You're Not Paranoid, You're Crazy," *The Atlantic*, November. Available online: https://www.theatlantic.com/magazine/archive/2015/11/if-youre-not-paranoid-youre-crazy/407833 (accessed March 27, 2021).

Kirstein, P. (2016), "Edge Networks & Devices for the Internet of Things," *Daedalus*, 145(1): 33–42.

Kitchin, R. (2014), "The Real-Time City? Big Data and Smart Urbanism," *GeoJournal*, 79: 1–14.

Kitchin, R. and Dodge, M. (2011), *Code/Space: Software and Everyday Life*, Cambridge: MIT Press.

Kitchin, R. and McArdle, G. (2016), "What Makes Big Data, Big Data? Exploring the Ontological Characteristics of 26 Datasets," *Big Data & Society*, January–June.

Kittler, F. (1999), *Gramophone, Film, Typewriter*, trans. G. Winthrop-Young and M. Wutz, Stanford, CA: Stanford University Press.

Kortuem, G., Kawsar, F., Sundramoorthy, V. and Fitton, D. (2010), "Smart Objects as Building Blocks for the Internet of Things," *IEEE Internet Computing*, 14(1): 44–51.

Kotis, K. and Katasonov, A. (2012), "An Ontology for the Automated Deployment of Applications in Heterogeneous IoT Environments." Available online: http://www.semantic-web-journal.net/sites/default/files/swj247_0.pdf (accessed July 12, 2022).

Kowalski, B. (2011), *Computational Logic and Human Thinking: How to Be Artificially Intelligent*, Cambridge, UK: Cambridge University Press.

Kuebrich, D. (1996), "Melville's Doctrine of Assumptions: The Hidden Ideology of Capitalist Production in 'Bartleby,'" *The New England Quarterly*, 69(3): 381–405.

Kulesa, T. and Dirks, S. (2009), "A Vision of Smart Cities: How Cities Can Lead the Way into a Prosperous and Sustainable Future," in *IBM Global Business Services*, 1–17, Armonk: IBM Corporation.

Lanzeni, D. (2016), "Smart Global Futures: Designing Affordable Materialities for a Better Life," in D. Lazeni, E. Ardévol and S. Pink (eds), *Digital Materialities: Design and Anthropology*, 45–60, New York: Bloomsbury.

Latour, B. (1984), *The Pasteurization of France*, trans. A. Sheridan, Cambridge: Harvard University Press.

Latour, B. (1987), *Science in Action: How to Follow Scientists and Engineers Through Society*, Cambridge: Harvard university press.

Latour, B. (1990), "Drawing Things Together," in M. Lynch and S. Woolgar (eds), *Representation in Scientific Practice*, 19–68, Cambridge: MIT Press.

Latour, B. (1999), "On Recalling ANT," in J. Law (ed), *Actor Network Theory and After*, 15–25, Hoboken, NJ: Blackwell Publisher.

Latour, B. (2005), *Reassembling the Social: An Introduction to Actor-Network-Theory*, Oxford: Oxford University Press.

Latour, B. (2010), *On the Modern Cult of the Factish Gods*, Durham: Duke University Press.

La Vaque, T. (1999), "The History of EEG Hans Berger: Psychophysiologist. A Historical Vignette," *Journal of Neurotherapy: Investigations in Neuromodulation, Neurofeedback and Applied Neuroscience*, 3(2): 1–9.

Law, J. (1992), "Notes on the Theory of the Actor-network: Ordering, Strategy, and Heterogeneity," *Systems Practice*, 5(4): 379–93.

Law, J. (2002), "Objects and Spaces," *Theory, Culture & Society*, 19(5–6): 91–105.

Law, J. (2012), "Technology and Heterogeneous Engineering: The Case of Portuguese Expansion," in W. Bijker, T. Hughes and T. Pinch (eds), *The Social Construction of Technological Systems*, 105–28, Cambridge: The MIT Press.

Lazzarato, M. (1996), "Immaterial Labor," in P. Virno and M. Hardt (eds), *Radical Thought in Italy: A Potential Politics*, 133–47, Minneapolis: University of Minnesota Press.

Lebedev, M. A., Tate, A. J., Hanson, T. L., Li, Z., O'Doherty, J. E., Winans, J. A., Ifft, P. J., Zhuang, K. Z., Fitzsimmons, N. A., Schwarz, D., Fuller, A. M., An, J. H. and Nicolelis, M. A. (2011), "Future Developments in Brain-Machine Interface Research," *Clinics*, 66: 25–32.

Lebedev, M. A. and Nicolelis, M. A. (2006), "Brain–Machine Interfaces: Past, Present and Future," *TRENDS in Neurosciences*, 29(9): 536–46.

Lebedev, M. A. and Nicolelis, M. A. (2009), "Principles of Neural Ensemble Physiology Underlying the Operation of Brain–Machine Interfaces," *Nature Reviews Neuroscience*, 10(7): 530–40.

Lee, Y., Chen, K., Cheng, Y. and Lei, C. (2011), "World of Warcraft Avatar History Dataset," in A. Begen and K. Mayer-Patel (eds), *MMSys'11 Proceedings of the Second Annual ACM conference on Multimedia Systems*, 123–8, New York: ACM.

Li, Z., O'Doherty, J. E., Hanson, T. L., Lebedev, M. A., Henriquez, C. S. and Nicolelis, M. A. (2009), "Unscented Kalman Filter for Brain-Machine Interfaces," *PloS one*, 4(7).

Lindley, J., Coulton, P. and Cooper, R. (2017), "Why the Internet of Things Needs Object Oriented Ontology," *The Design Journal*, 20: sup1: S2846–57.

Logan, S. (2017), "The Needle and the Damage Done: Of Haystacks and Anxious Panopticons," *Big Data & Society*, July–December.

Lorenzo, G. D., Pinelli, F., Pereira, F., Biderman, A., Ratti, C., Lee, C. and Lee, C. (2009), "An Affective Intelligent Driving Agent: Driver's Trajectory and Activities Prediction," in Proceedings from *2009 IEEE 70th Vehicular Technology Conference Fall*, Piscataway, NJ: IEEE.

Lupton, D. (2016), *The Quantified Self: A Sociology of Self-Tracking*, Malden, MA: Polity.

Lury, C. (2009), "From One to Multiplicity," in G. Ascione (ed), *Cultures of Change: Social Atoms and Electronic Lives*, Barcelona: Actar and Arts Santa Mónica.

Lury, C. and Day, S. (2019), "Algorithmic Personalization as a Mode of Individuation," *Theory, Culture & Society*, 36(2): 17–37.

Lury, C., Parisi, L. and Terranova, T. (2012), "Introduction: The Becoming Topological of Culture," *Theory, Culture & Society*, 29(4/5): 3–35.

MacKenzie, D. (2012), "Missile Accuracy: A Case Study in the Social Processes of Technological Change," in W. Bijker, T. Hughes and T. Pinch (eds), *The Social Construction of Technological Systems*, 189–216, Cambridge: The MIT Press.

Malabou, C. (2008), *What Should We Do with Our Brain?*, trans. S. Rand, New York: Fordham University Press.

Martin, L. and Secor, A. (2013), "Towards a Post-Mathematical Topology," *Progress in Human Geography*, 38(3): 420–38.

Martins, A. and Rincon, P. (2014), "Paraplegic in Robotic Suit Kicks off World Cup," *BBC News*. June 12. Available online: http://www.bbc.com/news/science-environment-27812218/ (accessed July 12, 2022).

Marx, K. (1993), *Grundrisse: Foundation of the Critique of Political Economy*, trans. M. Nicolaus, London: Penguin Books.

Massumi, B. (2002), *Parables for the Virtual: Movement, Affect, Sensation*, Durham: Duke University Press.

Massumi, B. (2015), *Ontopower: War, Powers, and the State of Perception*, Durham: Duke University Press.

McClanahan, A. (2009), "Future's Shock: Plausibility, Preemption, and the Fiction of 9/11," *Symploke*, 17(1–2): 41–62.

McCosker, A. and Wilken, R. (2014), "Rethinking 'Big Data' as Visual Knowledge: The Sublime and the Diagrammatic in Data Visualization," *Visual Studies*, 29(2): 155–64.

McKay, R., Langdon, Ro. and Coltheart, M. (2007), "Jumping to Conclusion? Paranoia, Probabilistic Reasoning and Need for Closure," *Cognitive Neuropsychiatry*, 12(4): 362–76.

Meillassoux, Q. (2008), *After Finitude: An Essay on the Necessity of Contingency*, trans. R. Brassier, London: Continuum.

Melville, H. (1853), *Bartleby, the Scrivener: A Story of Wall-Street*. Available online: http://www.bartleby.com/129/ (accessed July 12, 2022).

Merleau-Ponty, M. (2005), *Phenomenology of Perception*, trans. C. Smith, New York: Routledge.

Mezzadra, S. and Neilson, B. (2012), "Between Inclusion and Exclusion: On the Topology of Global Space and Borders," *Theory, Culture & Society*, 29(4/5): 58–75.

Michaelis, J. R. (2018), "Value of Information Driven Content Management in Mixed Reality Infrastructures," in T. P. Hanratty and J. Linas (eds), *Proceeding of Spies, Next-Generation Analyst VI*, Bellingham, WA: SPIE.

Miller, G. (2014), "Is This Mind-Controlled Exoskeleton Science or Spectacle?," *Wired*, May 16. Available online: http://www.wired.com/2014/05/world-cup-exoskeleton-demo/ (accessed July 12, 2022).

Millner, M. (2019), "Homo Probabilis, Behavioral Economics, and the Emotional Life of Neoliberalism," *Postmodern Culture*, 29(2).

Mills, J. (2003), "Lacan on Paranoiac Knowledge," *Psychoanalytic Psychology*, 20(1): 30–51.

MIT Sensible City Lab (2009), "MIT Researchers Develop Affective Intelligent Driving Agent," *MIT Sensible City Lab*. Available online: http://senseable.mit.edu/aida/downloads/AIDA_Press_Release.doc/ (accessed July 12, 2022).

Mitew, T. (2014), "Do Objects Dream of an Internet of Things?," *The Fiberculture Journal*, 23.

Moreno, V., Ubeda, B., Skarmeta, A. and Zamora, M. (2014), "How Can We Tackle Energy Efficiency in IoT Based Smart Buildings?," *Sensors*, 14: 9583–614.

Morton, T. (2013), *Hyperobjects: Philosophy of Ecology After the End of the World*, Minneapolis: Universitiy of Minnesota Press.

Muse Research (n.d.), *MUSE*. Available online: https://choosemuse.com/muse-research (accessed March 27, 2021).

MyEmotiv (n.d.), *EMOTIV*. Available online: https://www.emotiv.com/myemotiv (accessed March 27, 2021).

Nadler, A. and McGuigan, L. (2018), "An Impulse to Exploit: The Behavioral Turn in Data-Driven Marketing," *Critical Studies in Media Communication*, 35(2): 151–65.

Neidich, W. (2003), *Blow-Up: Photography, Cinema and the Brain*, New York: D.A.P. Available online: https://www.warrenneidich.com/blow-up-photography-cinema-and-the-brain/ (accessed July 12, 2022).

Newell, A. (1980), *Reasoning, Problem Solving and Decision Processes: The Problem Space as a Fundamental Category*. Available online: http://repository.cmu.edu/compsci/1575/ (accessed July 12, 2022).

Nicolelis, M. A. (2001), "Actions from Thoughts," *Nature*, 409(6818): 403–7.

Nicolelis, M. A. (2003), "Brain–Machine Interfaces to Restore Motor Function and Probe Neural Circuits," *Nature Reviews Neuroscience*, 4(5): 417–22.

Nicolelis, M. A. (2011a), "Wired-Up Brains Will Offer Out of Body Experience," *New Scientist*, 2813. Available online: https://www.newscientist.com/article/mg21028138-400-wired-up-brains-will-offer-out-of-body-experiences/ (accessed July 12, 2022).

Nicolelis, M. A. (2011b), *Beyond Boundaries: The New Neuroscience of Connecting Brains with Machines and How It Will Change Our Lives*, New York: Times Books.

Nicolelis, M. A. (2014), "Historic Moment: Eighth Volunteer Walks for the First Time with the Exoskeleton and Enjoys the Feeling of Walking Again," *Facebook Post*. Available online: https://www.facebook.com/207736459237008/videos/801662049844443/?comment_id=801675696509745&comment_tracking=%7B%22tn%22%3A%22R9%22%7D (accessed July 10, 2022).

Nicolelis, M. A. and Chapin, J. K. (2008), "Controlling Robots with the Mind," *Scientific American*, 18: 72–9.

Och, D. (2015), "Beyond Surveillance: Questions of the Real in the Neopostmodern Horror Film," in W. Clayton (ed), *Style and Form in the Hollywood Slasher Film*, 195–212, New York: Palgrave.

O'Doherty, J. E., Lebedev, M., Hanson, T. L., Fitzsimmons, N. and Nicolelis, M. A. (2009), "A Brain-Machine Interface Instructed by Direct Intracortical Microstimulation," *Frontiers in Integrative Neuroscience*, 3.

Olma, S. and Koukouzelis, K. (2007), "Introduction: Life's (Re-)Emergences," *Theory, Culture & Society*, 24(6): 1–17.

Pais-Vieira, M., Chiuffa, G., Lebedev, M., Yadav, A. and Nicolelis, M. A. (2015), "Building an Organic Computing Device with Multiple Interconnected Brains," *Scientific Reports*, 5.

Paranormal Activity (2007). [Film] Dir. O. Peli, USA: Blumhouse.

Paranormal Activity 4 (2012), [Film] Dir. H. Joost and A. Schulman, USA: Blumhouse.

Parisi, L. (2009), "Technoecologies of Sensation," in B. Herzogenrath (ed), *Deleuze/Guattari & Ecology*, 182–99, New York: Palgrave.

Pasquale, F. (2015), *The Black Box Society: The Secret Algorithms That Control Money and Information*, Cambridge: Harvard University Press.

Patton, L. (2018), "Hermann von Helmholtz," in E. M. Zalta (ed), *The Stanford Encyclopedia of Philosophy*. Available online: https://plato.stanford.edu/archives/win2018/entries/hermann-helmholtz/ (accessed July 12, 2022).

Peters, J. D. (2015), *The Marvelous Clouds: Towards a Philosophy of Elemental Media*, Chicago: The University of Chicago Press.

Pias, C. (2011), "The Game Player's Duty: The User as the Gestalt of the Ports," in E. Huhtamo and J. Parikka (eds), *Media Archaeology: Approaches, Applications, and Implications*, 164–83, Berkeley: University of California Press.

Pink, S., Mackley, K., Mitchell, V., Wilson, G. and Bhamra, T. (2016), "Refiguring Digital Interventions for Energy Demand Reduction: Designing for Life in the Digital-Material Home," in D. Lazeni, E. Ardévol and S. Pink (eds), *Digital Materialities: Design and Anthropology*, 79–97, New York: Bloomsbury.

Poincaré, H. (1913), *The Foundations of Science*, trans. G. B. Halsted, New York: The Science Press.

Poincaré, H. (2007), "On the Foundations of Geometry," in P. Pesic (ed), *Beyond Geometry*, 117–46, New York: Dover.

Ponder, G. (2012), "Nokia City Lens (Beta): A Closer Look. *Windows Central*." Available online: https://www.windowscentral.com/nokia-city-lens-beta-closer-look/ (accessed July 12, 2022).

Portal (2007), [Videogame], Bellevue, WA: Valve Corporation.

Portal II (2011), [Videogame], Bellevue, WA: Valve Corporation.

Portal Infinite Loop (2011), [Video file] Arctic Avenger, April 27. Available online: https://youtu.be/uKp8E3od_S0/ (accessed July 12, 2022).

Powel, D. (2013), "Mind-Controlled Prostheses Offer Hope for Disabled," *Washington Post*, May 6. Available online: https://www.washingtonpost.com/national/health-science/mind-controlled-prostheses-offer-hope-for-disabled/2013/05/03/fbc1018a-8778-11e2-98a3-b3db6b9ac586_story.html (accessed July 12, 2022).

Pradhan, M., Fuchs, C. and Johnsen, F. T. (2018), "A Survey of Applicability of Military Data Model Architectures for Smart City Data Consumption and Integration," in *Proceedings of 2018 IEEE 4th World Forum on Internet of Things (WF-IoT)*, 129–34, Piscataway, NJ: IEEE.

Ramakrishnan, A., Ifft, P. J., Pais-Vieira, M., Byun, Y. W., Zhuang, K. Z., Lebedev, M. A. and Nicolelis, M. A. (2015), "Computing Arm Movements with a Monkey Brainet," *Scientific Reports*, 5.

Rayes, A. and Salam, S. (2016), *Internet of Things: From Hype to Reality*, Switzerland: Springer Nature.

Reed, N. (2004), "The Specter of Wall Street: 'Bartleby, the Scrivener' and the Language of Commodities," *American Literature*, 76(2): 247–73.

Riemann, B. (2007), "On the Hypotheses That Lie at the Foundations of Geometry," in P. Pesic (ed), *Beyond Geometry*, 23–40, New York: Dover.

Rose, N. (2007), *The Politics of Life Itself: Biomedicine, Power, and Subjectivity in the Twenty-First Century*, Princeton: Princeton University Press.

Rose, N. and Abi-Rached, J. M. (2013), *Neuro: The New Brain Sciences and the Management of the Mind*, Princeton: Princeton University Press.

Rowell, J. T. and Streich, E. R. (1964), "The SAGE System Training Program for the Air Defense Command," *Human Factors*, 6: 537–48.

Ruckenstein, M. and Pantzar, M. (2017), "Beyond the Quantified Self: Thematic Exploration of a Dataistic Paradigm," *New Media & Society*, 19(3): 401–18.

Ryan, K. (1993), *The Incredible Machine*, Eugene, OR: Dynamix.

Sadowski, J. and Bendor, R. (2019), "Selling Smartness: Corporate Narratives and the Smart City as a Sociotechnical Imaginary," *Science, Technology, & Human Values*, 44(3): 540–63.

Sample, I. (2014), "Mind-Controlled Robotic Suit to Debut at World Cup 2014," *The Guardian*, April 1. Available online: https://www.theguardian.com/technology/2014/apr/01/mind-controlled-robotic-suit-exoskeleton-world-cup-2014/ (accessed July 12, 2022).

Santucci, D. M., Kralik, J. D., Lebedev, M. A. and Nicolelis, M. A. (2005), "Frontal and Parietal Cortical Ensembles Predict Single-Trial Muscle Activity during Reaching Movements in Primates," *European Journal of Neuroscience*, 22(6): 1925–40.

Satyanarayanan, M. (2001), "Pervasive Computing: Vision and Challenges," *IEEE Personal Communications*, 8(4): 10–17.

Sayad, C. (2016), "Found-Footage Horror and the Frame's Undoing," *Cinema Journal*, 55(2): 43–66.

Scholz, T. (2008), "Market Ideology and the Myths of Web 2.0," *First Monday*, 13(3).

Schwarz, D. A., Lebedev, M. A., Hanson, T. L., Dimitrov, D. F., Lehew, G., Meloy, J., Rajangam, S., Subramanian, V., Ifft, P. J., Li, Z., Ramakrishnan, A., Tate, A., Zhuang, K. Z. and Nicolelis, M. A. L. (2014), "Chronic, Wireless Recordings of Large-Scale Brain Activity in Freely Moving Rhesus Monkeys," *Nature Methods*, 11(6): 670–6.

Science in Portal 2: The Infinite Loop Squash (2012), [Video file] DoctorMelon, June 27. Available online: https://youtu.be/aRkphNk2yFM/ (accessed July 12, 2022).

Sedgwick, E. K. (2003), *Touching Feeling: Affect, Pedagogy, Performativity*, Durham: Duke University Press.

Sharon, T. and Zandbergen, D. (2016), "From Data Fetishism to Quantifying Selves: Self-Tracking Practices and the Other Values of Data," *New Media & Society*, 19(11): 1695–709.

Shaviro, S. (2009), *Post Cinematic Affect*, Winchester: Zero Books.

Shaviro, S. (2015), *The Universe of Things: On Speculative Realism*, Minneapolis: University of Minnesota Press.

Simondon, G. (1980), *On the Mode of Existence of Technical Objects*, trans. N. Mellamphy, London: University of Western Ontario.

Simondon, G. (1992), "The Genesis of the Individual," in J. Crary and S. Kwinter (eds), *Incorporations*, 297–319, Princeton: Zone Books.

Smith, S. (2014), "Mind-Controlled Exoskeleton Kicks off World Cup," *CNN*, June 13. Available online: http://www.cnn.com/2014/06/12/health/exoskeleton-world-cup-kickoff/ (accessed July 12, 2022).

Stantchev, V., Barnawi, A., Ghulam, S., Schubert, J. and Tamm, G. (2015), "Smart Items, Fog and Cloud Computing as Enablers of Servitization in Healthcare," *Sensors & Transducers*, 185(2): 121–8.

Star, S. L. and Griesemer, J. (1989), "Ecology, 'Translations' and Boundary Objects: Amateurs and Professionals in Berkeley's Museum of Vertebrate Zoology, 1907–39," *Social Studies of Science*. 19(3): 387–420.

Star, S. L. and Ruhleder, K. (1996), "Steps Toward an Ecology of Infrastructure: Design and Access for Large Information Spaces," *Information Systems Research*, 7(1): 111–34.

Stark, L. (2018), "Algorithmic Psychometrics and the Scalable Subject," *Social Studies of Science*," 48(2): 204–31.

Strengers, Y. (2016), "Envisioning the Smart Home: Reimagining a Smart Energy Future," in D. Lazeni, E. Ardévol and S. Pink (eds), *Digital Materialities: Design and Anthropology*, 61–76, New York: Bloomsbury.

Strum, S. and Latour, B. (1999), "Redefining the Social Link: From Baboons to Humans," in D. MacKenzie and J. Wajcman (eds), *The Social Shaping of Technology*, 116–25, Philadelphia: Open University Press.

Suryadevara, N. K., Mukhopadhyay, S., Wang, R. and Rayudu, R. (2013), "Forecasting the Behavior of an Elderly Using Wireless Sensors Data in a Smart Home," *Engineering Applications of Artificial Intelligence*, 26: 2641–52.

Terranova, T. (2012), "Attention, Economy and the Brain," *Culture Machine*, 13.

Thaler, R. H. and Sunstein, R. (2008), *Nudge: Improving Decisions About Health, Wealth, and Happiness*, New Haven, CT: Yale University Press.

Thaler, R. H. and Tucker, W. (2013), "Smarter Information, Smarter Consumers," *Harvard Business Review*, January–February: 44–54.

The Blair Witch Project (1999), [Film] Dir. D. Myrick and E. Sanchez, USA: Haxan.

The Elder Scrolls V: Skyrim (2011), [Videogame], Rockville, MD: Bethesda Softworks.

The Legend of Zelda (1986), [Videogame], Kyoto: Nintendo.

The Legend of Zelda: Breath of the Wild (2017), [Videogame], Kyoto: Nintendo EPD.

The Legend of Zelda: Breath of the Wild (n.d.). Speedrun.com. Available online: http://www.speedrun.com/botw#Any/ (accessed July 11, 2022).

Touch Titans' Mind Controlled Tesla P90D Ludicrous – Weekend Project (2016), [Video file] Touch Titans, April 4. Available online: https://www.youtube.com/watch?v=Ae6En8-eaww&feature=emb_logo (accessed July 11, 2022).

Vishmidt, M. (2018), *Speculation as A Mode of Production: Forms of Value Subjectivity in Art and Capital*, Boston: Brill.

Wark, M. (2007), *Gamer Theory*, Cambridge: Harvard University.

Weiser, M. and Brown, J. S. (1997), "The Coming Age of Calm Technology," in P. J. Denning and R. M. Metcalfe (eds), *Beyond Calculation*, 75–85, New York: Springer.

Wessberg, J., Stambaugh, C. R., Kralik, J. D., Beck, P. D., Laubach, M., Chapin, J. K., Kim, J., Biggs, S. J., Srinivasan, M. A. and Nicolelis, M. A. (2000), "Real-Time Prediction of Hand Trajectory by Ensembles of Cortical Neurons in Primates," *Nature*, 408(6810): 361–5.

What It Measures (n.d.), *MUSE*. Available online: https://choosemuse.com/what-it-measures (accessed March 27, 2021).

Whitehead, A. N. (1978), *Process and Reality: An Essay in Cosmology*, New York: The Free Press.

Wilke, C. (2017), "Seeing and Unmaking Civilians in Afghanistan: Visual Technologies and Contested Professional Visions," *Science, Technology, & Human Values*, 42(6): 1031–60.

Wilson, A. (2018), "Beyond the Neomaterialist Divide: Negotiating Between Eliminative and Vital Materialism with Integrated Information Theory," *Theory, Culture & Society*, 35(7–8): 97–116.

Witcher 3: Wild Hunt (2015), [Videogame], Warsaw, Poland: CD Projekt RED.

Wolf, G. (2019), "Know Thyself: Tracking Every Facet of Life, from Sleep to Mood to Pain, 24/7/365," *Wired*, June. Available online: https://www.wired.com/2009/06/lbnp-knowthyself/ (accessed July 12, 2022).

Xie, X. and Wnag, Z. (2018), "SIV-DSS: Smart In-Vehicle Decision Support System for Driving at Signalized Intersections with V2I Communication," *Transportation Research Part C*, 90: 181–97.

Yoran, G. (2018), "Applied Metaphysics: Objects in Object-Oriented Ontology and Object-Oriented Programming," *Interface Critique Journal*, 1: 120–33.

Zuboff, S. (2019), *The Age of Surveillance Capitalism: The Fight for a Human Future at the New Frontier of Power*, New York: Public Affairs.

Index

Printed in the USA
CPSIA information can be obtained
at www.ICGtesting.com
LVHW010531171223
766606LV00005B/277